There We Stood, Here We Stand

Eleven Lutherans Rediscover their Catholic Roots

By Timothy Drake

1stBooks – rev. 2/1/01

Dedication

I dedicate this book to the glory and honor of Jesus Christ and the Catholic Church, with love and gratitude to my parents who brought me up to believe in God. Thank you for the foundation you gave me.

Acknowledgements

First I would like to thank my family. Without the love and support of my wife, Mary, and her important work in the home, this book would not exist. I am able to do what I do because of what she does. I also want to thank my children, Elias, Isabel, Claire, Elena Grace, and baby Gabriel in Heaven. Thank you for your patience and your love, and for putting up with a father who is often locked in his office writing. I love you all.

I would also like to thank those who helped put this book together. I am grateful to Mark Dittman for his excellent proofreading and editorial skills. There's no one better at catching the small things. I also want to thank Ted Schluenderfritz for his creative design work on the cover, and Patrick Madrid for his creativity in providing the title for this book.

I also want to thank the Sisters of the St. Clare Monastery in Sauk Rapids, Minnesota for their continued prayers for this book and my work.

Last, but not least, I want to thank each of the men and women who were willing to contribute their stories for this book and for the world. It is my prayer that in sharing such personal journeys others may also come to know Christ's Truth and find their way home.

Contents

Foreword

Becoming More Fully Who We Are

As is the experience of most converts, even long after he entered into full communion John Henry Newman was regularly asked why he became a Catholic. He remarked, with perhaps just a touch of impatience, that it is not the kind of question one can answer adequately between the soup and the fish courses. I know a little of what he meant. It usually begins this way: "I'm sure it's a very long story and I know you've been asked this five thousand times, but why did you become a Catholic?"

My short answer is, "To be more fully who I was as a Lutheran." My longer answer I will perhaps have opportunity to set forth at book length sometime in the future. It strikes me that the fascinating essays in this book are, for the most part, expansions on the short answer. All the writers are grateful for what they received in the Lutheran communion that is true, good, and beautiful. Each finally, and often after much painful hesitation, acted upon the true and irrepressible intuition that, because there is only one Christ there can be only one Church, which is the Body of Christ, and therefore their baptism into the Church of Jesus Christ was, in fact, baptism into the Catholic Church, which is the Church of Jesus Christ most fully and rightly ordered through time.

We are called converts, although it is more precise to say that ours was a delayed fulfillment of the conversion that happened, by the grace of God, in baptism. In the words of the Second Vatican Council, we were when Lutherans "truly but imperfectly in communion with the Catholic Church," and now that imperfection has been remedied. That does not mean that we are perfect in understanding, obedience to truth, or holiness. Far from it. It simply means that we are where God intended us to be when in baptism he called us by name. I was received into full communion on September 8, 1990, the Nativity of Our Lady. I vividly recall waking up the next morning and realizing that something was very, very different. I tried to put my finger on it, and then it came to me: For the first time in many years, I was not beginning the day with the question weighing on my mind, Where do I belong in the Church of Jesus Christ? I knew where I belonged. I was there. I was home.

The essays in this volume represent a small but important part of a much larger story that is largely neglected. In recent years, through RCIA (The Rite of Christian Initiation for Adults), almost two hundred thousand adults per year have been entering into full communion with the Catholic Church. And that is only in the United States. In addition, others are received outside RCIA through private instruction. About half the adults coming into the Church each year are received through baptism, while the other half come from various, usually Protestant, communions and were already baptized. I hope that catechists and other leaders of RCIA will read this book. From anecdotal evidence, now reinforced by a study done by the National Conference of Catholic Bishops, we know that many adults coming through RCIA complain about an inadequate emphasis on doctrine and on the distinctive claims of the Catholic Church. It seems that some RCIA leaders think that emphasizing what is distinctively Catholic would offend ecumenical sensibilities. But surely that is a mistake. As is luminously clear in the following essays, people are earnestly searching for *the truth* about Christ and his Church. They are exploring the proposal of the Second Vatican Council that, if one is convinced that the claims that the Catholic Church makes for herself are true, then one is in conscience bound to enter and remain in full communion with her.

Of course, not everybody is a theologian, for which we can be thankful, and not every searcher is driven by exclusively theological concerns. As is evident in these essays, the Holy Spirit employs many means in leading people into the fullness of the Church – personal and family relations, vocational intuitions, aesthetic sensibilities, commitment to Christian unity, the quest for moral clarity and courage. Because God is one, truth is one, and the many paths of truth by which we travel lead to the fullness of truth in the Church that is "the pillar and bulwark of truth" (1 Tim 3:15). As the reader will see in these essays, Lutheranism at its best cultivates a stubborn insistence upon the truth of things. Personal story after personal story bears witness to how that graced stubbornness has led people into full communion with the Catholic Church.

The truth that leads to the Catholic Church does not exhaust the truth to be found in the Catholic Church. At first, a Lutheran may be concerned about whether Catholicism passes muster by Lutheran criteria of the truth – the criterion of "justification by faith," for instance. Once inside the Church, however, one discovers that the Christian reality cannot be exhaustively comprehended by any one formulation of doctrine or dogma. As the great G.K. Chesterton, himself a convert, observed, the Catholic Church is ever so much larger from the inside than from the outside. There are the riches of the fathers, the mystics, the traditions of spirituality, the seven sacraments, and devotional practices galore. And there is Mary. How could I have lived so long without understanding, really understanding, that, if Jesus is my brother, she is most surely my mother too?

Like the authors in this book, and like so many others who are finding or have found their way home in this new time of conversions, I am immeasurably grateful for all the grace of God I knew and I shared as a Lutheran. Like them, I hope that my witness will contribute to greater Christian unity by concentrating attention on the truth of Christ and his Church. Like them, by becoming a Catholic I am more fully, and yet very differently, who I was as a Lutheran.

The journey is not over. We pray in the third eucharistic prayer, "Strengthen in faith and love your pilgrim Church on earth." I have not left behind any with whom I travelled before. We travel together still. I have, by the grace of God, been joined to the company that is the center and the vanguard of the pilgrimage to our ultimate home. It is the company of the apostles, with the Pope, who is Peter among us; it is a ragtag company of forgiven sinners, a saintly company of heroes and heroines of faith, an everyday company of those gathered around the One who is, as he promised, sacramentally with us until the end of the age. It is, in sum and beyond dispute, the company of the one, holy, catholic, and apostolic Church. It is home on the way to home.

Richard John Neuhaus
Feast of St. Elizabeth Ann Seton
New York City

Father Richard John Neuhaus, a priest of the Archdiocese of New York, is president of the Institute on Religion and Public Life and editor in chief of First Things, *both based in New York. He is the author or editor of more than thirty books. Ordained a Lutheran pastor in 1960, he was received into full communion by John Cardinal O'Connor in 1990 and ordained a priest of the Catholic Church by the Cardinal in 1991.*

Introduction

One of These Things is not Like the Other

When my wife Mary, a lifelong Catholic, and I, a lifelong Lutheran, were first considering marriage we frequently heard the admonishment that, "Lutherans and Catholics are so alike today that there really is very little difference between the two." Well-meaning family and friends were trying to emphasize our similarities and make light of our differences to provide us some comfort in the decision we had made to spend the rest of our lives together. Yet, I asked myself, if the two are so similar, then why are they still divided?

While Mary and I had discussed the similarities and differences during our courtship it didn't take long into our marriage for those differences to rear their ugly head. Such differences included why Mary needed to attend a Catholic Church even if she had attended a Lutheran service, why I couldn't receive Holy Communion in a Catholic Church, as well as the usual Protestant misunderstandings regarding Mary, the Saints, and the Pope. It would be six years before I would fully understand the context of those differences.

Certainly, Catholics and Lutherans are similar in many ways. They are both liturgical. A visitor to both would find that the readings are the same on most Sundays. Both share similar prayers and share the sacraments of baptism, marriage, and Holy Communion. Both follow a Catechism.

However, to ignore the differences is to ignore the actions of Martin Luther nearly 500 years ago, and the more than 20,000 Protestant denominations that have arisen since the original split. To ignore this fact is to suggest that Catholicism and Lutheranism are more similar than they really are. This is a disservice to both.

This book is not meant to exaggerate those differences; it is meant to illuminate what is at the heart of Lutherans who have been moved to join the very Church that Luther had originally protested. Their stories highlight those differences, not as a way of dividing, but as a way of uniting. They demonstrate that there are real and substantive differences between Lutheranism and Catholicism - differences so profound, that once realized, they can provoke a conversion of the heart. As these stories demonstrate, sacramental, doctrinal, traditional, Scriptural, or practical differences are significant enough to provoke some to make the decision to embrace Catholicism.

We see small steps of ecumenism at work, trying to repair the break. At the heart of such efforts lay the unity which Christ himself so desires. The Joint

Declaration on Justification, issued by the Lutheran World Federation and the Roman Catholic Church in the fall of 1999, is one such example. The agreement, which is included as an appendix in this book, states that the condemnations that each side pronounced against each other in the sixteenth century no longer apply. While it represents a significant step, it is at best a baby step on the road to unity. Other differences remain.

Such differences are illustrated, for example, by the controversy surrounding the Evangelical Lutheran Church in America's (E.L.C.A.) "Call to Common Mission" – an agreement to enter full communion with the Episcopal Church. Such agreements have been reached between the E.L.C.A. and other Protestant denominations. In response, a counter-movement within the E.L.C.A., known as the Word Alone group, has erupted over differences in how the Lutheran and Episcopal denominations view the historic episcopate - the unbroken line of Church leadership, as evidenced by the bishops, reaching back to the days of the apostles. The Episcopal church accepts the historic Episcopate; the Lutheran church does not.

We are witnesses to events not very different from Luther's actions, or the actions of so many Protestant denominations that split after Luther. Each denomination, in turn, accepts or rejects Church teaching based upon its own interpretation of Scripture. The Word Alone group is merely the latest in a long line of successive splits that include denominations such as the Lutheran Church Missouri Synod, the Wisconsin Evangelical Lutheran Synod, the Church of the Lutheran Brethren of America, and the Association of Free Lutheran Congregations among others. In the end, one is forced to ask, "Where does authority reside?"

Those in this book have come to the conclusion that authority resides in Christ and the Church which He established. Their stories demonstrate that taking such a leap of faith is not easily or lightly made. In most cases it requires years of study, prayer, discussion, and discernment. The sacrifices that some make in their conversion process are truly inspiring. Some in this book have given up jobs and pensions. Others have given up their very vocation as minister. The decision for still others has meant separation from family and friends.

Reading, and re-reading the stories, I marvel at the ways in which the Holy Spirit works within individual lives. Each story is unique, and yet in their uniqueness they all bear something in common. The process of conversion is individualistic, unrepeatable and ongoing.

In my own search I found many books of conversion stories from an Evangelical or Jewish perspective, but very few examining it from a Lutheran perspective. This I found very surprising considering that it was Martin Luther, after all, who originally split with the Church. Of those that I found that did deal with the Lutheran-Catholic question, Louis Bouyer's *The Spirit and Forms of Protestantism* and Karl Adam's *One and Holy* were out of print.

In the end, my reading could only take me so far. I needed someone whom I could talk to who would understand my unique background and perspective as a questioning Lutheran. Remarkably, the Holy Spirit responded to my need by placing a previously unknown brother in my life. While I know that my own story is unusual, it is my hope that stories such as my own and the others in this book will serve to meet other Lutherans where they are at, and answer some of the unique questions with which so many Lutherans wrestle.

+

Tim Drake
December 29, 2000 – Feast of St. Thomas Becket

Married with Children

Father Larry Blake

I am a Catholic priest. I have been married for 18 years. This is my story. As young adults, my parents were not regular churchgoers. My father was raised as a Methodist and my mother was raised in the Swedish Lutheran Church. They were like a lot of people when I was born. While their home was in Braintree, Massachusetts, they were without a church home. I was born September 19, 1951, the oldest of six children. After my birth, my parents began looking for a church where I could be baptized. My father's family had connections with St. Chrysostym's Episcopal Church in Quincy, Massachusetts, and my grandmother attended church there. That is where I was baptized in November of 1951.

Not long after my baptism my parents began church shopping. The first time my mother brought my father to Salem Evangelical Lutheran Church, a Swedish Lutheran Church, he did not like it at all. The liturgy was all in Swedish, and he felt it just was not the place for him. In time, however, she prevailed. The church did offer worship in English and she was eventually able to get him to attend. So that is where they first began to get involved, and all of my siblings were baptized there.

Our religious training began with Sunday school and then later confirmation. My parents made a genuine effort to see that we were always in church every Sunday, sitting just behind the minister's family in the second row. As I look back on that time now I can see that this was a sign of growth and maturity in their own faith lives. The church was small and everyone knew one another.

It was a very liturgical church, and they placed a good deal of emphasis on the sacraments of baptism and Holy Communion. Holy Communion, especially, was surrounded with a great deal of solemnity. I sat in awe of this sacrament as a child seeing the gifts at the altar.

During my teenage years, my parents had become acquainted with some Baptist friends, and so we often spent Sunday mornings at Salem Lutheran and Sunday evenings at a Baptist church in Boston. This experience certainly aided my father in the growth of his faith. My parents would bring us there to participate in the church's strong youth program. We also attended a summer Baptist camp, complete with revivals, for a couple of summers. We found, as Lutherans, that it was good to be exposed to this tradition.

Through this connection my mother and a friend began a Wednesday afternoon children's faith formation program in our home. Children would come to our home, under the auspices of child evangelism, for a time of Bible study,

1

prayer, singing, and refreshments. I recall one evening, after an afternoon spent talking about personal salvation, asking my mother how I knew I was saved. Even with all that Baptist influence, she knew enough to return to the sacramental theology of her upbringing. She gave the good Lutheran answer that I had been baptized in the name of the Father, and the Son, and the Holy Spirit, and that God claimed me as His own in baptism.

Family prayer was strong during those years. Following supper, the family would gather in the living room and either my mother or father would read from the popular devotional, *Little Visits with God*. This was followed by prayer time before we went off to bed.

During high school we continued to be involved at Salem, which had merged with the Lutheran Church in America. I was very active in the Luther League youth program and shared a good relationship with my pastor. After two years of preparation I was confirmed during my sophomore year, 1966. We had been drilled in Luther's Small Catechism and I remember eight to ten of us sitting up in front of the church, facing the congregation on folding chairs. Our loving but serious pastor went up and down the row asking each of us to recite, from memory, portions of the Catechism. "Lawrence, can you tell us Luther's explanation to the second article of the creed?" he might have asked. That was our exam. Afterwards we were confirmed and received our first communion.

I recognize the importance of Communion at an early age

I always enjoyed being in church, but I remember particularly feeling joyous to receive communion. A white railing enclosed the altar and chancel and only the pastor and the servers went behind the railing. We knelt down to receive communion. Holy Communion was only distributed once a month, or on special holidays such as Easter Sunday or Christmas, and so I always looked forward to receiving communion after that.

In addition to my Sunday morning worship experience, the other formative part of my high school experience was my involvement in a Bible Club on the south shore of Boston. Alan Emery, a very successful businessman, and his wife, who felt that their ministry was to young people, led it. They were members of the Congregational Church and ran a Bible Club that was attended by between 40 and 60 young people every Thursday evening.

Everyone would crowd into their enormous living room and we would sing songs, listen to a spiritual talk, and hold a meeting. The focus of the evening was always the spiritual talk given by Mr. Emery. He had been a captain aboard a Coast Guard ship during World War II and he had the marvelous ability to tell stories about his life and stories from the lives of others. He would address topics such as living by faith in Jesus Christ or living a life of integrity.

2

The Emery's also had a home in New Hampshire, and throughout the winter and spring he would bring 10-12 students on retreat to his winter home. During my junior year I was elected president of the club. I remember going to Mr. Emery the night I was elected and said, "I can't do this. I can't get up in front of my friends and do this."

Mr. Emery put his hand on my shoulder and replied, "You know, Larry, I've seen many young men just like yourself. When they were called to this position they felt inadequate. Remember, though, that God gives you strength for every task that you are called to."

I served for two years. During that time I became aware, for the first time in my life, that my Lutheran faith was seen as somewhat of an oddity by most of my Baptist friends. I remember very clearly one of them once asking me if I believed in transubstantiation or consubstantiation. I knew enough to say that Lutherans believed that at the altar we received the body and blood, in and with and under, the bread and wine. One of my friends responded that that sounded "very Catholic."

Called to the pastorate

During the spring of my junior year I realized that I had a very strong calling to be in the ordained ministry. I felt that this was a way that God could use me. So, when I began searching for a college, the ones I considered were church-related. I considered Eastern Nazarene College, Wheaton, and Lenore Rhine. One night while visiting with my pastor, he told me about Concordia College in Moorhead, Minnesota. Of it he said, "It is a conservative school. There are a lot of Bible studies going on there. I think you should check it out. I think you would like it."

Our family did not have a lot of money for travel, and so my parents said that I could apply, but we could not afford to see it. They told me I would have to make my decision based upon what I read in their literature. In the end all three schools that I had applied at accepted me. Through prayer and meditation I decided upon Concordia. I graduated from high school in 1969, and in August I left home.

I landed at the one-runway airport in Fargo, North Dakota thinking that this must be the end of the world and wondering what I had done. It was quite remote and the taxi driver could hardly believe that someone would come halfway across the country to go to school in Fargo.

Fortunately, I found Concordia much to my liking. I was blessed with a good roommate and met many friends with a deep Christian faith, most of whom were also headed toward the ministry. It was good for me to be part of a group like that. In addition, there were Bible studies going on all over campus, and I linked up right away with an Outreach Teams organization. The outreach team worked

3

under the auspices of the college to provide music and worship leadership ministry at various churches throughout Minnesota and North Dakota over weekends. This was how I met my wife Diane. During the summer of my graduation I organized a team that traveled for 10 weeks in Montana, Idaho, North Dakota, Wyoming, South Dakota, and Minnesota. It was a wonderful experience and gave us the opportunity to witness to our faith in Christ numerous times.

We were required at Concordia to take a religion class every year as part of our core curriculum. In the fall of 1970, just five years after Vatican II, I had a class with an elderly adjunct faculty member from St. John's University in Collegeville, Minnesota. This was my first introduction to Catholic theology. In particular, I remember discussing with him the issue of celibacy for the clergy. He spoke about it as a gift to the Church and to the individual who accepts it. When I countered, "Well, aren't there many fine married Protestant clergy?" he responded, "Yes, and I most often hear from their wives about how difficult that is."

I graduated with a BA in sociology and a minor in Greek in 1973. Diane and I were engaged that fall, and I decided to work for a year in Moorhead while Diane was finishing up her degree. We were married in June of 1974 and I began my theological studies at Luther Seminary in St. Paul in September. When I started at Luther, the Lutheran Church of America operated Northwestern Lutheran Theological Seminary on the same campus. I also accepted a position in youth ministry at a local church to earn some money. The position offered a small stipend as well as free housing in the neighborhood.

My seminary years were good years. I spent my first year at Luther and then decided to transfer to Northwestern during my second year. I had hoped to be ordained into the Lutheran Church in America and therefore felt I should have contact with my colleagues who would be ordained there. The schools had separate scheduling as well as other differences.

These differences were made apparent to me, for example, in that I do not ever remember seeing a Luther professor dressed in clerics, whereas at Northwestern it was not uncommon to see faculty and the president dressed that way. The L.C.A. had a much stronger liturgical tradition than Luther. Northwestern had come from the old Northwest Synod of the United Lutheran Church before becoming part of the L.C.A. Its campus had a beautiful altar, complete with crucifix, baptistry, and organ. It was the first time that I realized there was a strain of Lutheranism that took seriously the liturgical part of the church. They used incense and they stressed the importance of the sacraments in the life of the church. I found this very enriching.

I also gained a deeper appreciation for and saw Lutheranism as a reform movement within the Church. Lutheranism, I felt, in its best expression would

4

move forward being a reform movement within the larger church. At some point there would be unity with Rome. I also had the sense that this is what the faculty believed. These years were a formative time that I have never forgotten. By the time I graduated the two schools merged to form Luther Northwestern Seminary, were sharing faculty, and were on the same schedule.

I was ordained for the Minnesota Synod of the L.C.A. in October of 1978 at my home church of Salem Lutheran. Coincidentally, my ordination occurred the same year that the Holy Father Pope John Paul II ascended to his seat in Rome. My first call was to Bethany Lutheran in Deer River, Minnesota. My responsibilities there also included serving at Suomi Lutheran church, a parish of Finnish background. During my time there I was approached by a third congregation, Jesse Lake Lutheran, that wanted to reopen. As a result I was on the road almost constantly.

My first experience of Catholic liturgy

The most significant event that took place during my time at Deer River was the result of a weeklong retreat I participated in at the Ecumenical Center at St. John's University in Collegeville, Minnesota. Visiting clergy were invited to come to St. John's for discussions on faith and life. I especially enjoyed my time there. More significant than the lectures, I was moved by the 1,500-year anniversary of the founding of the Order of St. Benedict that was taking place during my stay. We were invited to attend Mass at the Abbey and I found myself astounded by the beauty and universality of seeing these men who had come from around the world to take part in this event. The liturgy was second-to-none. It was an awe-filled experience. For the first time I realized how insignificant the time period tracing back to Luther was in comparison to the tradition that informed these men. The grandeur struck me, and for the first time I felt as if there was a whole section of Church history that I had missed out on in my training.

I accepted a position at St. Stephen Lutheran in Bloomington, Minnesota in 1982 and left Deer River shortly thereafter. Immediately after moving to Bloomington, as a result of being struck by the prayer life exhibited by the men at St. John's Abbey, I sought out men who were praying the liturgy of the hours. I discovered a group of Franciscans at St. Bonaventure and asked if they might let me come pray with them. They agreed, and during my time with them I felt that I was coming into contact with a long spiritual tradition of which I had been totally ignorant. I found this form of communal prayer to be a very powerful tradition and felt that God was leading me along all the way.

I spent seven years at St. Stephen and while there worked with two men who were of like mind on the Church at large. They too felt that the Lutheran church was in its best sense a reform movement within the Church at large and saw being reconciled with Rome as the ultimate goal. At St. Stephen we did things that I had not seen in other places. We had Holy Communion weekly, although not at every service, allowing the presider to take Communion each Sunday. We also had living Stations of the Cross during Lent, which was a new experience for me as a Lutheran. It was the first time I had worn a chasuble. After seven years, this got into my being. Slowly, I was coming to see the centrality of the Eucharist.

All three of us pastors left St. Stephen at about the same time. I left in 1989 to go to a smaller parish, Holy Cross Lutheran Church in Excelsior, Minnesota. Upon arriving at Holy Cross it was my inclination to try to recreate the environment we had had at St. Stephen. At the same time I became acquainted with the Franciscan priest in our neighborhood, Father Elstan Coghill, and we began to do some things together. My first summer there, we organized an ecumenical Catholic, Lutheran, and Moravian Church summer day camp experience for youth in Victoria. Father Coghill and I became close during that time and I found that my experiences at St. Stephen forced me to do some thinking.

What is the focus of Sunday morning?

I began to see that there was another way of looking at Sunday morning. Was the preaching the chief experience of Sunday morning? This is what I had been led to believe as a Lutheran pastor. Or, could the Eucharist be the focus of Sunday morning? What was it that was important about the Eucharist as the chief experience on Sundays? Father Coghill encouraged me to get into conversation with some people at St. Paul Seminary. Through the guidance of Father Coghill and Father Urban Wagner, one of the Bloomington Franciscans, I made my way to St. Paul Seminary in the summer of 1990. Enough of these questions were rolling around in my mind forcing me to wonder what the relationship was between all of the various Protestant churches and the Roman Catholic Church. I was beginning to think of the Roman Catholic Church as *the* expression of the Body of Christ on earth and wondered what the expression of all the other churches was to that Church.

I decided to explore these questions more formally by taking courses at St. Paul Seminary in St. Paul, Minnesota. My first course was a guided studies course on the Sacraments, and I found it fascinating. Through it, I was able to get in touch with the historical tradition of the Sacraments. This was something I had not learned as a Lutheran seminarian. Naturally, I found myself going back to Holy Cross beginning to think differently about Holy Communion and developing a deeper reverence toward that Sacrament that I had not had before. For instance, when the women in the altar guild removed the ciborium from the altar, it would go back into the cupboard until the next time Holy Communion was celebrated. Then it would be removed from the cupboard and put back on the altar. There was no sense that the Real Presence of Christ remains in the species. This was a source of tension in my life. My thinking was becoming more Catholic, but in practice I was still Lutheran.

I followed up the course in the Sacraments with a course on the Eucharist. In this course I was able to read through all of the literature about the Eucharist itself from the apostles through the Early Church Fathers, through the challenges that the Reformers put before the Church, as well as Trent and Vatican II. What was so clear to me upon this reading was that the Eucharist was the central Sacrament in the life of the Church. It had a place above all other Sacraments. I began to see the centrality of the Sacrament of the Eucharist in the life of the Church. It also became obvious to me that the language about the sacrifice and the Body and Blood of Christ was historical language as well. While it may have taken time for the theology to develop, the sense was always there that we have the Body, Blood, Soul and Divinity of Christ present at the altar. The sacrifice is Christ's sacrifice for us on the Cross. He does not die again, but the sacrifice is made present once again for us in the Mass.

At one point in my reading, I came across the debate between the theologians LanFranc and Berengarius in the 11th century. They were trying to articulate how Christ's body is truly present. They believed that it really could be present, but were troubled as to how Christ could also be present at the Right Hand of the Father. They argued that Christ can be truly present at the altar, but he does not resign his place at the Right Hand of the Father. He can be incarnate in the species of the bread and wine, and with the Father. At one point LanFranc, arguing about transubstantiation, states that "unless there is a change there is no Sacrament." Berengarius, however, could not go that far. He wanted to stop with a more symbolic presence. In essence, he was the predecessor to the Zwingliites and Calvinists, foreshadowing the arguments that came up in the Reformation 500 years later. My professor later recalled that upon reading this passage it was as if a light had gone on in my head.

I realized that when the Reformation did take place, Trent had to defend the historical teaching of the Church on the Real Presence of Christ in the Eucharist. While it had always been the teaching of the Church, Trent forced the Church to officially name it transubstantiation. I also realized that the Church did not have the luxury of trying to answer each and every Reformer's nuanced understanding at Trent. One could argue that Luther had a theology of Real Presence that was closer to the Roman Catholic Church than many of the other Reformers, but he stopped short of transubstantiation by using the phrase "in, with, and under the bread and wine." Hence, no change occurs. The Church, at Trent, could not name each position, but rather took a position over and against all the other theologies in saying that the Roman Catholic Church believes in transubstantiation.

Learning this was like a line in the sand for me. It helped clarify the issue. While the term "Real Presence" is used among Christian people, it means different things to different denominations. Only the Catholic Church believes in Body, Blood, Soul and Divinity.

Time for a change

Diane, at this point, had been tuning into the Eternal Word Television Network. In the fall of 1992 she asked me to join her in listening to the conversion story of former Presbyterian minister Scott Hahn. I found his talk fascinating and realized that there were other people whom walked along a similar path and were coming to a similar understanding. It was clear to me by the end of 1992 that a change was coming about within me and I would need to make a decision based upon that change.

I approached the Archdiocese and told the Chancellor that Diane and I felt fairly certain that we were going to make a decision to become Catholic, but that I needed to work out some employment first. I was put in touch with several pastors who might be able to help me find a job. In January of 1993, Father Tiffany of All Saints Catholic Church in Lakeville, Minnesota visited with our family regarding a job.

After much prayer and talking with Diane and several priest friends I submitted my resignation to the Lutheran Bishop in February of 1993. He was not in favor of my resignation and hoped I would take a call to another Lutheran church. He attributed the decision to frustration that things were not going as I wanted rather than seeing it as my desire to move into the Catholic Church. Reluctantly, he accepted my resignation. In March, I began working as pastoral minister at All Saints.

Diane and I were received into full communion with the Roman Catholic Church at St. John the Baptist Church in Excelsior by Father Allen McIntyre, who had instructed us in the Catholic faith. We were received into the Church at the Easter Vigil on April 10, 1993.

It was a wonderful experience, and many parishioners from Holy Cross Lutheran came to witness the event. We felt happy that they did not feel our conversion was a rejection of them as much as it was a desire on our part to be a part of this new Church.

My principal responsibilities at All Saints included bringing communion to nursing homes, visiting the sick, and working with the RCIA program. In RCIA, I was fortunate to have one young man who sought me out. He had been a graduate of St. Olaf College. I helped him prepare to be received into the Catholic Church in the spring of 1994. It was exciting work. That young man is now a seminary student preparing for the priesthood. Unfortunately, the Archbishop assigned an associate pastor to All Saints that spring, and so after only a year I lost my position as pastoral minister. This was something I had not prepared for.

I returned to the Chancery, sent out letters, and was accepted for a position in the Diocese of Winona working as a part of Bishop Vlazny's staff in June of 1994. Concerned that the Winona job might also be short-lived, I commuted from Victoria to Winona on Monday mornings and remained at the rectory where I lived during the week until Friday afternoons. My work involved helping parishes with their long-range and strategic planning. While there, I developed a plan to help consolidate some of the small, rural parishes and prepare pastors for that inevitability. My time of living with the two other priests at the rectory, and separation from Diane, made me realize that the Twin Cities was a better place for me to pursue my theological studies. In January of 1995 I talked to my boss, the Vicar General, and we agreed that I should finish out the work I was doing and return to the Twin Cities in the spring.

Once again Diane and I felt God's leading. The family was not uprooted during any of these transitions, and we were happy that we hadn't sold the house in Victoria. In May, 1995, I was accepted as parish administrator at the Church of the Risen Savior in Burnsville. My move back to the Twin Cities also brought me closer to the seminary where I could continue my theological studies.

In the fall of 1995 I approached Archbishop John Roach about putting a file together to send to Rome for consideration of ordination under the Pastoral Provision. He was happy to do so. The file included my work history, letters of recommendation, transcripts, baptismal certificate, marriage certificate, and ordination certificate. We were ready to submit the dossier when Archbishop Roach announced that he was retiring, and Bishop Harry J. Flynn, of Lafayette, Louisiana was named his replacement. Naturally, I was anxious. Would the new Archbishop be in favor of this?

In January of 1996, Archbishop Roach, Archbishop Flynn and I sat down together and Archbishop Flynn said that he would be very happy to help me. He said, "When I was in Louisiana, the Diocese next door had a married priest and from everything I heard it has worked out quite well." In the spring of 1996 the dossier was sent to the Congregation for the Doctrine of the Faith. Upon receiving the file they responded that it normally took three years before the case would be considered. However, because I had done significant theology work already, they said they could reduce it to two years.

The next two years were a time of waiting and preparation. Our family had become parishioners at St. Hubert's Church in Chanhassen in 1995. In addition, the rector at St. Paul Seminary had outlined several courses I should take, in the event that I should be accepted into the priesthood. So, I continued taking one

9

course per semester at the seminary, including courses in marriage and family, Canon law, preaching, and dogmatic theology. The spring of 1997 passed by and when the spring of 1998 passed by without word from Rome, I went back to the Archbishop to ask him about my case. In response, a second letter was sent to Prefect for the Congregation for the Doctrine of the Faith, Cardinal Joseph Ratzinger. The letter simply outlined the fact that I had finished all the theological preparation had been actively employed at a Twin Cities' parish, and that our family was actively participating as members of a Catholic parish. They responded in the fall of 1998 that they would take the case up immediately.

I am ordained to the Priesthood

Again, months passed without hearing from them. In the spring of 1999 a parish administrator position became available at St. Hubert's, our home parish. I was invited to apply, was accepted and began there in May of 1999. Not more than eight weeks later I received a phone call from Sister Dominica Brennan at the Chancery. She told me that they had received a letter from Rome and that I should come to see Archbishop Flynn in the morning. I said I would be there. When the bishop calls, you clear your calendar.

Archbishop Flynn told me that he had good news for me, as well as for the Diocese. The letter stated that I could be ordained first to the Diaconate and then to the priesthood under the Pastoral Provision. When Archbishop announced the news at a Presbyteral meeting with all of the Archdiocesan priests in attendance, the news was received with thunderous applause. I found such support reassuring.   ·

The Archdiocese made a media announcement shortly thereafter. One of the chief questions, of course, has been whether this signals a change in the rule of celibacy. Clearly, it does not. This is an exception to the rule requiring celibacy and does not undermine the good work of celibate priests.

We made preparations and in November I was ordained into the Diaconate along with the 4th year seminary class at the St. Paul Seminary chapel. By that time, plans were also underway for ordination. I had asked Archbishop Flynn if, since my ordination was taking place outside ordination for the 4th year class, if he would mind coming to St. Hubert's for the ordination to the priesthood. He said he would be happy to do so.

On December 11, 1999, with 1,500 parishioners and good representation from the presbyterate, I was ordained into the priesthood. I am humbled, honored, and feel tremendously privileged to serve as a Catholic priest. I am so appreciative of all the support I have received from the Archbishop, his staff, the Archdiocese, and my family. This journey has been beyond my imagination.

Before my ordination, Archbishop Flynn had two concerns. One was that I would have the opportunity to fulfill my priestly ministry, and the other that I would be able to draw an adequate living for my family. Since my position at St. Hubert's seemed to meet both concerns the Archdiocese decided that I should remain there. Therefore, I have continued to serve as parish administrator at St. Hubert's, while in addition carrying out sacramental duties.

While my assignment is a busy one, I have been able to balance work and family in a way I often did not do as a Lutheran pastor. In Church ministry, it's easy to say that because it is the Lord's work it is more important than anything else is. Archbishop Flynn said at my ordination, "You know you are now a priest and part of the fraternity of priests, but your first vocation, because it came first, is that you are married and have a commitment to your spouse and your family." With God's help I have been able to keep that in focus.

Father Larry Blake is assigned to St. Hubert Catholic Community in Chanhassen, Minnesota. His title is priest/administrator. He resides with his wife, three children and their dog, Penny in Victoria. Father Blake enjoys most outdoor activities and working out at the local gym.

From Missouri Synod to Magisterium

Audrey Zech

When I was a young Lutheran girl I wanted to become a Catholic nun. I scárcely knew any Catholics and certainly no nuns; but what I had read in novels and seen in movies and television gave me a vision of a life I wanted to share. The nuns I encountered in this way were selfless, dedicated, and devout, but not without their human weaknesses as well as a sense of fun. They were part of a church and a life that was ancient, vast, and to me, mysterious. I felt drawn to this holy calling.

It seemed clear, however, that the door to this life was closed and locked to me forever, because I was not Catholic and never could be. I was part of the Lutheran Church - Missouri Synod (L.C.M.S.), and even as a child I was taught that while my church was in many ways very close to the Church of Rome, there were certain key points of doctrine on which we were deeply divided, and on these there could be no compromise.

Yet here I am today, a Catholic, having been received into full communion with the Church of Rome on April 3, 1999. I thank God every day for the privilege of being a Catholic. It is a blessing beyond compare, a deep joy, a chest filled with treasures too vast to enumerate. But how did I get here? I can only say it was divine mercy. For some reason God chose to call me at this particular time to embark upon a venture of discovery and change, a journey with Himself as companion and Himself as goal. Similar to J.R.R. Tolkien's Hobbit, I couldn't plan for this journey because I didn't know I was going, and though I hadn't sought adventures, I suddenly found myself in the middle of them.

Contrary elements found a happy co-existence in me, because despite my yearning to be a Catholic nun, I was, in reality, a hard-core Lutheran. Reformation Day was special to me, and I thrilled when joining the congregation in belting out lusty renditions of "A Mighty Fortress." I admired Martin Luther for standing up for what he believed, despite the danger. He was a hero; he was my hero. "Thank God," I thought, "for Martin Luther, who brought truth to light. Thank God that I am a Lutheran."

The small town near our family farm had five churches, all Protestant. The church my family attended was a big, old, beautiful structure, with lovely tall stained glass windows and a high white and gold altar that incorporated a life-size statue of Jesus. Some non-members referred to this church as "the Catholic church".

I spent grades four through eight in Lutheran parochial school, which I consider a great blessing. In daily worship we became familiar with many hymns, and in our impromptu choirs I learned to sing harmony. We were taught Bible history and the basics of the Christian faith, and in confirmation class, while studying Luther's *Small Catechism*, we learned the importance of doctrine and memorized a great many Bible verses. After confirmation and eighth-grade graduation, I moved on through the "Walther League" years of high school, and then through college, finishing with a B.A. in English.

A crisis in the synod

When I was in my early twenties, the crisis in the Missouri Synod was coming to a head. While the two sides in the conflict would disagree over its cause and content, there was a high-intensity focus on biblical interpretation, especially the use of the historical-critical method. Authority was a key issue. Who has the right to determine what Scripture says and what the church is to believe and teach? Can "truth" be decided by majority vote? Can clergy be required to subscribe to documents other than the historic Lutheran confessional writings? For those unfamiliar with the history of that crisis, I suggest reading *No Room In the Brotherhood* by Frederick W. Danker.[1]

In January of 1974 the majority of students and faculty of Concordia Seminary in St. Louis walked out and started a new seminary, Concordia-Seminary-in-exile, known as Seminex. The parish of which I was then a member became informed about the situation and took a supportive stand on behalf of the Seminex students and faculty. In reading the various literature about the crisis, I wanted to know more about the topics under discussion, and to understand better what was at stake. I bought a copy of *The Book of Concord*, the compilation of Lutheran confessional documents binding on all ordained Lutheran clergy, and read it cover to cover. My conviction at the end was that the central and overarching theme of these writings is justification by faith.

Meanwhile, I became involved in the national support group for Seminex, called the Evangelical Lutherans in Mission (E.L.I.M.). As the breach between the L.C.M.S. and the Seminex supporters widened without hopeful signs of reconciliation, E.L.I.M. voted to create synods for those parishes who chose to join, and the synods would be connected by an "umbrella organization," the Association of Evangelical Lutheran Churches (A.E.L.C.). These entities would support Seminex and call its graduates to ministry. I was full of enthusiasm for this cause, and served as officer and board member of our local conference when the A.E.L.C. formed in the Twin Cities (St. Paul/Minneapolis) metropolitan area.

---

[1] Clayton Publishing House, Inc.: St. Louis, 1977.

I become a pastor

As I grew more acquainted with the Seminex professors through their writings on current church events, and by reading the accounts of how they risked everything to be true to their beliefs, I wanted to know them personally, to study under them, and, ideally, to emulate their faithful and courageous stance. This led to my enrolling in the Master of Divinity program at Seminex in St. Louis in 1979 in order to become a pastor. There I spent some of the best years of my life.

In worship class we studied the history of the liturgy, which meant, of course, a close look at Catholic liturgical theology and practice. I delighted in making the acquaintance of terms such as *baldachino* and "humeral veil". In many ways the seminary's worship life incorporated so-called "Catholic" elements. Daily noon Eucharist was referred to informally by some as "Mass", and the Lutheran calendar of saints was observed at chapel, sometimes with special festivities. Most major services were held at the Episcopal Cathedral downtown, Christ Church Cathedral, which lent itself to our elaborate liturgies, with deacon and subdeacon in dalmatic and tunicle to match the celebrant, processions and incense, bowings and crossings, kissing of the Book, and a profound reverence for the Sacrament being celebrated.

My interest in and love for the Liturgy led to my serving at these occasions in the various roles of acolyte, torchbearer, crucifer, and thurifer. As a close friend of the sacristans I was privileged to assist behind the scenes in all aspects of the service. I was also one of those who regularly served as assisting minister at our daily noon Eucharist in chapel. Once, while visiting a Lutheran parish out East, I stood in as acolyte and had the privilege (a rare one in Lutheran churches) of ringing the bell at the Consecration. All of this drew my heart very close to the Catholic liturgical heritage.

Meanwhile, in my Confessions and Luther Studies classes I was being strengthened in my already firm conviction of the "rightness" of Lutheran doctrine. Furthermore, I loved the Lutheran heritage and I loved Martin Luther. I read his writings for my own enjoyment. I resonated with his struggles to find a gracious God. Luther spoke my language, and his pastoral writings were of great help and comfort to me. When I became a pastor, Luther became my pastor.

I graduated from Seminex in 1983, and because my name was at the end of the alphabet, I was literally the last person to receive the M.Div. from Seminex in St. Louis, before it "deployed" to three other seminaries. Eventually I was ordained in the A.E.L.C., where I served a term call doing the things I liked best.

Doctrinal changes lead me elsewhere

When three Lutheran church bodies, the Lutheran Church in America (L.C.A.), the American Lutheran Church (A.L.C.), and the A.E.L.C. merged in

1987, I was grandfathered in as a clergyperson in the new church body, the E.L.C.A. (Evangelical Lutheran Church in America). On leave from call, eventually I applied for a study leave and began brushing up on languages, ancient and modern, in preparation for post-graduate work. I was accepted by the school of my choice for Ph.D. studies in Bible and Semitics, but family concerns and a lack of financial aid for first year candidates at that school caused me to set that plan aside for the time being. Meanwhile, things were happening (or not happening) in the E.L.C.A. that caused me no little concern. I was hearing frequent references to the counter-cultural nature of Christianity; yet it seemed to me that the E.L.C.A., particularly on certain issues, was veering more and more toward the secular mainstream, where there is little objective truth (and that little is not often articulated), and where personal "rights" and individual preferences tend to overshadow any considerations of objective truth.

On the ecumenical front, it looked to me as though Lutheran doctrine was not consistently being given its due in the discussions. What the Reformation churches have been able to affirm mutually about the Lord's Supper did not seem to me sufficient to warrant entering into the intimate relationship of altar and pulpit fellowship that full communion would allow.

Finally, because of issues of both doctrine and morals, I felt I could no longer in good conscience remain in the E.L.C.A. But where could I go? Others were facing the same dilemma, and some spoke of looking into the Orthodox Church, while others leaned toward the Episcopal Church. Still others debated returning to the Missouri Synod. Where could I go?

From Lutheran church friends I had heard about the Eternal Word Television Network, a Catholic satellite network broadcasting throughout the world. In March of 1997, I moved from out-state Minnesota to St. Paul, where I was now able to receive EWTN on a UHF channel. This was the start of a whole new life. It was as water to a thirsting soul and nourishment to the faint. I was seeing devout Catholics talking about their Church and their faith, *happy* to be Catholic. In a strange sort of way, as I watched these programs, I was "being encountered", if you will, in such a way that I can only describe it as being *healed.*

It was here that the doctrinal tide began to turn for me. I was impressed by the pervasiveness of Scripture in what I heard, and there were whole series devoted to Bible study. Who says Catholics don't use the Bible? The Scriptures were opened to me in new ways, answering questions that had puzzled me for years.

Then there were the broadcasts of Daily Mass. Besides the blessing of a reverent liturgy, there was the sermon, every day, a long sermon! Again and again I heard long, wonderful, insightful, Scriptural sermons. Who says Catholics can't preach?

There was a wide range of programming, and I soaked up everything; I could hardly turn off the television. I knew that I wanted to share what all these people had in common: the Catholic Church.

I began to read Catholic theology written *by Catholics*. The more I probed, the more I saw how Catholic teaching is solidly grounded in Scripture and Tradition and fits together like pieces of an intricate puzzle, combining to form a picture of great beauty and coherence. I started reading *The Catechism of the Catholic Church*, which I found to be eloquent in its simplicity and elegant in its language--a truly beautiful work. I read stories of converts: Ronald Knox, Cardinal Newman, G.K. Chesterton, and contemporaries like Thomas Howard and the folk found in *Surprised By Truth* and *Journeys Home*. I read papal encyclicals and the documents of Vatican II. I savored Aidan Nichols and Romano Guardini; I was braced by Cardinal Ratzinger and Hans Urs von Balthasar. I worked through Matthias Scheeben's two-volume *Mariology*. One simply outstanding presentation of Catholicism that I would recommend to everyone is Karl Adam's *The Spirit of Catholicism*.

Drawn by ecclesiology

The areas of doctrine which drew me most strongly to Catholicism were, first of all, its ecclesiology, including necessarily the Papacy and the Magisterium, the Priesthood, and the Communion of Saints; secondly, the Sacraments; and thirdly, the Catholic Church's emphasis on personal holiness. Not only does the Church call her members to holiness, but she aids them in this quest.

One of these aids is devotion to the Blessed Sacrament in the form of Eucharistic adoration outside the Liturgy. For those unfamiliar with this term, it refers to the Consecrated Host, Our Lord Himself, present in the tabernacle, or enthroned in a monstrance which is placed in a church or chapel for adoration. I began to practice this devotion on December 16, 1997, when by a series of circumstances I was led to a church I had never visited in a small town. The series of events that brought me there could seem trite, even silly, but I share Pope John Paul II's conviction that "there are no accidents." I saw a sign outside the church announcing "Adoration--Thursday, All Day". I had no idea what to expect, nor of proper protocol, but I found the chapel and went in. I have to say that I wept the whole hour. I knew I was in the Presence of Christ, and I knew that I was spiritually naked before Him, but that mattered not a whit, or shall I say, rather, it was all to the good. I was there seeking the Lord, and He was seeking me.

In subsequent visits I found myself repeatedly blessed, at times in very surprising ways. Whether at prayer, in meditation, or in pure adoration, it was active engagement with the Incarnate God. Those who go to visit Our Lord are "hosted" by Him in a most gracious manner. While we come to worship and adore Him as God, He may reveal Himself also as Compassionate Friend, as Beloved Elder Brother. He condescends to be present there with us, and I give thanks when I can be there with Him.

Regarding the Eucharist, accepting the doctrine of Transubstantiation was not a problem for me. I suppose I was a consubstantiationist, believing that Christ was truly present though the bread was still bread and the wine remained wine. However, I always believed that the Real Presence stayed with the bread and wine, so that proper handling of the elements during and *after* Communion was of the essence. My seminary experience was one of great reverence for the elements and for reverent treatment in cleansing the sacred vessels and linens, which was a good bridge to Catholic doctrine and practice.

Finally, in June of 1998, I knew I had to break with Lutheranism, and on Father's Day I began visiting Catholic churches for Sunday Mass. That first Sunday, as I knelt in the pew during Communion, I longed with all my heart to be able to receive Our Lord with the others. But as the people around me returned to their pews, I became aware of a sense of Our Lord's Presence, not only spiritually, but physically, in the people around me. I was surrounded by Our Lord's Holy Presence!

On the following Sundays I attended a different Catholic church each week, and then returned to some for a second look. I heard some good sermons, although as a former Missouri Synod person they were all far too brief for my taste. Some liturgies were more elaborate than others, though the ones I attended generally used the basic form from the hymnal, easy to follow because it was so similar to the Lutheran liturgy to which I was accustomed.

By what some would call a coincidence but I would again call God's guiding hand, I learned of a church in downtown St. Paul that had been given a good report by an acquaintance who had attended. It was the Church of St. Louis, King of France. I did not go there immediately, but the first Sunday in August I thought I would give it a try. The interior had been newly renovated and was immaculate in white, blue and gold. It had marvelous stained glass, lovely statues, and a high white marble altar. Although spacious, it had a feeling of intimacy. There was a new, elegant pipe organ and fine music. The congregation participated in the singing to an impressive degree. The altar boys, while very young, were well-trained and reverent. And clouds of incense! Yet the vital thing to me was the reverent way in which the priest celebrated the Mass. *That* is what gave validity to all the rest.

It was the custom at that parish for the priest to greet the people after Mass. The priest that day was the pastor, Fr. Paul F. Morrissey, S.M., who greeted me most cordially and kindly. I felt welcomed and knew that I would return, because my search was ended: This place truly felt like home.

17

In September I met with Fr. Morrissey to discuss the possibility of my entering the Catholic Church. Because doctrine is of such importance to me, I hastened to add that in spite of my experience of being drawn to the Church, I had serious reservations about being able to join.

In order for me to pursue in depth the matters of concern to me and in light of my seminary training, we felt that rather than follow the pattern of RCIA I would benefit more by a one-on-one tutorial. Father arranged for me to meet with Joseph Michalak, who at that time was the parish's lay theologian and an adjunct professor at the University of St. Thomas in St. Paul. We met bi-weekly for two-and-a-half-hour sessions. Joe's excellent grasp of Catholic theology enabled him to get quickly to the heart of my concerns and explain things to me in a helpful way. If anyone had happened to pass the door of his office during our talks, they might have heard me exclaim, "But that's heresy!" However, as I came to understand the thought behind certain terms, phrases, and dogmas, I came to see them, not as heresy, but as reasonable truths, whose coherence exuded, I might even say, a certain beauty. In short, it all fit.

Catholicism as a whole

As we talked and as I probed more deeply into various matters, I saw that certain teachings that cause problems for those outside the Catholic faith do so mainly because they are looked at in isolation and at face value. This way of looking at doctrine may work for Protestant teaching but it cannot for Catholicism. For one thing, any Catholic teaching never stands alone. You cannot say "Immaculate Conception--take it or leave it." Each doctrine has its own place, but within the whole realm of Catholic teaching, and each teaching has lines of connection to other doctrines that are connected to yet others. So you cannot take Purgatory apart from the Communion of Saints, and you cannot separate the Communion of Saints from Christ and His Church. You cannot take the Immaculate Conception apart from the Virgin Birth nor from the Incarnation nor the Two Natures in Christ. This is so with every single part of Catholic doctrine: Each is like a piece of a vast puzzle, with its own specific place in which only that piece will fit, each interlocking with the next, to make one inclusive and beautiful picture.

Another factor in Catholicism is the depth of each doctrine, a depth often hidden. I found this to be true in my probing, and specifically, for example, in Marian dogmas. I was trying to acquaint myself with them but didn't understand how the Church arrived at certain claims. I went to a library and checked out Matthias Scheeben's *Mariology* and plunged in. It became clear to me that Tradition is a great treasure and foundation of Catholic teaching. I had had no difficulty accepting the value of Tradition along with Scripture, but now I was seeing its activity in a new light. As I read Scheeben's work, I said to myself,

18

"Just look at the depth and detail of thought that has gone into the formation of these dogmas. They didn't emerge full-grown like Venus from the sea. People thought and debated and lived with and worked over and worshipped with these ideas through the centuries, and because of how they fit with the other doctrines, they complete the picture." It is therefore legitimate for a Catholic to assent to "all the truths which the Holy Catholic Church teaches," knowing that God has been working by the Holy Spirit through the teaching office of His Church to bring to light the fullness of Truth.

Catholic piety was another factor that drew me to the Church. One September day in 1998 I went to a local Catholic Church to see an exhibit of a replica of the Shroud of Turin. It was tastefully done, with a series of pictures and diagrams explaining the marks on the Shroud and various historical backgrounds on Roman methods of flogging and crucifixion. Also, there was a life-sized crucifix, to show in particular the position of Christ's arms, and the many wounds from the flogging and the Crown of Thorns, and thus the direction the flow of blood would take that would explain the stains on the Shroud.

A kneeler had been placed in front of this crucifix, which I didn't really notice at first. My Protestant mind had seen the crucifix as simply part of the exhibit. It was when I saw people going over to it and kneeling in prayer that I caught on. At first I felt rather stunned to see people going up and kneeling to pray, so obviously, in front of everyone. I thought, "Only a Catholic could do that." But these people were entirely unselfconscious about it. I began to realize that for them a crucifix was first and foremost an object of devotion, and that one's first response had to be the acknowledgement of Our Lord depicted there.

This kind of unselfconscious devotion is one of the beauties of Catholic piety. A person may enter a church at any time of the day to pray without being thought strange; they may weep, murmur, or whisper their prayers; they may bow or genuflect or make any gestures of devotion; they may gaze raptly at the Crucifix or Tabernacle or pore over a prayer book, and no one looks askance.

In the course of my discussions with my tutor, Joe Michalak, we looked at the Lutheran-Catholic Joint Declaration on Justification. I came away with the sense that the differences are often matters of focus and emphasis. For Lutherans, justification focuses on forgiveness of sins, while for Catholics it is more a matter of relationship. The Lutheran forensic model has God declaring the sinner righteous by imputing to him the merits of Christ; while for Catholics, by the merits of Christ the sinner actually is made righteous. The righteous God wants to be more than an impartial judge to us; He wants an intimate personal relationship. He doesn't just send us on our way out of the courtroom cleared of all charges against us. Rather, He takes us home with Him for dinner, and works to build and strengthen the bond between us, that it may continue and flourish.

Now certainly Lutheran theology includes a relationship of love and acceptance by God of the sinner, but it has seemed to me that the primary focus in speaking of justification has been on the act and means of God's forgiving our sins and not on the ensuing relationship. I realize that I am oversimplifying here, but I'm trying to describe a difference in emphasis between the Lutheran and Catholic approaches. It seems to me that the Catholic emphasis is the more accurate one, and, moreover, the Catholic synthesis takes up the Lutheran concerns as well.

As I debated within myself about becoming one with the Church of Rome, my thoughts echoed the concern of Cardinal Newman: If I was wrong the first time, might I not be wrong again? Also, I was troubled by the thought that I would be acting contrary to what I had been taught by all my Lutheran mentors, especially my seminary faculty, whom I held in profound respect. These were men (and one woman) of great faith, keen intellect, and delightful wit, whom I admired, trusted, and loved. How could I think that I could know better, that I could turn away from much of what they had taught me and embrace Rome? This was a difficult struggle. I knew that I could not "know better" than they. All I knew, finally, was that for whatever reason, God had taken hold of me and showed me the Catholic faith in ways that convinced me that the Catholic Church was the fullest expression of His Church. Having reached that point I had no choice but to seek entrance.

My personal conversion

In the course of my Catholic journey, I never saw my coming into the Church as a simple change of denominations. I felt all along as if I was *being converted*, being changed from the "Old Adam," or Eve, as it were, into a new person. I felt as if I were living in another dimension. There was a strong sense of God's leading me throughout. I have never prayed so often, so long, so fervently, as I have throughout this journey: For I knew that whatever my will might desire, it would be as dust and ashes unless it was God's will also.

To speak of conversion in one's life is a very personal sort of thing, and I include the following occurrence because it helps me to explain my thoughts on a certain aspect of Catholic theology. When people speak of a conversion experience, they may be referring to a specific moment in time when something changed for them in a sudden and decisive way. Others may experience a gradual change that brings its own profound and lasting effects. I would say that for me it was both. At a point within a two-year conversion period, I experienced a moment that has had tremendous consequences for me.

For whatever reason, all my life I had found it all but impossible to believe that God loved me, except in a general sort of way, as He might love a rock or a squirrel or a tree, or anything He had made; but only on rare occasions could I feel or believe that He loved me for myself. I can't say that this is a side effect of Lutheranism, because certainly plenty of other Lutherans feel secure in God's love, and speak confidently of it to others. I'm thankful to say that I was able to believe in God's love for others and to declare it to them, but I rarely felt that that love included me. My salvation depended, then, not on God's love working on my behalf, but rather on His being faithful to the new covenant He had made in Christ. He was *obliged*, in effect, to forgive me and save me, because He had made this covenant and was legally bound to live up to His own decree. He might save me, but that didn't mean He loved me. He was simply fulfilling His own law of justice.

God works in His own mysterious way and time, with a power that could shatter stone, yet so tender that it is like a caress. I was sitting by the window on a June evening in 1998 reading a mailing from EWTN. It spoke of the indelible seal of the Holy Spirit imprinted upon us in Holy Baptism, and of God adopting us as His sons and daughters, with the right to call Him Father. How many times throughout my life had I heard those teachings? Yet that evening I heard them as never before. I can only think of it as a revelation. Suddenly I *knew*, knew for a fact and believed in my heart, that God loved me, He had created me as me and He had chosen me to be His own adopted daughter--because He loved me, just as I was. The Creator of the starry night--the God Who holds the planets in their courses--who rules the winds and makes the earth bear fruit--this God wanted me so close to Him that He made me a part of His family. Words cannot express my feelings then or now about this intensely personal realization.

I don't know why this moment of conversion was placed within my larger journey into the Catholic Church, but it has been a great blessing in some specific ways as well as in the overall grace that it bestowed. This sense of God's love has given me a better understanding of the teaching on divinization. That very word--divinization--always had sounded unredeemably heretical. Only God could be divine; and yet, as I learned to know of God's intense love for us, His desire to have us know Him and draw near to Him, it began to take shape in a new way. For better or worse we become like those with whom we spend our time. The more time we spend with God, the better we are able to grow into His likeness, the more we are conformed to the image of Christ. The more we focus our eyes on God, the deeper we enter into relationship with Him. The deeper and closer the relationship, the more we find our will conforming itself to His. Surely that is one of the attributes of the Holy Trinity: that the Three Persons are united in Their will. The more that our will is drawn into God's will, the closer we share in His divine life.

I continued to meet with Joe Michalak for tutorial sessions during the autumn of 1998 and into the winter, and I met again with Father Morrissey for some helpful discussions. We talked of my being received into the Church at

Easter. He suggested that during Lent I make a week-long retreat, focusing on conversion. This I did, at New Melleray Abbey in Peosta, Iowa. By focusing on conversion, with the Lenten daily readings echoing and reechoing the theme, "Repent, change, turn to God," my interior experience was one that I can only describe as "profound." Many wonderful and unexpected blessings were granted to me during my stay at the abbey. Perhaps the greatest blessing of all was Fr. Bernard, a priest at the abbey, who patiently and kindly listened to what may have been the world's longest first confession.

Holy Week that year, 1999, had unusual significance for me as the time drew near to be received into the Church. At the Easter Vigil on April 3, I joined several others in being received into the Church, being confirmed, and making my First Holy Communion. The vigil itself, which is always like a time of heaven on earth, was especially so that night, in its holy beauty, mystery, and power. And now, at last, I was a Catholic! Apart from my baptism, this was truly the most exciting and wonderful thing that had happened to me in my entire life. I deemed it the greatest privilege to be received into full communion with Rome.

Why did God call me into the Catholic Church? He may and certainly does invite conversions in various ways, in various people, acting powerfully in their lives to fulfill His purposes in a particular way and time. As for me, He called me to conversion and into the Catholic Church in all her fullness and splendor of truth. Here I find unexpected joys and blessings, far greater than I could have imagined. I mentioned earlier the doctrines that drew me most strongly to the Catholic Church. Others have written of them far better than I could hope to do, so I refer you to their works. However, I would like to share some thoughts.

At one point in my journey I wrote in my journal that, "I feel a part of something so vast yet so intimate." This is how I see the Communion of Saints. One evening, while I was still a Catholic-wanna-be, I had gone to an adoration chapel. As I entered the building a woman was on her way out, and as she passed me she said, "Would you please pray for my intention?" I was greatly pleased and moved by this request. It struck me how closely we are related to one another in the Body of-Christ. If one member suffers the whole Body shares, literally, in that suffering; and as Christ's Mystical Body, together we share in the sufferings of Christ. Even so, one person's sin weakens the Body, while another's charity builds it up. We dare not think that we stand or act alone. This is a great responsibility, but also a great comfort. When we are weak, we can draw on the strength of the rest of the Body, and that includes not only those members on earth but also those in heaven interceding for us as well.

Understanding Mary

One area that was slow in developing for me was Marian devotion. Although I had played the role of Mary in a country school pageant in second grade (with a mantle made of an old sheet dyed a lovely shade of blue), she never seemed like a real person to me. Nevertheless, she held a certain attraction for me, and I bought some Marian icons that I hung where I could look at them often.

Our Lutheran churches gave Mary the limelight for the Annunciation, a prominent role at the Nativity (It would be difficult not to!), and a lesser role on the other occasions where she appears in the New Testament. One had the sense that some of Jesus' own words to her and about her were meant to show her relative unimportance.

When I entered the "active phase" of my Catholic journey, I was open to Mary and Marian devotion, and in fact desired it for myself. I had noted that all the saints I'd read about seemed to share a great devotion to the Blessed Virgin. They had imitated her in giving themselves completely into God's service, entrusting their lives to His will and purpose. It seemed that the combination of the saints' holiness and their devotion to Mary could not be mere coincidence.

I began to read books on Marian piety and doctrine. I really didn't have much difficulty with the doctrine. What surprised me was the pervasiveness of her presence in Scripture, especially the Old Testament. Specific references to Mary in the New Testament are few, but now I was discovering her in typology in both the Old and New Testaments. She was the Second Eve, the Ark of the New Covenant, the Woman Clothed with the Sun. Why had I never seen this before? It was like a picture being shaken up in a snow-globe and all the pieces floating down and landing perfectly in place. It all fit, and it brought out meanings in the texts in remarkable ways.

Besides this kind of reading and study, I was memorizing Marian prayers and hymns, which I used in my own devotions. However, Mary still didn't seem like a living presence. After I had been a Catholic for over a year, I decided that the only way to get to know a person was to spend time with her and talk with her, so I began saying a decade of the Rosary every morning. I used books of meditations for the Mysteries and took my time with it. I learned for myself what every other Rosary-praying person already knows: There is an inexhaustible depth to the meaning of the Mysteries of the Rosary.

Furthermore, I discovered the reality of what I had often heard that the Rosary brings us closer to Christ. Not only was I getting acquainted with Our Lady; I was seeing Our Lord in ways I had never really pondered before. I was drawn into His Passion, suffering with Him; but I found myself also among the mockers and spitters, the scourgers and nailers, the weeping women and the disciples sleeping in the Garden.

As I walked with Our Lord's Mother through the key events of His life, she became more and more real to me, both as an historical person and as a heavenly intercessor. I could see that if one desires to become another Christ (alter Christus), one can do no better than to imitate Mary. She modeled in herself Our

Lord's life of perfect self-emptying, of giving herself body and soul into the Father's holy service, uniting her will with His. Anyone who has ever given up anything out of love for another knows that the will involved in that act is not passive. Self-giving is an active service, and Mary, like Our Lord, gave her all in love.

Perhaps chief among the treasures of the Church are the Sacraments, whose scope encompasses the ordinary life of a Christian. The Sacrament of Holy Orders is the link between Christ's authority and how it is exercised in the Church, confirming Christ's own presence and activity in the Sacraments. What could be a greater, more undeserved privilege and a more sobering responsibility than to stand *in persona Christi* to the people under one's charge?

The value of confession

As a Lutheran, I had often wished that our churches would practice sacramental confession. However, the Lutheran churches and pastors who offer this sacrament are few and far between. Yet in his *Large Catechism*, Martin Luther gave "A Brief Exhortation to Confession," in which he spoke of it as a healing medicine, precious as gold. He was rightly upset over the abuse of this sacrament, but he strongly urged its practice, saying that a Christian should be happy to run a hundred miles to go to confession.

The healing power of this Sacrament is incalculably great. While one may confess one's sins directly to God, and should, there is only one's subjective awareness as to whether one is heard, accepted, and forgiven. If faith is weak or emotions tend toward guilt, one is left trying to muster up a sense of God's mercy. Scripture passages treating of God's grace and forgiveness can be helpful, but still they are self-applied.

In Sacramental Reconciliation there is a real and living presence so close we could reach out and touch it in the person of the priest. There is an ear that hears our confession. There is a mouth that speaks words of counsel and comfort. There is a person who accepts us. When burdened by sorrow, guilt, and shame, we hear the Gospel proclaimed and the Absolution pronounced with the authority of Christ Himself. Whatever our subjective emotions, we can go away in the knowledge that our sins are forgiven; the Sacrament is efficacious. What better healing, what better renewal, could possibly be obtained for the Christian, to restore him to God, to comfort his soul, and to aid him in amendment of life and growth in holiness?

That Christ makes Himself so available to us in the Sacraments is a marvelous thing. That Our Lord should desire intimate fellowship, even union with us, is one marvel; how He brings it about is yet another. Here we find Catholic sacramental theology in full splendor, with visible earthly elements playing a vital role in conveying heavenly goods.

If the Sacrament were only a spiritual union or communion, we would be left wondering if we were properly disposed at the time and really were receptive beneficiaries of Christ's Presence. In the Catholic Eucharist we need not wonder. We received Him, and we know it, because we physically received Him into our very mouths and bodies. How we respond may leave something, even much, to be desired; but there can be no doubt *that* we did indeed receive Our Lord. As we contemplate His physical presence in us, we apprehend the spiritual union He desires, a union so intimate and pervasive that we cannot separate ourselves from Him.

One thing I've noticed coming into the Catholic Church is that God somehow seems "bigger" and "more". I might compare it to viewing an old, old painting that has been restored. The grime of centuries has been removed, revealing the original colors as bright and rich. I'm seeing details that were formerly obscured. Now I see God more glorious and transcendent, yet more concerned with the details of human life. He is more majestic and powerful, yet more condescending. His wrath is fiercer, His mercy more abundant. His judgment is stricter yet His grace is richer. His expectations of us are higher, but the greater is His patience with our human frailties. His love for us is deeper and more tender; and His desire to draw us to Himself makes Him ever more ardent to seek us and unite us to Himself.

People might wonder how a woman could give up the status of ordained minister to enter a Church where that is not an option. They don't understand that my so-called loss is as nothing compared to what I gain. What I had before was good; what I have now is beyond compare.

Audrey Zech is currently on the staff at Luther Seminary Bookstore in St. Paul, Minnesota. Her steady diet of nutritional theological reading is supplemented by occasional lighter fare in the form of classic fiction series such as Horatio Hornblower and the Laura Ingalls Wilder books. Audrey also enjoys playing with foreign languages, swimming (in a lake, of course), and collecting rocks.

Are You a Religious Person?

Anthony L. Gerring

In June of 1991, that simple five-word question prompted a reconsideration of my beliefs that six years later led me from the Lutheran Church-Missouri Synod (L.C.M.S.) into the Catholic Church. At the time the question was asked, I had not the slightest hint of where God would lead me and I'm sure that had I known, you probably would not be reading this story. In fact, had anyone told me in 1991 that I would be received into the Catholic Church at the Easter Vigil Mass in 1997, I would have laughed and dismissed the idea as utter nonsense.

I was born in Wyandotte, Michigan in 1966 on the 420th anniversary of Martin Luther's death. When it was time to begin kindergarten, my parents sent me to the same Lutheran elementary school in Wyandotte my father had attended as a boy. My family had a long history at the German Lutheran church in Wyandotte going back to about 1920. The Gerrings were German Lutherans from Hungary who had immigrated to Ohio just after the turn of the century and later moved to Wyandotte seeking work. My paternal grandmother's parents were Donauschwaben German Catholics from Slawonia and the Banat. They too had immigrated to the USA just after the turn of the century, first going to St. Louis and then eventually settling in Wyandotte. In 1921, they left the Catholic Church because a priest did not visit their eldest son who was suffering from typhoid fever and was near death. As a result, a neighbor lady took my great-grandmother to see her Lutheran pastor who offered to pray for the boy. When the illness passed, much to their surprise, my great-grandfather and his family converted to Lutheranism and he began sending his children to the Lutheran school.

From the earliest days of my elementary education, I was taught the Old Testament stories of the patriarchs, kings and prophets and the New Testament stories of Jesus, the Apostles and the early Christians. The Bible was always central to our studies, as was Martin Luther, the monk who challenged the Catholic Church with his Ninety-five Theses in Wittenberg on October 31, 1517, igniting what Lutherans and other Protestants call the Reformation. As members of L.C.M.S., we also learned about Rev. Carl F. W. Walther and the nineteenth-century German Lutherans who organized the Synod in Missouri. And we were told that all Evangelical Lutherans in agreement with our Synod were Christ's true, visible church on earth.

From the time I began kindergarten, my family was always involved in our church. My father served on various boards and my mother volunteered in the hot lunch program at our school. My siblings and I went to Sunday school and vacation Bible school and we had several perfect attendance awards over the years. Around sixth grade or so, I became an acolyte and was very honored to serve at Sunday worship. We also participated in many other activities and social events, including Christmas pageants, school picnics, field trips, special worship services during Advent and Lent and one of my favorites, potluck dinners.

One of the highlights of the school year was the annual Reformation Day celebration, held on or near October 31st. In order to commemorate the day in 1517 when Martin Luther posted his Ninety-five Theses, all the Lutheran elementary schools in our area gathered together for a joint worship service. Each year, the service was held at a different church and I always looked forward to visiting another church and seeing all the kids. The highlight of our worship occurred when we all joined together to sing Luther's hymn "A Mighty Fortress is Our God." Our triumphant singing always made me proud to be a Lutheran.

After graduating from eighth grade in 1980, my parents sent me to a Lutheran high school in Detroit. In addition to the college-oriented academic subjects necessary for graduation, the school also required all students to take four years of religion courses. The classes covered such topics as the Old and New Testaments, church history, comparative religion, and the beliefs of Lutheranism and the L.C.M.S. Most of our religious training took place in religion class or in our chapel services that were held in the school gym.

Following the alternative crowd

During my first two years in high school, I had not really participated in extra-curricular activities at the school. However, when I started my junior year, I got involved in the school band, the drama club, and cross-country running. I also started attending the dances held at our school and soon became a fan of musical groups such as the B52's, Duran Duran, Billy Idol, Adam Ant, and U2. By the end of my senior year, I had collected numerous record albums of other "alternative" groups. On the day before my high school graduation in June 1984, I bleached the top of my hair to a light blond color. The next day, I went to my graduation in black leather pants with my now blond hair ratted and sticking out everywhere. A few of my classmates thought it was weird while a few others who were heading in the same direction thought it was great.

Throughout the summer of 1984, I continued to become more interested in the alternative music scene. I met a few other like-minded people at a local dance hall, bought more of the music and dressed a little more obnoxiously. When I began attending college in the fall, I began frequenting many of the alternatives, late nightclubs in the Detroit area. My adventures often kept me out until three or four o'clock in the morning, especially on the weekend. Of course, neither school nor church was my highest priority at the time.

In November 1984, I met my future wife, Karen, while standing in line to buy tickets to see U2 at the Fox Theatre in Detroit. Karen and her sister Diane had attended a nearby Catholic high school. The following month, we met at the concert and after the show met Bono and other members of the band and got their autographs and a few photos together.

Over the next few years, I continued taking classes, working and going to various clubs in Detroit and though my church attendance was not perfect, I had not completely stopped attending. As my interest in alternative music grew, so did my record collection that soon amounted to over several hundred albums. Much of the music contradicted my beliefs at the time, though I tried to dismiss the contradictions with the thought that it was just entertainment. At the same time, my appearance had gone from bad to worse. Soon, I had a black leather jacket with a skull painted in the back, my hair was partly shaved and partly ratted, and I wore black leather combat boots everywhere I went.

Karen and Diane and I became closer friends and we often went to concerts together or hung out at the local clubs. However, in the summer of 1987, a friend of ours began experimenting with cocaine. Since we refused to have anything to do with drugs, we quickly had a falling out over the issue. About the same time, I began noticing some changes in the alternative music scene, including some flirtation with neo-Nazism and even occultism. Besides, I also found myself growing tired of the whole late night music scene. The smoke filled halls were increasingly bothering me and the loud music gave me headaches and left my ears ringing for hours after leaving. As a result, I began intentionally distancing myself from some of my previous acquaintances and began taking my studies more seriously.

Luther's attitude toward Jews troubles me

The following spring, I signed up for a history class on the Reformation. On the first day of class, our professor explained the requirements and suggested a few topics for the final paper. Among the topics she suggested was Martin Luther's attitude toward the Jews. The moment I heard the name Martin Luther, I knew what my topic would be. While I had studied his life in high school, this seemed a good way to learn more about my boyhood hero. However, as I began doing the necessary research and read what Luther actually wrote about the Jews, his comments began to trouble me.

In 1523, just six years after posting his Ninety-five Theses, Luther wrote a pamphlet entitled *That Jesus Christ Was Born A Jew* in which he denounced the way the Jews had been previously treated and he asked his fellow Christians to begin showing them love. Not only was he convinced that this message would win the Jews over to Lutheranism, but he hoped that they would join him in his attack on the Catholic Church. However, over the next ten years Luther failed to

28

win the Jews to his side and his disappointment over this failure eventually turned into bitter anger against the Jewish people.

Despite what he had previously written, by 1543, Martin Luther's anger toward the Jews prompted him to begin writing tracts attacking them. In his first, called *On the Jews and Their Lies*, he repeated all the same stories he had denounced twenty years earlier. He also warned that Lutherans who continued to tolerate or protect the Jews would participate in their "abominations" before God. Finally, he closed by urging that their synagogues and schools be burned, their houses similarly destroyed, their prayer books and Talmuds be taken away, that Rabbis be forbidden to teach on peril of their lives, that they be denied safe-conduct passes for traveling, and that all their money and gold be confiscated. He did urge Lutheran rulers to give the Jews an opportunity to convert. However, if they refused, then he believed that the civil rulers should "drive them out like mad dogs." Within the same year, Luther issued two additional tracts on the same topic.

Clearly, Luther's writings against the Jews violated Christ's teaching to "love your neighbor as yourself." Moreover, his writings prompted me to question the esteem with which I held Luther. How could it be that the man God had chosen to rediscover the pure Gospel after having been obscured for so many centuries could become so hateful? At the time, I didn't think about it too deeply and merely chalked it up to sin. After all, Luther had written these statements many years after having overcome what I thought were the false teachings of the Catholic Church and the Pope. What did it really matter, I thought? Many godly men have fallen into sin and Luther was certainly no different. As I finished my paper, I concluded with the thought that it was "sad to know that the great reformer, Martin Luther, could not show love to the Jewish people."

In 1990, I finally graduated with a liberal arts degree. Later that fall, I began taking graduate classes at another local university. However, by the following June, I had decided to seek a full-time job and responded to a newspaper advertisement for a company in Detroit. A few weeks later, I went for an interview and was subsequently offered a job. On my first day in to work, someone asked me rather innocently, "Are you a religious person?" The question caught me by surprise. Was I religious? My first thought was "Of course, I'm a Lutheran." As I thought about it, however, I had to honestly admit that I had not been very serious about being a Lutheran during the last few years. I never really did answer the question, though it bothered me for the next few days. The more I thought about it the more I realized that I wanted or perhaps needed to become more serious about practicing my faith.

Hooked on Kresta

Around the same time, Karen's sister, Diane, mentioned that her pastor had accepted a job working for a local Evangelical radio station as a talk show host. A few years earlier, Diane had begun attending an independent Evangelical church and had been encouraging her sister, Karen, who I had been dating, to become more serious about living her own faith. So, I began tuning in my radio at work to listen to Al Kresta on the local Christian radio station. Kresta hosted a talk show called "Talk from the Heart" which aired on Monday through Friday from 1 to 4 p.m. During that time, he interviewed Christians and non-Christians alike about everything imaginable and he did so from an explicitly Christian perspective. Over the next several years, I tuned in almost daily to hear some of the brightest Christians in the country talk about the Bible, evangelization, history, politics, economics, and some of the most controversial issues of our day. Soon, I found myself searching local bookstores for a few of the authors or book titles mentioned on the radio. Since I had studied history in college, I was especially interested in the historical development of secularism and materialism and the loss of faith and morals in Western society as well as the history of Christianity in general.

About the same time, Karen and I began talking more seriously about marriage and in the late summer of 1991, we became engaged and set a date for our wedding. Karen's parents wanted her to marry in the Catholic Church and though I wasn't happy about it at the time I agreed and we began taking a marriage preparation course with one of the priests at her parish. When he learned I was Lutheran, the priest mentioned that my pastor could participate in the wedding if I wished. I chuckled a bit at his suggestion and told him that I was Missouri Synod Lutheran and that I doubted my pastor would be willing. At the end of our class, Karen signed the required papers agreeing to raise our children in the Catholic faith. In November 1992, we were finally married and the following month we moved into our first house together. By the spring of the following year, however, I had easily convinced Karen to leave the Catholic Church and become Lutheran.

After visiting various L.C.M.S. churches in our area, we finally settled on a little mission church about thirty minutes from our home that was trying to reach out and evangelize people who would not usually attend church. The congregation met in an old school building and used recorded, contemporary music instead of an organ. Even more unusual for the L.C.M.S., the pastor wore only a sport coat and there were no candles, traditional liturgy or hymn books. After attending for about six months, my wife and I inquired about joining and began taking a new member class. Soon after completing the class we both became involved in various activities in the church.

However, we quickly learned that there was some dissension and disagreement at our new church over the pastor and his methods and the church was somewhat divided. The following year, I was asked to serve on the board of the congregation and though I was somewhat hesitant, I agreed. Soon after, I happened across copies of various Lutheran publications at the church and began reading them whenever the opportunity arose. One newsletter, the *RIM Report*, was published by Renewal in Missouri, a group of L.C.M.S. pastors who viewed the charismatic movement favorably and were pushing for dialogue with Synod officials in St. Louis. Another publication, the *Christian News*, was published by a staunch, independent Lutheran pastor in Missouri who was seeking affiliation with the L.C.M.S. Among other things, the *Christian News* reported on internal issues in the L.C.M.S. as well as the conflicts over charismatics, the church-growth movement, contemporary worship, joint worship with other Lutheran and non-Lutheran groups, open and closed communion, and a host of other issues. It didn't take long to realize that many of the articles in the *Christian News* were directed against the very L.C.M.S. church Karen and I attended.

As a result, I borrowed a copy of the *Book of Concord* from my father and began studying the Lutheran Confessional statements of the sixteenth century. The Confessions are the symbolic books of the Evangelical Lutheran Church and the L.C.M.S. accepts the doctrinal positions of the *Book of Concord* as binding statements of the Lutheran faith. Interestingly, charismatic Lutherans in the L.C.M.S. appealed to the Confessions to defend their understanding of worship as did the more traditional Lutherans who wrote for the *Christian News*. Considering their often contradictory positions, the primary point of their disagreement was authority: who has the authority to state the "correct" Lutheran position on worship? Clearly, since Luther and the other original Lutherans were no more, it was impossible for any contemporary Lutheran body to issue a binding statement on all Lutherans as Martin Luther had done. Moreover, since there was no explicit statement prohibiting "contemporary" worship in the Confessions it was impossible for any one group of Lutherans to issue a binding statement on all other Lutherans as Luther and the sixteenth century Lutherans had done in the Confessions. This situation seemed puzzling, but I didn't think it was troubling enough to warrant further consideration at the time.

The Lutheran church and birth control

Around June 1994, after hearing an interview on the radio about the subject of abortion and eugenics, I began reading a hard-hitting book called *Grand Illusion: The Legacy of Planned Parenthood*, by George Grant. The book was a real eye-opener. Grant obliterated every myth I had unknowingly accepted about birth control, sex education, abortion and population control and revealed the atheistic and anti-Christian origins of these modern movements as well as their

31

interconnections. His book also proved to be a turning point in my spiritual life, though I did not realize the full impact at the time.

The term "birth control" was first coined in 1914 by Margaret Sanger, the founder of the American Birth Control League that later became known as Planned Parenthood, now the largest abortion provider in the United States. Sanger, who had an intense hatred of Christianity, agitated endlessly to gain popular acceptance of birth control because she believed this would undermine Christian morality and the Christian faith. Indeed, as she wrote in her first newspaper, the *Woman Rebel*, in 1914: "Birth control appeals to the advanced radical because it is calculated to undermine the authority of the Christian Churches. I look forward to seeing humanity free someday of the tyranny of Christianity no less than Capitalism." Sanger also denounced marriage and defended assassination and her views were deemed so radical that the U.S. Post Office soon suspended her postal privileges and she was indicted for violating federal anti-obscenity laws. She answered the charges by fleeing to Europe.

Grant also revealed the connection between Margaret Sanger and the Nazi Party. After returning from Europe in late 1915, Sanger began stressing the eugenic benefits of contraception, a tactic recommended by her European associates. In 1920, Sanger wrote a book called *Women and the New Race* in which she urged women to take control of their destiny: "The most merciful thing that the large family does to one of its infant members is to kill it" (p. 67). Four years later, in 1924, she wrote that she stood for the "sterilization of the insane and feeble-minded and the encouragement of this operation upon those afflicted with inherited or transmissible diseases." That same year, on the opposite side of the Atlantic Ocean, a troubled young man wrote similar words in his own book: "No diseased or weak person should be allowed to have children." Adolf Hitler was the man and *Mein Kampf* was his book. Hitler's words were no coincidence. In fact, Sanger was a member of the American Eugenics Society and during the 1920's, Hitler and his followers had become avid readers of American eugenicists, some of whom were published in Sanger's magazine. By the early 1930's, however, the influence had come full circle. In April 1933, *The Birth Control Review*, a magazine published by Margaret Sanger's organization, published an article entitled "Eugenic Sterilization: An Urgent Need," written by Prof. Dr. Ernst Rudin. In addition to his academic posts in Germany, Rudin also served as Hitler's Director of Genetic Sterilization and he founded the Nazi Society for Racial Hygiene.

As Grant unfolded this story page after page, I began to investigate the issue of birth control in light of historic Christian teaching and was somewhat astonished at what I learned. Prior to 1930, when the Anglican Church approved of birth control at its Lambeth Conference, all Christians taught that birth control was immoral and sinful, including every pastor and theologian in the L.C.M.S. In fact, this had been the consistent Lutheran teaching going back to Martin Luther, who believed that birth control was a sinful violation of the natural law ordained by God at the creation of the world. This understanding was not unique to Luther as it had been the universal Christian teaching going back to the first century. Nor was this position ever viewed as contradicting the strong Lutheran stand on *Sola Scriptura*. Rather, Luther and subsequent Lutherans, including Carl F. W. Walther, found support in the Bible for their traditional understanding of the natural law.

In fact, in 1927, Concordia Publishing House, the official publishing arm of the Missouri Synod, published the Concordia Cyclopedia that included this statement in an article on birth control:

"The president of the American Birth Control League is Mrs. Margaret Sanger, and she and several of her associates also edit a periodical in the interest of her theories. -- The Bible very emphatically does not sanction movements of this kind. Ps. 127, 3-5; Ps. 128, 3; 1 Tim. 2, 15; 5, 14, and other passages are in force to-day as they ever were" (p. 84).

Another vocal Missouri Synod critic of artificial birth control was Dr. Walter A. Maier, a professor at the Synod's Concordia Theological Seminary, located in St. Louis, Missouri. Maier also served as the speaker of the popular Lutheran Hour radio program from about 1930 to 1950. In early 1931, he issued a sharply condemning statement in response to an endorsement of the use of contraceptives by married couples issued by the Federal Council of Churches (a forerunner of the present National Council of Churches): "Birth Control, as popularly understood today and involving the use of contraceptives, is one of the most repugnant of modern aberrations, representing a 20th century renewal of pagan bankruptcy."

In 1939, another L.C.M.S. publication, the *Concordia Pulpit*, echoed this same thought. Also published by the Missouri Synod's Concordia Publishing House, the *Concordia Pulpit*, Volume XI, contained sermon outlines for L.C.M.S. pastors for 1940. Included in the volume was a "Series on the Christian Marriage Relation" which contained the following sermon notes:

> "The main purpose of marriage is the propagation of the human race. God Himself clearly stated this purpose: 'Be fruitful,' etc. (Both a command and a blessing bestowed upon the human family.) Also Ps. 128:3,4; 127:3-5. . . . Various sinful methods of birth control. Abortion. ... Second sinful method, the sin of Onan, Gen. 38:9. Very common practice. (Catholic priest in this city told the writer that in the confessional he has learned this to be the most common practice among his people; guilty of the sin of birth control.) Today use

of mechanical devices prevalent. Reasons: greed, career, enjoyment of life, lust, fear of labor and pain in childbirth. Additional proof for our position: voice of conscience; terrible consequences of this unnaturalness, such as impaired health physically and mentally. Some who are not Christians place these practices on the same plane with self-abuse. Bernard Shaw: 'Contraceptive practices are reciprocal masturbation.' St. Augustine: 'Contraception makes a prostitute out of the wife and an adulterer out of the husband.' Companionate marriage has been termed 'licensed prostitution.' Dr. Howard Kelly, perhaps America's ablest gynecologist, neither a Lutheran nor a Catholic, uses these words: 'All meddling with the sexual relation to secure facultative sterility degrades the wife to the level of a prostitute.' The preacher will be chiefly positive in this matter and show forth the blessings of parentage. . . ."

Considering that these strong and clear statements were in complete accord with the teachings of Martin Luther and Carl Walther, I wondered how this teaching had changed in the L.C.M.S. As I studied further, it became clear that because of Luther's stand on "faith alone," the Lutheran Confessions emphasized theological issues rather than Christian morality. For instance, the Book of Concord includes few, if any, statements relating to some of the most pressing moral issues of our day: contraception, abortion, and homosexuality, largely because Luther and subsequent Lutherans lived in a society that was steeped in Catholic moral teaching. Thus, Luther and the early Lutherans took for granted that Christians would hold the traditional positions on such issues and they never really included such issues in their confessional statements. The thought that Christians could somehow accept contraception, abortion or homosexuality would have been utterly implausible for them.

Thus, the Lutheran Confessions did not include statements against contraception, abortion and homosexuality because the traditional teachings were not challenged. The L.C.M.S. did not take an "official" stand in opposition to abortion until 1971, though prior to that time, Missouri Synod pastors and theologians had simply accepted and taught the traditional teaching against abortion as it had been handed down since the time of Luther. Likewise, Lutheran pastors and theologians had consistently issued strong statements against birth control for over four hundred years. However, because there had never been an "official" Lutheran statement on contraception, most L.C.M.S. pastors and theologians began to change their views on the issue when more "progressive" ideas started to become more widely accepted in American culture during the 1940s and '50s. In addition, one man in particular helped push for the acceptance of birth control in the L.C.M.S., Alfred M. Rehwinkel, a professor of ethics and church history at Concordia Theological Seminary in St. Louis.

In the early 1940's, Rehwinkel began critiquing the traditional Lutheran stand against birth control, a position he advanced more vocally over the next twenty years. As a result, the previous condemnations of contraception that had appeared in various L.C.M.S. publications and church sermons and academic lectures began to fall silent and many pastors began to quietly advocate contraception. In 1959, Rehwinkel finally put his views in print in a book entitled *Planned Parenthood and Birth Control in Light of Christian Ethics*. In it, he defended Margaret Sanger's motives and work, calling her a "brilliant young woman" (p. 32) and a "sensitive soul" (p. 34). Rehwinkel also went on to write that,

> "[a]fter a long and bitter struggle within her own soul she finally resolved to take up a singlehanded battle against the Anthony Comstock law and to do all that was in her power to change public opinion on this subject. She began by publishing a small paper, the *Woman Rebel*, as a means of getting her ideas before the people. But as she continued in her crusade, she realized more and more that she was not yet adequately equipped for the task, and so she resolved to go to Europe and study the methods employed in England, France, and especially Holland. She visited Europe in 1913 and again during the war years of 1914 and 1915. The most valuable help and encouragement she received from Dr. Rutgers in Holland. Armed with the new information she had acquired in Europe, she returned to America ... The struggle was a hard and bitter one. Very few men or women had the courage to share with her the odium of public disapproval, though they might share her general ideas. ... But Margaret Sanger was determined to carry on until ... public opinion had been enlightened" (p. 34-35).

Rehwinkel also described how Sanger opened a birth control clinic in New York in 1923 and how, since 1936, most states had begun allowing physicians to give contraceptive advice to their patients. His biography of Sanger was deeply flawed and presented a wholly inadequate picture of Sanger and her motivations. It seemed as though Rehwinkel had fallen victim to the story presented in Sanger's 1931 book, *My Fight for Birth Control*, which he had quoted from.

Having thus set the stage, Rehwinkel went on to provide the theological argument that allowed the Missouri Synod to accept birth control in good conscience. Contrary to previous Lutheran theologians and even Martin Luther himself, Rehwinkel insisted on separating the natural law from the moral law. Then, he argued that only an explicit verse from Scripture could prohibit contraceptive birth control. Finally, he argued that since there was no explicit teaching on birth control in the Bible, it therefore was not immoral. This same line of reasoning was later used by other Lutherans to change their stance against abortion since there is no explicit Scriptural teaching against abortion and the word "abortion" is not found in the Bible.

As a result, the drift of the Missouri Synod in the 1950's accelerated during the 60's, and Rehwinkel's arguments for contraception met with less and less opposition. Increasingly, lay L.C.M.S. members, like most of their Christian counterparts in other traditions, jumped on the cultural bandwagon and began using various means of artificial birth control. Many pastors simply went along for the ride, arguing that since the L.C.M.S. was so committed to *Sola Scriptura*, the argument that Scripture was silent was now valid. In the early 1970's, the L.C.M.S. was rocked when conservatives finally succeeded in ousting those who had been leading the Synod in a leftward direction for over thirty years. However, while more traditional Lutherans regained control of the Synod, the L.C.M.S. had already moved so far away from the historic Lutheran position against contraceptive birth control that even they could not or would not reinstate the original teaching.

As I considered the change on this issue, Maier's words echoed in my mind: "one of the most repugnant of modern aberrations, representing a 20th century renewal of pagan bankruptcy." This clearly was the original position held by all Lutherans for well over four hundred years. Only two plausible explanations remained: either the Lutherans and all earlier Christians who opposed birth control during the previous nineteen hundred years were wrong that the Bible supported the traditional teaching against birth control, or the Lutherans who now argued that the Bible was silent on birth control were wrong. Given the choices, it was easy to come down on the side of the original Lutheran teaching against birth control. Obviously, Martin Luther, Carl F.W. Walther, Walter Maier and every other Lutheran before the early twentieth century would have agreed.

The acceptance of contraceptive birth control was a decisive break with the historic moral teachings of Lutheranism and Christianity. As I considered this fact, however, the Missouri Synod's position that other Lutheran bodies were morally compromised on abortion became quite troublesome since I now believed that all Lutheran church bodies, including the L.C.M.S., were morally compromised for accepting birth control. Moreover, given the strong stand Martin Luther took on agreement in doctrine, it also became all too clear that if Martin Luther and Carl F. W. Walther were alive today, they would surely denounce the L.C.M.S.'s present position as pagan, grossly immoral, and unworthy of anyone calling themselves Lutheran. The words of the prophet Isaiah came to mind: "Woe to those who call evil good and good evil" (Isaiah 5:20).

Was the L.C.M.S. truly pro-life?

With these troubling thoughts in my mind, I turned to another issue mentioned in the book *Grand Illusions*. In a section covering the medical risks of birth control, Grant mentioned that the contraceptive Pill actually caused abortions by preventing a human embryo from implanting in the uterine lining of the womb. He also documented how Margaret Sanger was a driving force in the development of the birth control pill in the 1950's and how her organization had financed research undertaken by the American Medical Association that eventually led to the development of the Pill. It didn't take much to confirm that Grant was right once again. Many contraceptives could prevent a fertilized egg from implanting in the womb, thereby causing a very early abortion.

Again, I was faced with a dilemma. Though the L.C.M.S. had a strong pro-life position, the Synod had never issued any official statement against the Pill. Thus, a pro-life Lutheran who took the Pill might have multiple chemically induced abortions throughout her life and never know the truth while a pro-choice atheist who never took the Pill might never have a single abortion. Were it not for the evil involved, the absurdity would have been laughable. Though Karen had never taken the Pill, we had used other contraceptives and we immediately stopped from that moment on. We had been discussing the idea of having children anyway and it seemed clear to us that God had arranged this discovery for the moment when we were the most ready to accept it.

While I attributed the acceptance of birth control among the various Lutheran churches to sin, much as I had done with Luther's attitude towards the Jews during my college days, I had also learned that only the Catholic Church still officially held to its teaching against birth control. And, unlike the Lutheran churches, the Catholic Church had a long line of official documents stating and restating their position. While I found this all very intriguing, yet I still believed the Catholic Church was full of errors and that Lutherans had the best understanding of Christianity, despite the shift on birth control. The thought that the Catholic Church might possibly be what it claimed was something that was too fantastic to believe. However, this issue did prompt me to admit that perhaps the L.C.M.S. might very well be wrong in other ways as well.

About the same time Karen and I changed our minds on the issue of birth control, the dissension over our pastor finally broke into the open when a few families decided to leave the church. To make matters worse, I increasingly found myself agreeing with some of the criticisms of contemporary worship and church growth techniques I read in the *Christian News* and was beginning to have second thoughts about the whole orientation of our church. A few weeks later in September 1994, Karen and I stayed after Sunday worship for a congregational meeting at which there was more discussion about our pastor and the future of our church. As we listened to the various opinions expressed during the meeting, it became clear that the situation was only getting worse and I became disheartened by the whole affair. By the time the meeting ended, I had made up my mind to leave the church and I asked our pastor if I could speak to him for a few minutes. After explaining my sadness over the difficulties and disagreements in our church as well as the changes in my own thinking, I told him that I was resigning from the board and that Karen and I would be leaving. He urged me to wait and stick it out for a while more, but I had made up my mind.

On the following Sunday, we attended a Missouri Synod church near our home. It was a more traditional Lutheran church and the liturgy and order of the service were a welcome change. The Lutheran Hymnal (TLH) I had grown up with was still in use and it brought an immediate connection with the church of my youth. Soon after, we transferred our membership and began attending a few church functions in order to get to know some of the folks at our new church. We also signed up for a Bible class held in the home of another member, and I volunteered to help with the church newsletter.

Around this time, my sister-in-law mentioned that my favorite Christian talk-show host, Al Kresta, had decided to convert to the Catholic Church. I couldn't believe it. Al Kresta was becoming Catholic? The first thought that came to my mind was, how could such a serious and intelligent Christian do such a thing? We all had a good laugh about it at the time, though I did wonder how and why he had converted.

In the spring of 1995, I began having a few discussions with some coworkers on an internal company bulletin board about the issue of abortion. As I had become somewhat conversant with the arguments for and against abortion, it was easy to point out the many logical difficulties in the pro-abortion positions of my coworkers. While such debates rarely changed the minds of those who participated, such discussions offered an opportunity to demonstrate the strength of the pro-life position to the many other people who read our debates. Indeed, I was pleasantly surprised by the number of people who contacted me in private to thank me for taking a vocal stand against abortion and I realized that there were many who agreed with me though they felt unable to participate in such controversial debates.

Over the next few months, I purchased a few additional pro-life books in order to learn better how to defend the pro-life position. As our debates continued, however, it became clear that the root of the pro-abortion position lay in the rejection of absolutes. Yet, since the assertion that there are no absolutes is itself an absolute statement, such an assertion is self-contradictory and illogical. As I came to understand this truth, I also came to understand the importance of understanding the philosophical presuppositions of an argument.

Which Lutheran denomination is authentic?

Throughout the early spring of 1995, I began searching the Internet for information about Lutheranism and found a few interesting web sites, including Project Wittenberg and the home pages of various Lutheran churches across the United States. However, as I began reading through the information, the divisions within Lutheranism began to trouble me as well. For one reason or another, there were several smaller Lutheran bodies in the U.S. that had broken away from the L.C.M.S. in the past and these groups each claimed that both the Missouri Synod and the Evangelical Lutheran Church of America (E.L.C.A.) were too liberal on one issue or another. Among the issues raised was that the L.C.M.S. had allowed women to vote at voter's meetings and that the Synod had softened its earlier position that the Pope was the anti-Christ.

To make matters worse, it seemed that none of the smaller Lutheran groups were in complete agreement with each other either. All of a sudden, I was filled with a host of questions about Lutheranism and the L.C.M.S. How was I to know which one of these groups were authentically Lutheran and which were not? And, what if their claims about the L.C.M.S. were valid? How was I to know what authentic Lutheranism actually was? And, if all of the Lutheran bodies had collapsed on the issue of birth control, were there any contemporary Lutherans who could really claim to be the heirs of Martin Luther? While I pondered these difficulties, I began to pray that the Lord would help me know His truth about these various issues.

Soon after, another issue arose while reading about the canon of Scripture. As a boy in elementary school, I was taught that there were sixty-six books in the Old Testament and twenty-seven books in the New Testament. These books made up what we called the Canon of Scripture. However, while reading an article on the Canon in the Lutheran Cyclopedia, published by Concordia Publishing House, the author indicated that the books Lutherans call the Apocrypha had been "used ... by the framers of the Book of Concord," who made "no pronouncements on the extent of the OT Canon" (Lutheran Cyclopedia, p. 132). I read and reread the words again to make sure I understood them. Yes, it said that the Apocrypha were "used" by the Lutherans and that they made "no pronouncement" on the books of the Old Testament canon.

After researching the issue for a few weeks, it quickly became apparent that when the Book of Concord was compiled, the early Lutherans never included a list of the books they believed were part of the canon as had other Protestants in the sixteenth century. And, as I searched through articles and essays on the canon and the Apocrypha, I encountered several Catholic arguments that seemed to present a strong case for including these books in the Scriptures. In fact, I soon found myself in agreement with the Catholic position. Since the early Lutherans had made no statement on the issue, it seemed that I could accept the books included in the Catholic Bible as part of Scripture without compromising my Lutheranism.

As I continued to study the Lutheran Confessions, I began to suspect that Martin Luther would have a difficult time recognizing late twentieth-century Lutherans as his heirs. Not only had contemporary Lutheran church bodies abandoned the historic Lutheran position against birth control, many had also abandoned the teaching against abortion. Likewise, I also realized that most contemporary Lutherans had altered or done away with the original Lutheran position on private confession and the original Lutheran esteem and honor for the blessed Virgin Mary as the Mother of God.

Indeed, according to the sixteenth-century Lutherans, private confession and absolution was to be retained (Augsburg Confession, Article XI) because it was useful to the conscience (Augsburg Confession, Article XXV). Martin Luther held that private confession was not a sacrament, though he did strongly insist that the practice was spiritually beneficial and should be retained. Apparently, he also went to private confession throughout his entire life. However, during the era of Pietism in the late seventeenth and early eighteenth century, private confession was attacked as being too "Catholic" and was replaced with the more common general confession found in almost all Lutheran churches today. Since that time, there have been a few attempts to reinstate private confession in keeping with the Lutheran Confessions, but such attempts have failed largely as a result of the resistance or refusal of average Lutherans in the pew. So, despite the intentions of Luther himself, the practice has for the most part disappeared. While a few Lutheran pastors might offer private confession and absolution, it is unlikely to ever be a widespread practice within Lutheranism again because few Lutherans would claim the authority to enforce such a decision.

Likewise, Christ's mother, Mary, was originally held in high esteem by Luther and the early Lutherans. Indeed, the Lutheran Confessions call her "the blessed Virgin Mary" (Augsburg Confession, Article III); and "the pure, holy, [and always] Virgin Mary" (Smalcald Articles, Part First); and state that "she is truly the mother of God, and ... truly remained a virgin" (Formula of Concord, Epitome, Chapter VIII); who is "most worthy of the most ample honors" (Apology of the Augsburg Confession, XXI, 27); and who "prays for the church" (Apology of the Augsburg Confession, XXI, 27). Again, however, the emphasis and esteem of the sixteenth-century Lutherans was attacked by the Pietists as too "Catholic" and along with the influence of other Protestants in Europe and North America, this emphasis has largely disappeared as well.

While pondering these issues in early 1996, I happened upon a biography of Luther that revealed another little known fact. In 1539, Martin Luther, Philip Melanchthon, and Martin Bucer all personally approved the bigamous marriage of one of their allies, Philip, Landgrave of Hesse, as a matter of political expediency. Apparently, Philip led a rather promiscuous and immoral life though he had converted to Lutheranism in 1524 and was one of the signers of the Lutheran Augsburg Confession in 1530. When the bigamy was finally exposed, Luther dismissed the whole affair as necessary for the cause of "the Christian Church." I noted that the Pope, who Luther accused of being the anti-Christ, refused to grant Henry VIII a divorce regardless of the political fallout and Luther, the great reformer of Christianity, approved of a bigamous marriage out of political expediency. I wondered how the anti-Christ could stand firm in defending marriage while the "Great Reformer" had so easily approved of such obvious sin? The irony was more than unsettling and I began to suspect that there was more to the Catholic Church than I really knew.

As I continued reading Catholic apologetics, one of the things that surprised me the most was that the Catholic explanations were not nearly as outrageous as I thought they would be. As a result, I began comparing more and more Catholic material with my Lutheran beliefs. I also began checking out the Catholic sections of various bookstores in my area and even purchased a few books as well. Since I still had quite a bit of bias against the Catholic Church, I thought it best not to say much about my reading selections and even carried my Catholic books around in a brown paper bag, lest someone see me and think I had gone mad.

Over the next six months I read several more Catholic books and many more essays and soon found myself agreeing with much of what I was reading. Indeed, the Catholic positions on grace, justification, faith, and Scripture seemed more intellectually coherent than the Lutheran positions. As I began to understand my own Lutheran presuppositions about Scripture, I also began to see the beauty and truth of the Catholic positions. While I still had an emotional reaction against the idea that the Catholic Church might just be Christ's true Church, I knew that I could not let my emotional prejudices stand in the way of the truth.

Another issue I tackled was the Catholic criticism of the philosophical roots of Martin Luther's theology. During his academic training, Luther was greatly influenced by the nominalistic philosophy of Ockhamism, named after William of Ockham, a fifteenth century English Fransican. Ockham rejected the reality of universal concepts or ideas and taught that only individual objects have real existence. Subsequent scholastics adapted Ockham's basic ideas into a philosophy known as nominalism, from the Latin word nomina, meaning name. They held that abstract ideas or universals have no objective existence or reference but exist only as names. However, as I grappled with these ideas, it seemed that nominalistic philosophy was incapable of dealing with the supernatural reality that God was the objective reference of all universals.

As I continued my studies, I learned that the scholastic nominalists were actually the philosophical and theological "liberals" of Luther's day. By the sixteenth century, many of the Catholic scholastics that taught Luther had adopted nominalistic philosophy and integrated it into their theological outlook. They taught Luther that God was arbitrary, cruel and threatening and that God destined some for heaven and some for hell without any objective reason.

However, Luther, reacting against such a corrupted and unbearable idea of God, used the same nominalistic philosophy he was taught to formulate his own theological positions against the scholastics with which he disagreed. For example, Luther taught the doctrine of imputed righteousness that holds that grace is God's divine pronouncement of righteousness upon a soul corrupted by sin. That is, Luther taught that grace was not a "medicine for the soul" to aid in the growth of righteousness, but was simply God's judicial pronouncement on a sinner. Luther claimed to find this idea in the Scriptures. However, were it not for his nominalistic philosophy, he would never have thought of grace in such terms.

Going where I had no intention of going

During the summer of 1996, as I grappled with these criticisms of Luther and his theology, I experienced a profound sense of depression at the implications of my studies. I had a growing sense that God was leading me in a direction in which I had no desire to go. Yet, a few weeks later while discussing my struggles with Karen, I mentioned my frustration about such uncertainties and told her that if God wanted me to follow the truth where ever he led, even if it meant into the Catholic Church, then that is what I would do. A week later, as I was reading an essay called "The Necessity of Being Catholic" by a Catholic convert named James Akin, I came upon this statement: "A person who has a desire to be saved and come to the truth, regardless of what that truth turns out to be, has an implicit desire for Catholicism and for the Catholic Church, because that is where truth and salvation are obtained. By resolving to pursue salvation and truth, he resolves to pursue the Catholic Church, even though he does not know that is what he is seeking. He thus implicitly longs to be a Catholic by explicitly longing and resolving to seek salvation and truth."

Akin's words made me choke. Here was a convert to the Catholic faith stating exactly what I had just said to my wife a week earlier. Yet, I still could not emotionally bring myself to accept what he said. My Missouri Synod up-bringing kept telling me that the Catholic Church was wrong, plain and simple. When I later mentioned Akin's essay to my wife, she remarked: "I always knew you, Mr. Lutheran, had an 'implicit' desire to be Catholic," and she burst out in laughter. Of course, I didn't find the situation very funny at all at the time.

Around September, 1996, I went and told my Lutheran pastor about the issues that I had been struggling with for almost two years. I was really hoping he would give me a good reason to remain Lutheran as the thought of becoming Catholic made me very uncomfortable. We talked for a few hours, he gave me a few books to read, and he confirmed that Lutherans could, in fact, hold the Apocrypha as inspired Scripture, if they were so inclined. We talked about a few other issues, but by the end of our discussion, it seemed clear to me that he wasn't telling me anything I had not already dealt with before. We met together several more times over the next three months, but in the end, he couldn't convince me that the Lutheran positions were correct.

By December 1996, I had become intellectually convinced that the Catholic Church was all that it claims to be - Christ's true Church on earth and that the Pope had the unique charism of infallibility when speaking dogmatically on faith and morals. However, I was still struggling with the implications of acting on that belief and how my family would react to the news. Yet, when I remembered Christ's words: "Anyone who loves his father or mother more than me is not worthy of me" (Matthew 10:37), I knew what I would eventually have to do.

The final straw broke one evening during an Advent service at our Lutheran church a few days before Christmas. My ten month-old daughter had become a little fussy just as our pastor began his sermon so I carried her to the back of the church so as not to disturb the congregation. While I held her in my arms and listened to the pastor's sermon, I found myself mentally disagreeing with what he was preaching. At that moment, as I looked at my little daughter lying in my arms, I realized that I had ceased to be a Lutheran. Though I had fought against the final decision for several months, I realized that I no longer accepted the tenets of Lutheranism and that it was time to move on to whatever God had planned for me.

A few weeks later, after further prayer and discussion with my wife Karen, I called my Lutheran pastor and made an appointment to talk with him about my decision. At the same time, I also called Al Kresta at the Evangelical radio station where he worked and explained my dilemma. I also asked him if he knew any good priests in my area who might be willing to talk with me. He listened to my story and offered to check with a friend about a priest in my area. A few days later, I met with my Lutheran pastor and thanked him for all his advice and his willingness to talk and pray, and then told him of my decision. He was somewhat surprised, as he sincerely thought I would remain a Lutheran.

A few days later, I also went and broke the news to my parents. I knew my father would take it hard and would not be happy at all. For a few days, I even thought about remaining Lutheran rather than face him with the news of my decision to convert. However, after praying about the issue, I knew I had to follow Christ wherever he might lead. In the end, telling my father turned out to be one of the most difficult things I have ever done in my life.

A few weeks later, I found myself driving to an appointment at St. Stanislaus Kostka Catholic Church in Wyandotte to meet a Catholic priest. Mr. Kresta had called the previous week with the name of a priest, Rev. John Hedges, whom a friend had recommended. So, I called Rev. Hedges and talked with him briefly and we scheduled a meeting to discuss my situation.

As I drove to the rectory about a week after my thirty-first birthday, I reflected on all that had happened to bring me to this point in time. I never in a million years would have thought that God would lead me to the Catholic Church, and yet here I was, on my way to talk with a priest about becoming Catholic. When I finally arrived at the rectory I introduced myself to Father Hedges and told him all that had happened to me since 1994, how I had been reading about Lutheranism and Catholicism, how I had talked to my Lutheran Pastor and how I had finally become convinced that God was calling me to become a Catholic.

Much to my relief, he listened very patiently to my ramblings and then asked me about some of the books I had read. Providentially, he was familiar with one of the books as he had used it in a course he taught at a local Catholic university. After talking for almost three hours, he finally told me that I would not have to take a class on the Catholic faith since I had already read far more than was required for the class anyway. He also asked me if I had any particular issues or doctrines that I struggled with. I thought about it for a few seconds and responded by saying: "No. Besides, even if there were, it wouldn't matter because I accept that the Church is all that it claims to be, Christ's true Church on earth, and that is good enough for me."

Father Hedges' next words took me by surprise. He said that since Easter was only about a month away, I could enter the Church at that time by making a public act of faith if that was my desire. I remember thinking that I didn't want to do anything wrong, so if I had to wait until later, I was willing. Shortly after my meeting with Reverend Hedges, my wife was reconciled to the Church. On March 29, 1997, I made my first confession and Karen acted as my sponsor when I was received into the Catholic Church on the Easter Vigil.

Since then, the Lord has poured untold blessings upon us. Of course, since becoming a Catholic, I have become even more aware of my sinfulness and my own weaknesses due to some of the bad attitudes and habits developed in my earlier years. Yet, our merciful Father has helped both Karen and I to grow tremendously in faith and love for Him, each other and our family since becoming Catholic and have found the Sacrament of Reconciliation to be very beneficial in our spiritual lives. Martin Luther was certainly right about something: God is indeed a mighty fortress!

Tony Gerring and his wife, Karen, have three children under five plus one in the hands of God and are members of St. Stanislaus Kostka Church in Wyandotte, Michigan. Tony enjoys being a father though he often wishes he was as patient as Job. In the wee hours of the evening, he likes to peck away at his computer doing genealogy and writing and editing Catholic apologetics articles. He also likes to tinker around his house and usually fixes more than he breaks, which makes his wife happy. He hopes to live on a farm someday soon. And, whenever he begins to sing Martin Luther's famous hymn, "A Mighty Fortress is Our God" at his church today, the corners of his mouth turn up into a little smile at the mysteriousness of God's ways. Gerring currently works in the development office of Ave Maria College in Ypsilanti, Michigan.

My Pilgrimage to Rome

Sally Nelson

The first truth about being human -- first to be taught by Sacred Scripture, and the first in order of its most basic nature -- is that each human person is created in the image of God. The second truth is that this image has been marred by sin. The third truth is that Jesus Christ is the Way by which God is at work to restore His image in us, for which purpose He makes use of the Church which Christ Himself established.

The process by which an individual is being transformed by God to more nearly reflect His image is called conversion. All people -- including even those who do not acknowledge God -- are at varying stages of conversion; but no person's conversion is complete in this lifetime.

My own awareness of God and of my need for conversion began with a relatively high level of ignorance. I was unbaptized and considered myself an atheist at age seventeen. Yet in another way, there was an openness to God in that I was raised to consider that service to humanity was an ideal to strive for, and beyond this there was a vague instinct that the underpinning of such service must be love.

My parents had both been raised in Protestant denominations, but left any observance of the Christian faith shortly after their marriage. My father became a Unitarian minister, a sect that is both un-Christian and non-creedal, at times belligerently so. This gave him both the freedom to develop whatever philosophical framework he liked and a platform from which to preach it to others. This was during the 1950's and 1960's and the civil rights and anti-war movements significantly shaping his preaching and writing.

My knowledge of these years is vague and second-hand, since I was the last addition to the family, born at Sacred Heart Hospital in Eugene, Oregon in 1964. Given the entirely unpredictable direction my life has taken, I've speculated that the nuns must have done some praying over my crib before I was taken home, thanks be to God.

When I was about five years old, my father retired from active ministry and moved with my mother and their two youngest -- my brother Bruce and myself-- to a cabin in the woods of Wisconsin. This was property my parents had owned since World War II and it had served since that time as a summertime retreat, but now they wanted to have the experience of living there year round, which we did for two years. The great advantage of this home was its lack of electricity and ergo, no television or artificial daylight. It was also relatively isolated and I think

46

it was there that a sense of self-sufficiency was begun in me, a sometimes positive and sometimes negative force in my life. If I have any capacity for contemplative prayer, this too was begun in that environment that invited quiet reflection and rewarded careful observation, rather than demanding immediate reaction to constant stimulation.

When I was in third grade we moved to the farm near Wausau where most of my growing up years would pass. This, a one-time dairy farm that my father hoped would one day provide self-sufficiency in food and energy, also was a place that afforded me all the space I required for time alone and in silent reflection -- a tendency that my parents didn't always feel comfortable with, but yet has ever since been one of the most important factors of my personality.

Initially, my parents maintained a loose affiliation with the Unitarians in Wausau, but soon became members of the Religious Society of Friends, or Quakers. They had long admired the Quakers for their simple life, idealistic view of humanity, and their intense involvement in works of peace and justice. Since many Quakers are humanist rather than Christian, this did not necessarily represent an ideological shift for my parents.

I often attended silent meetings with Mom and Dad, and although I recall being only vaguely interested in the theology, I still have many affectionate memories of those Quakers I came to know -- people of gentleness and genuine conviction that I found more interesting and easier to be with than most of my own peers.

This sense of having little in common with my schoolmates is not insignificant -- it led to a fair degree of misery when the personality and interests that had developed in me met with a negative response in other young people, and this response in turn collided with an unyielding stubbornness in myself in regard to any compromises that might be made. This mutual antagonism culminated in my dropping out of school as soon as I was legally able.

Finding a purpose in my life

There followed earnest but fruitless attempts to find some sort of mission and purpose for my life, leading me to work with a peace organization in Philadelphia and attend a disc jockey school in Minneapolis. At seventeen I found myself back in my parents home, enduring with little grace my first experience of being humbled in self-estimation and self-confidence. Yet the experience apparently broke me open somewhat, to hear, faintly, the voice of God. I can yet recall with great clarity the moment when I stood gazing out my bedroom window and the thought came to mind unbidden, unlooked for, "Is there a God?".

I had never been interested in that question before, assuming the answer was negative. But now it burned in me with an insistent urgency that, since I could

47

not wipe it out entirely, I sought to control. This, I proposed, would be undertaken as an experiment, an inquiry with a certain structure, a beginning, and therefore, an end. I recorded my thoughts in a journal, beginning with a grandiose flourish: "I am Sally Nelson, atheist. I am right now investigating my atheism, discovering its origins, probing its substance to find out if it holds or falls. Are my beliefs rooted in truth or fallacy? This I desire to know, and shall endeavor to resolve in what follows. As to what does follow, it is a record of my investigations."

There follows a month's worth of such intellectual attempts to control the whole event, interspersed with moments of intense longing for a God whose existence I denied and passionate rage when this longing was unsatisfied. When reading an excerpt from St. Augustine's *Confessions* many years later, I would understand him perfectly when he said, "You have created us for yourself, Oh God, and our hearts are restless until they find their rest in You." Although at the end of this month I would make a pretense of wrapping up my investigation and setting it aside, yet this divinely inspired restlessness would drive me on relentlessly until I gave up the pretense and was left nothing but a wounded soul desperately seeking its Creator.

In this state I wrote to a local pastor, one chosen at random from the church ads in the local paper. How good God is! In this intensely vulnerable state, I would have been easy prey for any bent on conforming me to their own agenda, yet I stumbled upon a man who was the very essence of a good and decent pastor -- Ken Melby, then pastor of Immanuel Lutheran Church in Wausau. Ken recognized from the first meeting that what was taking place was of the Holy Spirit, and his task was simply to facilitate what God was accomplishing in me. This he did with great compassion and sensitivity, patiently answering questions and allaying fears, until the time was finally right for him to ask me if I wanted to be baptized. I did, with all my heart I did, and this grace was given me on October 30, 1983. (A lovely piece of irony is the fact that this was Reformation Sunday, a date Ken thought would be appropriate, since my searchings and struggles reminded him of Martin Luther).

Even before my baptism the people of Immanuel embraced me in love as one of their own, as my frequent visits to Sunday worship were making me known to many of them. But it was with baptism that I took my place in the assembly of children before the Father's throne, as well as receiving formal membership within the congregation.

The next four years I remember as being a time of steadily deepening in the faith, a time relatively free of conflicts, or of conflict that could be easily borne in baptism's state of grace. I was in college at this time, working towards the bachelor's degree necessary for admission to seminary. Yes, I had experienced "the call." For me this was a concrete event, a moment in time of being overwhelmed with images of myself performing the tasks of ministry, along with a strong sense that this was something being offered to me. I was free to reject this offer, but only in the sense that a lover is free to say "no" to the beloved -- it was so far from my will and desire that it seemed impossible. The same had been true at my baptism -- always we are free to reject our Lord, but such freedom seems worse than any slavery, worse than death itself. And so it is.

Onto the seminary

I began my studies at Luther Northwestern Seminary in St. Paul in the summer of 1987. This, too, was a period of deepening in faith, and a time of growing into a mature theology. I was extremely fortunate to have this experience at one of the finest Protestant seminaries in the country, learning the trade at the feet of men and women of outstanding scholarship and vibrant faith. I was humbled, also, to find myself in the company of other students with a multitude of gifts, degrees, and experience. Yet my pride did not suffer in this setting, but rather was given food to grow on as my class became increasingly confident in our certain knowledge of the truth and our ability to deliver that truth with accuracy and vigor. In retrospect I now see that in many instances our professors were setting up straw men for us to swat at, and that in our pride we strutted like kittens who think they are tigers.

But I love to deck myself in tiger stripes, so seminary was a good fit for me, and I enjoyed myself immensely while gaining a first-rate education. I also had the intoxicating experience of living, studying, and working in the midst of a large group of people with whom I shared a sense of common mission in the world.

Nevertheless these four years were not unalloyed joy. Far from it -- it was during this time that I first became seriously ill with clinical depression/anxiety disorder. I was diagnosed during my third year and Prozac helped me to return to a normal life, but with an unprecedented sense of my own vulnerability and potential fragility. This new self understanding pushed me further out of my self to seek a deeper than intellectual connection with the people around me. This growth was unfortunately small, being satisfied with simply getting back on my feet, back to where I had been before.

My first calling

In 1991 I graduated from seminary and moved to Lancaster, Minnesota to be pastor of Sion Lutheran Church. I arrived with all manner of apprehensions -- what would it be like the first time a parishioner died, how would they accept their first female pastor, would I know how to be whatever it was that I was supposed to be, etc. Yet I find myself smiling whenever I think of those years -- the people met me with such loving acceptance that loving them in return was

49

the most natural thing I've ever done. And it is in loving that we will be found faithful, whatever our calling.

Most of the time, of course, our acts of love are done in the mundane, which for me meant spending time gossiping with the farmers at the cafe, going to high school football games, eating their food at potlucks, feeling anxious for the small person with a bit part in the Christmas play. And on Sunday after Sunday praying for our sick, passing on announcements of choir practices, singing hymns they hated and I loved or I hated and they loved, and feeling the burning in my bones for them to hear the gospel of Jesus Christ as something new, something life giving, dead raising, hope reviving.

We grew accustomed to one another, in the space of four years, which is what made me the right person to baptize their children, wed the young couples, preach the Resurrection, all the "big" things we thought of as ministry when apprehending it in seminary. And in the spring of 1995, it was to my door that a distraught sister came to tell of her husband finding a man dead of a gunshot to the chest, a man well known, well-loved, a pillar of church and community. A man who, it was revealed, had been molesting his granddaughter and chose this as a way of avoiding the light that was now being shown on what he had done in darkness. His burial was the Monday of Holy Week, and on Tuesday the funeral home called to tell me of the sudden death of my neighbor -- another pillar, but one who didn't leave us feeling our love had been betrayed. His burial was the Saturday before Easter Sunday.

For ten days my time was consumed from dawn to late night by the intense needs of people in desperate grief and shock, the planning of funerals, the preparation and praying of Holy Week and Easter. After the last Alleluias of the Church's most triumphant moment had been sung, I locked the doors and went home to a heavy dreamless sleep. That evening I returned to the church and knelt before the altar to pray. I found myself prostrate and sobbing, weeping for my people. Then, unable to speak eloquent words, with not even the strength to stay upright and with none to see or admire, that was the finest hour of my ministry.

An extra burden lay on my heart that day, for I knew that God was calling me into the Catholic Church. Recognizing the voice of the Beloved calling me nearer to Himself, I knew great joy in His caresses, mingled with pain and apprehension in the thought of leaving the people that had been given me to love. I knew that I could not hope for any to understand, and feared that in their confusion they might feel let down, betrayed.

It had begun some months before, the sudden, insistent movement of the Holy Spirit in my heart as I read through some books I had just "happened" to purchase, without any real sense of why. One was *Butler's Lives of the Saints*, when I was constantly filled with the conviction that the Lutheran church did not have the means to produce people like this -- good, decent people, yes -- but not the transcendent, luminous holiness reflected in these pages. The other book I was reading I now believe to be the greatest publication of the 20th century, and probably of at least the last thousand years -- *The Catechism of the Catholic Church*. Aside from Sacred Scripture, there is no surer witness to the Truth which is Christ available to us in our time, and the constant echo in my heart as I read was, "This is true, it is all true".

In sharing these events with a friend of mine from seminary, we agreed that it was more than a simply strange situation, that at the time of our graduation from Luther, I would have easily been the one in our class voted "Least Likely to Become a Roman Catholic."

Before these sudden movements in my heart, I hadn't experienced any disillusionment with Lutheranism, and had certainly never had any inclinations towards Catholicism. There was no one trying to persuade me of the truth of Catholic teaching, neither did I know any Catholics well enough to be persuaded by their way of life. There was nothing, nothing but the call of the Beloved, the call that could have been rejected, but as at baptism, as at the invitation to ministry, such rejection was unthinkable, as unthinkable as death itself.

Meeting Our Lord

Once it was obvious to me that becoming Catholic was inevitable, I knew that I needed to talk with a priest. But who? I looked up the local Catholic parishes in the telephone book, and deciding not to contact the one nearest to Lancaster, I called St. Stephen's, about thirty miles distant. Within a week I was sitting in the office of Father Dennis Wieland, telling him I was being drawn to the Catholic Church, then explaining that I was pastor of the Lutheran church in Lancaster. Once again, I was fortunate to have found a faithful shepherd who would not exploit my vulnerability to push his own agenda, but instead recognized that the Holy Spirit was at work and his task was but to facilitate what was being accomplished in me.

The second time I met with Father Dennis, I felt compelled to ask him to teach me how to pray. He seemed uncertain at first how to address this request, then said he felt strongly that what I needed was to pray before the Blessed Sacrament. He explained to me what this was, then took me over to the church, introduced me to my Beloved, and left me there.

I was uneasy there, aware of a heightened sense of longing, but fearful that this longing would only bring sadness and frustration. I strove to open myself to God's presence, but experienced only the old aching dryness. Finally in anger I got to my feet and turned to storm down the aisle and out the door. But at the door I paused, unwilling to leave in such a state of mind. I returned to the tabernacle, knelt and found peace, the quiet assurance of His Presence. As I drove away, it was with the conviction that I had to be where this Sacrament could be found.

Nearly every day I drove to St. Stephen's to spend time with Christ in the Blessed Sacrament. It was no ecstatic experience for me; more a great peace, a sense of the Presence that was all to me, a longing being met with its fulfillment. After a month or two I started to come to the weekday Mass, and grew in the sharpness of my desire to be able to receive Jesus in Eucharist. As Father lifted Him before us and declared, "Behold the Lamb of God, who takes away the sins of the world. Happy are we who are invited to share in His supper", in that moment I knew with assurance that I *was* invited, that all that remained was my response.

My introduction to Eucharistic adoration culminated on the Feast of the Sacred Heart of Jesus, when Father Dennis followed celebration of the Mass with Exposition of the Blessed Sacrament. Such sweetness! I knelt, prayed, adored, and abandoned self to Him -- all drawn forth spontaneously by the powerful, gracious Presence of our Lord. Then was the beginning of my devotion to the Sacred Heart. And then was the time that I truly began to understand a sense that had begun even before I was baptized, the sense that Christ has called me to live a single life, and that He would Himself provide the intimacy and support I would otherwise gain through marriage. As a Lutheran, there was no room for the single life as a calling of the Holy Spirit, but only as an aberration from the norm. And as a Lutheran, although I didn't feel drawn to the married state, still I experienced a sense of incompleteness, a lack within me that was not filled by the status of being a pastor, or by meaningful employment, or the respect of the community, or by anything else within my experience. But now, simply being in the Presence of Christ in the Eucharist, that lack and incompleteness was finally resolved -- here I could purposefully live a dedicated single life that would be truly fruitful. In so many ways drawing near to Rome was truly a "coming home" -- the faith that had begun in Lutheranism was beginning to find its fullness in the riches and wonder of the Catholic Church.

I resign from Sion

Shortly afterwards, I mailed a letter to each household of Sion, announcing my resignation, to be effective at the end of August. Although I explained the reason for my leaving in the letter, and let them know that I stood ready to meet with any whom had any questions about it, still I didn't expect that anybody would understand, and I anticipated having to deal with anger and feelings of betrayal. How little I trusted that relationship of love that there was between us! These lovely people were far more gracious than I could have ever expected, showing me love and care even in the midst of their own pain of loss. It was still a difficult time, as we prepared to say good-bye, but the parting was on the best of terms -- mutual love and respect.

In resigning from Sion, I did not know what I would do as a Catholic to earn a living. As it turned out, about a month after my resignation, the pastoral associate at one of the parishes Father Dennis was pastor of had to resign for health reasons. Father Dennis asked me if I would like to fill that position. In prayer coming to see this as God's purpose for me at that time, I said yes, and began work at St. Rose of Lima about a month after being received into the Church by confession of faith and the sacrament of Confirmation.

I had thought that I didn't have any ego invested in the title of "pastor," but I did find that I missed the immediate respect, the sense of a clearly defined and recognized role that had been mine. It was a blow to my pride to go from loved and respected pastor to one who was referred to as being "not even a nun." It was a struggle to keep focused on the work that was mine to do, the people given me to love, when I felt that they were always looking past me, hoping for something better to come along.

In telling of these experiences, I am aware that I must hasten to add that I tell of them as God's action to humble my pride, not as a criticism of the Church I love. It is necessary to emphasize this in a time when so many are falsely accusing the Church of hating and oppressing women. What is most disturbing to me is the assumption of many that since I am a woman, I must therefore be disloyal and schismatic. They assume that I disregard the Church's great love for women and her cherishing of the "feminine genius" to rail over what Christ in His sovereignty has not given to the Church -- the ordination of women. There is so much that people lose by choosing irrational anger and bitterness over a simple rejoicing in God's goodness and providence.

It is Lent as I write this, in the year of the great Jubilee. Over the past few years I have often thought how I would, if circumstances allowed, love to make a pilgrimage to Rome during the Jubilee year. Circumstances however did not allow such a journey, as I am unemployed. But I think that this is not to be deplored. I am unemployed because in God's providence I have been making instead a pilgrimage to Calvary, to be more nearly conformed to the image of the suffering Christ.

In the past two years the illness of clinical depression/anxiety disorder has made itself felt again in my life. Although Prozac worked for me before, this time it was ineffective, as were nearly a dozen other medications that have been tried. It seems that finally a workable combination has been found and now I am beginning to climb out of the deepest darkness I have ever known, with the help of many who work in the psychological unit at the local hospital. I first became familiar with them when I was voluntarily admitted last fall, after getting so worn down by the illness that the darkness engulfed my everyday. I was discharged after a week, having had a very positive experience and thinking myself on the mend. In reality, I quickly experienced relapse upon relapse, being readmitted twice more (the third time being brought in by the police when I hadn't the wherewithal to make it on my own), then to the state hospital in Fergus Falls for a month's stay. After that was a lull of two months, followed by two hospitalizations in quick succession, each initiated by Dr. Grant (my psychologist) signing a 72-hour hold on me.

Those are the external facts of the situation. The internal reality was a twisting storm cloud of dark imagery, confused thinking, terror, despair, pain, and a numbing, crippling weariness. My life was thoroughly out of my control -- I could not function in the realm of work, personal relationships, or even the simplest social interactions. Depression is not a case of the blues, it is a debilitating illness that can destroy a person's life. The anxiety that often accompanies it is not a case of nerves, for me it has been a white noise of racing thoughts that overwhelm all the circuits in my brain, until the rational part simply shuts down and leaves me flooded with the dark and irrational, hyperventilating and shaking, often unable to even speak without great difficulty.

And through it all, undergirded by the prayers of many and praying that I might be united with the cross of Christ, I can say that this has been one of the richest experiences of my life, bringing about a mystical union with Christ, which has in turn meant union with all of suffering humanity. Did Christ strain and falter under the weight of the cross? Even so my own weariness bore me down to the ground many times. Did Christ taste the bitter gall? I knew the bitterness of the many useless medications I swallowed. Christ cried out the words of the twenty-second Psalm from the cross, and I cried them too -- My God, my God, why have you abandoned me? -- kneeling on the floor of my hospital room.

When Dr. Grant signed the first hold on me, I had to strip off my garments in the presence of a nurse, putting on the paper ones instead. Then the door of the bare room was locked, and I was alone and entirely impoverished -- of the most elemental freedoms, of my work, of my financial independence, of outward dignity, of any cause for pride, of anything that I could have claimed as my own. And when I look back on that time I see it infused with light, an experience of total union with Christ's death, a moment when my soul apprehended great grace.

Years ago in seminary I tried to read the writings of St. John of the Cross and understood nothing of the little I read. Shortly after coming into the Church I tried again, and had to put it aside again. The last time I was in the hospital I came across "The Soul's Union With God" in the back of my breviary, and it was delightfully, joyfully obvious.

Oh night that was my guide!

Oh darkness dearer than the morning's pride,
Oh night that joined the lover
To the beloved bride
Transfiguring them each into the other.

Sally Nelson is single and currently living in Thief River Falls, Minnesota. Vocationally, Sally is undergoing a time of formation with the hopes of one day being admitted to the Order of Consecrated Virgins. Sally hopes to soon be working for the Church again, perhaps in the area of writing and speaking.

Rejoice, Sing, Exult, Sound the Trumpet

Jim Cope

"Rejoice, heavenly powers!
Sing, choirs of angels!
Exult, all creation around God's throne!
Sound the trumpet of salvation![2]

On Easter Vigil, 2000, rejoicing and exulting with the Church in heaven and on earth, my lovely wife Marcia and I entered the Catholic Church. Our entry into the Church was made easier by the kindness and support we received from our outstanding parish priest, Father David Zink.

"Why did you decide to enter the Catholic Church?" "That must have been hard after thirty-six years as a Lutheran pastor?" "Was this something you have been thinking for some time about doing?" Some said, "I couldn't believe it when I heard it," and others said, "I guess when I heard it, it didn't surprise me." These are some of the kinds of questions and comments that I received when I announced that we were going to enter the Catholic Church. I have conscientiously tried to give an "explanation," "a reason for (my) hope"[3] to everyone who asks. My struggle has been to find a way to answer that is gentle, reverent, and kind but at the same time is honest and bears witness to the fullness, beauty, goodness, and truth which I have found in the Catholic Church. My earnest hope is that the inquirer will come back for more conversation and that someday we will be one not only in Christ but also in his body the Church.

I must confess that when I was asked to write this piece, I agreed to do it with a feeling of ambivalence. On the one hand, I want to see all people come to a knowledge of the truth and to find the oneness and communion that God desires that we have with himself and with one another - a oneness and communion realized in the sacrifice of Christ and made manifest in the One, Holy, Catholic, and Apostolic Church. On the other hand, I am hesitant to speak of my pilgrimage to the Catholic Church because it is personal, the fruit of a growing intimacy with God. Our conversion stories have value only to the extent that they bear witness to the goodness and loving kindness of God and aid others

---

[2] Easter Proclamation, April 22, 2000
[3] 1 Peter 3:15 (NAB)

in their journey of faith; that is, only to the extent that others "see your good deeds and glorify your heavenly father".[4]

Shall I say that God called me from the foundation of the world, that this was part of his plan from eternity? Did it begin with Adam and that "happy fault," that "necessary sin which gained for us so great a redeemer"?[5] Or should I begin with the redeemer himself who suffered, died and rose again that we might life and have it abundantly? Did my coming to the Church Catholic begin on that day centuries ago when an ancestor acted willfully and broke the unity of the Church for which Christ prayed so fervently?[6] Or perhaps it was my mother's ancestral fear and distrust of the Catholic Church that, from my earliest youth, gave the Church in my mind certain fascination and mystery? Then again maybe the seeds were planted on the day of my baptism and reawakened on a lonely Korean road when I became conscious of my sinfulness and turned to God for mercy and forgiveness? Could my theological education have played a part in my becoming Catholic? The Lutheran education I received was articulated against the Catholic teaching with which Lutherans disagreed?

Unlike some converts, I have never experienced any anti-Catholic feelings. As far back as I can remember the Catholic Church seemed mysterious and fascinating. While serving with the American Army in Korea I experienced my first conscious tug toward things Catholic. A young Catholic soldier was going through a spiritual crisis and would sit in front of his tent contemplating the crucifix. I was so drawn to the crucifix that at the first opportunity I bought a crucifix for myself. As a young pastor I was strongly influenced by the liturgical movement and became a conscious part of a movement in the Lutheran Church that referred to itself as Evangelical and Catholic. Some people called us High Church Lutherans - their term, not mine.

I understood the church to be the sacrament of communion with God. I placed great emphasis on the sacraments, held firmly to the doctrine of the real presence of the body and blood of Christ in the Eucharist, practiced private confession, and understood myself to be the icon (image) or representative of Christ in the midst of the people whom I served. For sixteen years I celebrated a daily mass in my parish and I have for many years prayed the Daily Office. I thought of myself as Catholic and considered all the people in my parish as my responsibility regardless of the church to which they belonged. My Catholic identity was not an unmixed blessing, for although I was drawn to the Catholic Church my belief that I was already Catholic kept me for many years from considering entering the Catholic Church. It was only in the late 1980s that I realized that we who called ourselves Evangelical and Catholic were not in fact

---

[4] Matthew 5:16 (NAB)
[5] Easter Proclamation
[6] John 17:11, 21-23 (NAB)

Catholic and that wanting to be Catholic and thinking of myself as Catholic did not make me Catholic. I also realized that the unity of the Church for which I so desperately longed was not going to happen and that the kind of church that most Protestants would be willing to belong to would not be Catholic in any recognizable sense.

Grateful for the gifts of the Lutheran church

It is not my desire to say anything negative about the Lutheran Church because I am deeply grateful for the many gifts the Lutheran Church has given me. But honesty requires that I speak of some of the negative things that were happening because this negativity caused me to critically reexamine my Lutheran heritage, and that reexamination helped me to see that Luther and the Lutheran Church had gotten many things wrong. The church, in order to proclaim the Gospel to the world, must be open to encounter and dialogue with the world. It is sometimes the case that the world enters the Church instead of the Church being an effective sign of contradiction in the world. When the world enters the Church, then the Church becomes worldly and fails in its God-given mission of calling the world to repentance and purification.

In 1970 the Lutheran Church in America decided to ordain women. This radical break with tradition, made on other than theological grounds, was the first event that pushed me toward a critical reexamination of Lutheranism. Then "inclusiveness" became the watchword of the hour. "Inclusiveness" is not a bad word and could be understood in much the same sense as the word "Catholic." "Inclusiveness", however, came to mean opening our arms to unrepentant sinners and thus became a denial of the universal invitation to all men to "repent and believe the Gospel."[7]

As unbelievable as this may sound, at one point in the formation of the Evangelical Lutheran Church in America a vote was taken to determine whether to continue to use traditional Trinitarian language or to find a more "inclusive" language to speak of God. I am pleased to report that the Lutherans chose to keep the traditional Trinitarian language (e.g. Father, Son, and Holy Spirit), but the very idea that anyone could conceive of bringing this question to a vote was more than I could comprehend. Then there was the issue of abortion. The acceptance of abortion in the Lutheran Church was clothed, as it is in our culture, in the language of "choice" and of a woman's "right" to the control of her body.[8] There were other issues I could mention, but the ones which I have named are enough to give you a feel for what was happening in the Lutheran Church and to indicate why I was moved to reexamine the tradition in which I had been

---

[7] Mark 1:15 (RSV)

[8] See Romans 14:7 At best, our control of our bodies is a very limited control and must be rightly ordered to the will of God.

raised and educated. These were painful times, but I am grateful that they are behind me and that I am where I am today.

I discover the fullness of Truth

It was not the negative things happening in the Lutheran Church so much as the fullness of the Truth which I found in the Catholic Church that brought me to the decision to become a Catholic. Four events profoundly influenced my movement toward the Catholic Church.

The first was Vatican Council II. I watched with joy as that Council unfolded and I longed for the day when the Church would again be one as Christ had so fervently prayed that it would be. At that time I was not thinking of becoming Catholic but I was hoping to see the unity of the divided Church restored. Also the Council's twin goals of *aggiornamento*, (opening the window) and *ressoursement* (returning to the sources) had a powerful appeal to me.

The second event was the first visit of Pope John Paul II to the United States. Before his visit the notion that a nation could receive a pastoral visit had never occurred to me. I was very deeply moved by his visit to our nation and I realized that he was the only pastor in the world that could make a pastoral call on the United States. This realization caused me to reevaluate the Petrine office and I came to understand the necessity of such an office in the Church. I also realized that the doctrine of papal infallibility was a gift of God to the twentieth century, for it protected the Catholic Church from the wild excesses that were ravaging the Protestant denominations and kept the Catholic Church firmly anchored in Tradition.

The third was the publication of *The Ratzinger Report*.[9] Vitterio Messori, at one point, asked Cardinal Ratzinger, what is the remedy "to the crisis in the understanding of the Church, to the crisis of morality, to the crisis of women."[10] Cardinal Ratzinger answered with one word: Mary. Mary! Yes that is the answer, so simple and yet so profound. To God's invitation to Mary to be the mother of "the Son of the Most High," Mary responded, "I am the handmaid of the Lord; let it be to me according to your word."[11] Mary's utter openness and docility to the will of God is the attitude that is so desperately needed today. I realized that I needed to sit at the feet of our mother, personified in the Church, and learn from her how a little brother of Jesus is to live in this world. Meditation on Mary flowered into a love for Mary and a devotion to her. The real source of my conversion to the Catholic Church I attribute to the

---

[9] *The Ratzinger Report: An Exclusive Interview on the State of the Church*, by Joseph Cardinal Ratzinger with Vittorio Messori. Ignatius Press, San Francisco, 1985.
[10] Ibid., p. 104f
[11] Luke 1:38 (RSV)

intercession of Mary and to the prayers of all those who asked her to intercede for me.

Humanae Vitae influences me

The fourth influence in my becoming Catholic was the reading of *Humanae Vitae* (On the Regulation of Births), the Encyclical Letter of His Holiness Pope Paul IV. By the time I received my theological education, the Protestant Churches had uncritically accepted the use of contraceptives in the control of births. This issue was never discussed in my seminary education or, to my knowledge, in any publication or at any conference of the Lutheran Church. After I read *Humanae Vitae*, the Pope's teaching seemed to me to be so obvious as to be self-evident. The core of his teaching was that every conjugal act has a two-fold significance: a unitive or bonding significance and a procreative significance and that these two aspects are inseparably connected and must be maintained in every licit conjugal act.

The Pope then went on to warn that the artificial regulation of births would result in dire consequences: it would encourage "conjugal infidelity," bring about a "general lowering of morality," lead to a "loss of respect for women" and cause men to look on women "as a mere instrument of selfish enjoyment and no longer as a respected and beloved companion." All of this, the Pope said, would lead to more broken marriages and he warned that governments would be tempted to use coercive methods in solving population problems. Every one of his prophecies was fulfilled! With a little reflection, it became obvious to me that once contraception is accepted, it becomes impossible for the church that accepts contraception to claim that any sexual act between consenting persons is wrong. If married couples, by means of contraception, can render the act sterile; that is, engage in it for the pleasure alone, then no meaningful reason can be given why unmarried persons and homosexuals persons should not be free to engage in sexual acts. In fact, once contraception is accepted no valid and meaningful reason can be given as to why even adultery is wrong. I am aware that many would want to argue this latter point, but I think that this point, while not expressly articulated in our society, is intuitively understood and acted upon. Finally where contraception is accepted, the violent and murderous act of abortion is required to assure that the sexual act will be sterile for those who wish it to be sterile.

By the time I was in my mid-fifties, I had come to the conclusion that the Catholic Church taught the truth in matters of faith and morals, that the Petrine office was essential to the life of the Church and was founded by Christ himself, that Mariology was essential to a sound and correct Christology and that Mary by her fiat modeled the "yes" that God seeks from each of us and yet I did not enter the Catholic Church. Why? I was afraid. Was I lacking in faith? I couldn't figure out how I was going to support my family if I resigned my pastorate and entered the Catholic Church. So, I continued to serve as a Lutheran pastor until I felt I could live on my retirement. The wait was painful, but there was one positive result that I believe was a fruit of waiting. Ten years ago I carried in my heart a residue of bitterness toward the Lutheran Church. That bitterness is now gone. For that I thank God.

Today Marcia and I look forward with joy to serving God in the Catholic Church and we pray that someday our children, my brothers and sister, and many dear friends and former colleagues, all "great saints in the making,"[12] will be in full communion with the Catholic Church.

Jim Cope retired in the fall of 1999 and lives in west central Ohio with his wife Marcia and their youngest daughter Rebecca. Jim is currently looking for a way to use his skills, training, and experience to serve the Catholic Church. He admits his most pressing question is, "How may I serve?"

---

[12] An expression used by our parish priest, Father David Zink.

The Grass is Greener

Arthur Bowman

When my father set out from the Midwest for California in 1949, he was heading for greener pastures. The Midwest was too burdened with toxic residue from his growing up years. California was all the rage and so that is where he headed. His first stop was Riverside, California. He phoned home one evening to announce that he was going to buy a chicken ranch. My mother prevailed against this far out project and so he began his search anew, this time in the northern part of the state. Soon he found both a job and a house and sent for us--my mother, brother, sister and me.

California was home until I went off to college. Eventually I would adopt the Midwest as my physical and spiritual home, but it was in California that my faith was given the beginning shape that would one day take the full form and substance of Roman Catholicism.

I grew up going to an evangelical church. I was in church every Sunday morning and evening. Dutifully I attended Bible camp in my pre teen years, graduating to Youth for Christ with the dawning of adolescence. The spiritual air I breathed was that of the pietist revivals that had filled the souls of many of the early Swedish immigrants to America. The evangelical church I attended was good enough for them and thus for me. As far as I was concerned First Covenant Church in San Jose, California was the way church was supposed to be. All that was to change.

The first inkling I had that there was another world of church came when I began the study of California history in the fifth grade. One cannot study California history without learning about Father Junipero Serra and the California missions he founded up and down the west coast. My introduction to the Catholic Church had commenced. My interest in things Catholic was increasingly whetted with each succeeding visit to one of the missions built by Father Serra. I would have chosen him to be my patron saint had I not joined the Roman Catholic Church on the feast of St. Jerome. A tree in the back yard was decommissioned out from under the shadow of Martin Luther and blessed with Father Serra's name, however. I am getting ahead of my self now, but step by step I was being led down a path that would one day lead me to Rome.

My first meeting with a bishop

My interest in the Roman Catholic Church was ushered forward when our neighbors, the Boscios, were visited by a Bishop from Africa. The Boscio's eldest son was a priest serving the church in Africa. As an honor to his parents, Father Boscio's Bishop scheduled a visit to the Boscio family while on his tour of America. As the day neared for the Bishop to arrive, an invitation went out from the Boscio's to all the neighborhood to join them in welcoming the Bishop to their home. We neighborhood Protestant's grew restless as no one among us had ever met a Bishop before. To a person we wondered, "How shall we address the Bishop?" Some said that it would be proper to bow before the Bishop and kiss his ring. At this suggestion, Protestant sensibilities were put on alert. I remember arguing tooth and nail against such a greeting, yet all the while being somewhat intrigued by the possibility.

I cannot recall whether or not I knelt and kissed the Bishop's ring. I would not hesitate now to do so, but then it was a gesture I had no way of putting in context. My guess is that I shook his hand as I gazed in perplexity at his serene countenance.

No more bishops or religious dignitaries interrupted the next several years as adolescent yearnings occupied my days and nights: football, basketball, baseball, girls, trips to the beach, fooling around. Things religious were put on hold, but stirrings of the spirit from time to time hinted that all was not settled.

Attracted by liturgical music

My college years seem in hindsight rather prosaic. There were minor flirtations with Marxism, Zen, and Existentialism. One revelatory experience does stand out, however.

I did not typically hang out with music majors, but one evening in the dorm I happened to join one of their music bull sessions. One of the more avant-garde of their group had just purchased a long playing record and was anxious to have us hear it. I was curious so stayed to find out what it was that so excited him. The recording was "Twentieth Century Folk Mass."

A new world opened to me as I listened to liturgical church music unlike anything I had ever heard. It thrilled me that there were churches where such music was played. So entranced was I that I went right out and bought my own copy, poor though I was. My first exposure to classical liturgy, albeit in a rather modern musical style, was to have effects beyond which I could ever have imagined. Nowhere in my evangelical background was there anything to approximate the "Twentieth Century Folk Mass." I knew then and there that a window had been opened and a fresh breeze had blown over me, but as there was no steady reinforcement, I did not pursue my new-found love of liturgy until many years later.

As I now reflect on my spiritual life during my college years, I believe that I had exhausted the resources available to me in evangelicalism. I knew I was saved so that issue had been dealt with. But where to go from there? The energy in evangelicalism was spent in winning souls for Christ. Those who were saved were urged on to help win others for Christ. The saved were left with that one task and not much more. Being in the presence of God would be taken care of in heaven. While on earth, it was best to spend one's energy getting as many souls as possible onto the heaven bound train.

Because I did not have the resources at that time to move beyond evangelicalism, I stayed put. I didn't try out different churches even though I was exploring new philosophical and theological territory. I remember when John Robinson's book "Honest to God" hit the bookstores. I raced to purchase my copy. I was more hungry for things of God than I had realized. Robinson's book did little to satisfy this hunger, but my eagerness to buy and read it helped me to realize that I was searching for something to feed my soul.

After graduating from college with majors in Philosophy and Psychology, I moved from Chicago, Illinois to St. Paul, Minnesota and enrolled at St. Thomas College. For the first time in my life I was out of the evangelical nest and on my own. Although I did not explore the opportunities to grow in my religious life at St. Thomas, things Catholic permeated the atmosphere there and breathing it in was easier than I could have imagined. I was being softened. My part-time job in the library softened me more. My job was to file daily reports being sent to the library from Rome where Vatican II was in progress. Before I would file the reports I would spend a little time reading them. Nothing seemed dubious or devious. My interest in things Catholic grew.

We head West

After receiving my Master of Arts degree, I married Barbara Widboom of Worthington, Minnesota, who had recently graduated from the University of Minnesota. Together we set out for my home state of California to teach school. A teaching deferment held out the promise of my being deferred from going to Vietnam. The deferment was soon deferred.

My desire to go to seminary and prepare for the pastoral ministry surfaced just as my teaching deferment was lifted. I am sure that the admissions office of he seminary to which I applied looked at my application somewhat skeptically, thinking they had another draft dodger seeking an easy out from the war in Vietnam. My motives were honest, however. My love for the church and my desire to share the joy of the Christian faith were the prime movers in my applying.

Accepted by North Park Theological Seminary into their Bachelors of Divinity program, Barbara and I left for Chicago in the summer of 1966. My intention was to become a pastor in the Evangelical Covenant Church of America. I knew being a Covenant pastor would prove to be a challenge as I could not in good conscience embrace the church's pietistic ethos. If I could manage pastoral positions where strict evangelical piety did not hold sway, I had a fighting chance. With a little help from my superiors I could hopefully avoid those places where push might come to shove.

I loved my four years of work in the seminary. The collegiality, the academics, the lively discussions; I embraced them all. The Old Testament books of Amos and Hosea came as a revelation. Church history opened to my mind's eye one new vista after another. With a lively sense that I now had all the answers and all the tools, I journeyed off to be the intern pastor of the Covenant Church in Beverly, Massachusetts. I couldn't have been happier. The more liberal Covenant Churches were to be found in the East and thus I would be right where I could be myself, feeling right at home. And so it proved to be.

When I returned to Chicago from Beverly, Massachusetts for my last year of seminary, Barbara was pregnant with our first child. Barbara would not be able to work outside the home so I was left with only one alternative-work and study. Through the recommendation of a classmate, I was offered a job as an assistant to the pastor of an inner city Lutheran Church. I had never been in a Lutheran Church before, much less worked in one, but the hours dovetailed well with my class schedule and the work looked challenging so I jumped in feet first.

My introduction to Lutheranism at Holy Communion Lutheran Church whetted my appetite for things Lutheran. I had never worshipped in a formal liturgical setting before but with each passing week at Holy Communion Church I fell more deeply in love with formal liturgy and the sacrament of Holy Communion. Where before I had sat in the pew waiting for the crackers and grape juice to be passed, now I could get up out of the pew and go forward to kneel before the altar and have bread and wine given to me with the accompanying words, "The body of Christ; the blood of Christ." I knew that this way was right and true. How could I ever go back to sitting in the pew and waiting for the quarterly celebration of the Eucharist? At the singing of the liturgy my spirit rejoiced. I knew it would be just a matter of time before I left the Evangelical Covenant Church for the Lutheran Church.

I believed it only right and fair to serve a Covenant Church upon graduation from seminary. The Covenant Church had nurtured me in the faith and I felt obligated to see if I could be a good fit as a pastor in one of her churches. I gave my best effort as an associate pastor at First Covenant Church in Youngstown, Ohio, but with each passing season I realized I was a fish out of water. I soon contacted the Bishop of the Illinois Synod of the Lutheran Church in America and began the process of transferring my ordination. Soon I was serving a Lutheran congregation in Illinois.

Leaving behind the church of my youth was difficult. I value loyalty and I was not being such. Family is important to me and I was separating myself from my family. But a greater desire had taken hold of me, the desire to be part of the fullness of the church. Father Serra and St. Francis and Teresa of Avila and Mother Teresa were my brothers and sisters and I wanted to be one with them in the church. As a Protestant they would be only distant relatives for me. I desired to be in more full communion with them.

After three years as a pastor in The Evangelical Covenant Church in America, I transferred my ordination to the Lutheran Church in America. I didn't become one with all the saints, but I was getting closer. As a Lutheran pastor, of all the special celebrations during the Church Year that called forth my most creative energy, All Saints Sunday stands out. I had not experienced this celebration in the Covenant Church. As a Lutheran, I had my first taste of being in communion with the saints. Years later when my wife, Barbara was received into the Roman Catholic Church at the Easter Vigil, tears rolled down my cheeks as we sang the litany of the saints. Unknowingly, my deep desire to be in communion with the saints was moving me in the direction of becoming a Roman Catholic.

Though my evangelical background kept me bereft of much of what was part and parcel of pre Reformation Christianity, I will always be grateful for the gifts I did receive. I am grateful for solid biblical preaching, rousing hymnody, passion for evangelism, and the witness of Christian men and women who nurtured me in the faith as I grew to manhood: Bruce Stephenson, Mac Martinez, Paul Anderson, Lloyd and Eunice Robeck, Bud LaMedrid, Warner Swanson, Gust Berquist, and others known only to God. Leaving the church of my youth also meant leaving the friends I had come to love while in seminary, friends who I would be able to lean into when times got tough. I would be an unknown among the Bishops of the Lutheran Church in America, so getting recommended for a call to a church could prove difficult. My support system in the church would have to be built from scratch, never an easy task.

I was young and energetic so I plowed ahead. There were moments when I yearned for the security of the familiar, but with the newness of Lutheranism enlivening my imagination at every point, I barely noticed. Relating as a Lutheran to members of my immediate family did and does require special graces, however. I wondered if my status as a Lutheran pastor would be threatening to family members and old friends from my Covenant days. The issue remains an issue I am quite sure. Sensitive to the confusion of others as to the why's and wherefore's of my exodus from the Covenant Church, I determined that I would not aggressively make my reasons for becoming a Lutheran known. I would wait for questions before I would begin to tell my story.

Change was and is disruptive for all concerned. Yet change is often the only way new life can begin. Some people seem to change just for the sake of change. Change is a good way to get out of a rut. Whenever I have come to the place where I believed change was necessary, I have sought spiritual counsel so that I might examine my motives and see if there was anything in my desires that was hidden from my understanding. Was I a rebel? Was I fighting some unconscious battle with authority? Was I trying to solve some deep-seated psychological problem? Through excellent counsel I became aware that my desire to move beyond the religion of my youth was never change for change's sake nor was it a need to work out unconscious and deep seated psychological problems. It became more and more clear to me that the issue I was dealing with were God's call to be part of the Roman Catholic Church, the church that Jesus Christ founded upon the rock which was Peter. Step by step I was being led by the Holy Spirit to know and do what God intended.

Going home

As a Lutheran pastor I served six congregations, thirty years of pastoral ministry. Ultimately, however, being a Lutheran meant being half way home, a lighter shade of green. The Covenant Church had started me out on my spiritual journey; the Lutheran church had helped me along the way; but eventually I came to the place where I realized that as a Lutheran I would end up short of the high calling of Jesus Christ. To get to my spiritual home I would have to commit myself to the Roman Catholic Church.

I left the Lutheran church both from disillusionment and from illumination. I enjoyed my work as the senior pastor of a large Lutheran Church in Minnesota. But as I became more and more familiar with the Roman Catholic Church I became disillusioned with things Lutheran. The grass seemed so much greener on the other side of the fence. The Roman Catholic Church's connectedness through her Bishops all the way back to Peter seemed solid and right. The moral authority of the Roman Catholic Church on abortion, homosexuality, and marriage was unequivocal. The teaching authority of Roman Catholic Church was not vested in majority votes at church conventions but in the Magisterium of the Church. This I believed was how the Church should bear witness to the Gospel of Jesus Christ.

When the Evangelical Lutheran Church in America offered coverage for abortions in it's health care policy for church employees, I felt myself slipping away from being a loyal son and pastor. With each passing attempt to allow for the ordination of practicing homosexuals, I slipped further away. But it was not so much the liberal social positions taken by the E.L.C.A. that finally convinced me that I could no longer remain a pastor. The stumbling block was the ecclesiology of the E.L.C.A. My deepening awareness of the different understandings that Lutherans and Roman Catholics have about the nature of the Church led to the conclusion that the difference between the two is not one of degree but of kind.

I had always thought that Roman Catholics were different from Lutherans on the basis of a more formal liturgy, devotion to Mary, celibacy for the clergy, and the place of saints. These differences are real, but not as substantial as the issue of authority. For Roman Catholics the locus of authority resides in the Pope and the Bishops. As this truth became more and more real to me I could no longer tolerate Lutheran Church Conventions made up of special interest groups detailing what Lutheran belief and practice should be. Theoretically, a Lutheran Church Convention could vote Easter off the Church calendar.

The issue of authority in the church most importantly extends to the meaning of ordination and the validity of the sacraments. The Lutheran Church's lack of both a teaching Magisterium and a single authority figure caused me to become suspect of what authority the Lutheran Church really possessed, if any. I shared with a friend an analogy that helped me to make sense of how a priest in the Roman Catholic Church is different from a pastor in the Lutheran Church. "Suppose," I said, "that someone pulled your car over on the highway and wrote on a piece of paper that you were speeding and had to pay a fine of one hundred dollars. If the person who pulled you over were a state trooper legally authorized by the state to issue you a ticket, it would all be legitimate. You would have to pay the ticket or be held in contempt. But what if the person issuing the ticket had no authority to do so other than his personal whim? The ticket would be invalid because it was not authentic. You could ignore it with impunity. The person who stands at the altar and consecrates the bread and the wine is either legitimate or illegitimate. The state has its ways of legitimizing someone to issue traffic tickets. The Church has its ways of legitimizing someone to consecrate the bread and the wine. Those not legitimized have no real authority to either issue traffic tickets or to consecrate the bread and wine at the Eucharist. The Church legitimizes persons to consecrate the bread and the wine through the Bishop who himself was legitimated by a Bishop who can trace his legitimacy back to Jesus Christ, who consecrated Peter to be the first Pope." I had come to the place where I believed I was a Christian layman. My pastoral office was not legitimate.

In saying, "My pastoral office was not legitimate," I do not believe that all I did as a pastor in the Lutheran Church was to no avail. God uses Christians from Protestant denominations to do his will. But what Protestant pastor's do is not a full expression of what God intends for the clergy of his Church. Because Protestant pastors are not in full communion with the Roman Catholic Church, they have no legitimacy to offer the sacrifice of the mass. If I believed other than this, I would still be an ordained pastor in the E.L.C.A. Because a good friend helped me to see that as a Lutheran pastor I was a "lay Christian," I could not keep up the pretense.

And so on the Feast of St. Jerome, I was received into the Roman Catholic Church. Joining me at Mass were several members of the American Chesterton Society. These friends, some of whom had similar pilgrimages from evangelicalism to Rome, were a great support. Our shared mentor, of course, was present, albeit from afar. G.K. Chesterton's writing and witness had gently nudged me day by day to take the final step into the Roman Catholic Church. Chesterton's name is attached to a growing Norwegian Maple tree in our back yard. I pray that some day G.K. Chesterton will be sainted for he has been both source and inspiration for many to know the joy of being in communion with Rome.

I was home. No bells or whistles. No opening skies. A place to pray. A place to confess my sin. A place to receive the Body and Blood of Jesus Christ. A place that called for my obedience to the teaching of the Holy Father and the Magisterium. A place to be in communion with all the saints. A place to become more acquainted with someone almost a stranger, the Blessed Virgin Mary. A place where the fullness of God was and is pleased to dwell.

As I now seek to find my place in the ministry of the Church, I have been fortunate to belong to a parish where the priest has affirmed me and the gifts God has given me. I hope to teach, to catechize, to work with sponsors of those preparing for marriage, to one day serve on the parish council, and maybe one day assist parishes administratively during pastoral vacancies. The office of the Bishop in the diocese of St. Paul-Minneapolis has welcomed me warmly and encouraged me in my efforts. I trust God will direct my paths as he has in the many years of my pilgrimage to the green, green grass of home.

Art Bowman served as a Lutheran pastor for 30 years. Both he and his wife, Barbara, were received into the Catholic Church during the Jubilee Year, 2000. They have three sons and Art is presently working with their eldest son in a startup company. He is serving as a catechist for others preparing to join the Church and is making preparations to serve the Church in some structured way in the near future.

Real Churches Don't Kill Babies

Jennifer Ferrara

"**R**eal churches don't kill babies." My trek to Rome began in the spring of 1996 the day I read this line by Pastor Leonard Klein. This was his critique of the decision of the Church Council of the Evangelical Lutheran Church in American (E.L.C.A.) to reject its own health care provider's carefully worked out restrictions on payment for abortions. Instead, the Church Council decided to cover the cost of any and all abortions procured by E.L.C.A. employees and their dependents. As I read Klein's editorial on the topic, I began to hyperventilate; I knew my life as a Lutheran pastor was never going to be the same.

Prior to this point, I had never seriously considered becoming Roman Catholic. The thought did briefly cross my mind when Richard John Neuhaus made the transition in 1990. He was a Lutheran pastor and the *de facto* leader of the evangelical catholic cause with which I identified myself. Evangelical Catholics view Lutheranism as a reform movement within and for the one Church of Christ. They believe Martin Luther never intended to create a permanently separated communion of Christians. Therefore, Lutherans have a responsibility to work toward reconciliation with Rome. If such an understanding of Lutheranism ever had a chance of becoming the predominate view among Lutherans, Neuhaus' departure seemed to dash all such hopes. He forced me and others to confront the fact that Lutheranism's separated ecclesial existence is accepted by most Lutherans, not reluctantly for the sake of the Gospel, but wholeheartedly as the preferred state of affairs. In other words, Lutheranism has become, perhaps always has been, just another Protestant denomination among Protestant denominations.

After a short time of feeling angry and depressed, I chose to ignore the implications of Neuhaus' move. The idea of following him to Rome was incomprehensible. He was an unmarried male and intended to become a priest. I was a married, ordained female. Though I knew nothing of his thoughts upon the subject, I felt he had betrayed the cause of women's ordination. In the fall of 1990, I began to take graduate level courses at the Lutheran Seminary in Philadelphia. Once again, I was happy to be a fourth-generation Lutheran pastor steeped in the traditions, theology and ethos of Lutheranism. I was not contemplating conversion at all.

A storm shakes my inmost calm

Leonard Klein's editorial, which appeared in *Lutheran Forum*, shattered the relative calm of my life. He labeled the decision of the Church Council of the E.L.C.A. to fund abortions schismatic: "The E.L.C.A.'s inability to honor an ancient moral consensus of the Church and the widest witness of the most vibrant Christian communities to the present, along with the collapse of morality into subjectivity, would appear to make it something other than the One Holy, Catholic and Apostolic Church confessed in the creeds." I knew the phrase "culture of death" because it appeared in journals such as Neuhaus' *First Things*. However, I had never read John Paul II's encyclical *Evangelium Vitae*. I did and was awestruck. The leadership of the E.L.C.A. has replaced claims for authority with calls for openness and dialogue, and these are often barely disguised attempts to bludgeon theological conservatives into changing their positions. One only need look at the Division for Church in Society's 1993 social statement on human sexuality to see what I mean. It states, "As Lutherans, we offer guidelines but we also affirm our Christian freedom to make responsible decisions specific to our life situations." It proceeds to explain not everyone's life situation falls into the categories of marriage or celibacy, the other situations being cohabitation and homosexual relationships. From our enlightened perch, we can see both Scripture (especially St. Paul's writings) and Church Tradition are hopelessly out of touch with modern views of human sexuality. Two thousand years wiser, we now know "mutual commitment" and "not the license or ceremony" is what counts. By contrast, in *Evangelium Vitae*, I encountered the constancy of the Church's moral teachings on sexual morality and human life stated in the loving and compelling way that is a hallmark of Pope John Paul II. Like a person coming to terms with the death of a loved one, I saw my church body had fallen captive to the culture of death.

We live in strange and unsettling times when many in our churches have ceased to recognize the most basic of Christian beliefs in God as Creator and Redeemer. When we reject human life at any stage in its development, we reject the triune God and begin to live as if he did not exist. Pope John Paul II explains: "It is precisely in the 'flesh' of every person that Christ continues to reveal himself and to enter into fellowship with us, so that rejection of human life, in whatever form that rejection takes, is really a rejection of Christ." As John Cardinal O'Connor has said, "The culture of death is a culture without God." I was part of a church whose leadership rejects God.

As a pastor, I had encountered the horrible reality of abortion face to face. Several of my parishioners opted to have abortions. Though I told these women abortion is murder, I sounded as if I was offering an opinion. I failed to explain that abortion is "really a rejection of Christ." I failed to tell them such action would put their very souls at stake. I failed to be the voice of a Church and

Tradition that regards abortion as the murder of God's most innocent creatures. However, I also recognized that to take a firm stand on abortion was extremely difficult in a church that offers no authoritative stance on a single matter having to do with sexual ethics or the sanctity of human life. My friend and fellow pastor, Patricia Ireland, admitted to having similar experiences with parishioners who had had abortions. Together we confessed our failure in an open letter published by *Lutheran Forum*. In the letter, we pleaded with the bishops of the E.L.C.A. to take up their proper role as judges of doctrine and morals and condemn the decision of the E.L.C.A. Church Council to fund any and all abortions. We also said if they failed to take such action, we would have to decide if we could continue to serve the E.L.C.A. Needless to say, the bishops took no action.

At times, I wondered if I was insane. Why did this abortion issue bother me so much when my orthodox colleagues, many of whom were far brighter and more theologically astute than I, did not seem to care? To be more precise, no one with whom I spoke thought it reason enough to leave the E.L.C.A. I talked to several renowned Lutheran theologians, and they all told me, in so many words, the Roman Catholic Church has problems too. When I pressed them to explain those problems, they pointed to women's ordination, the Marian doctrines and the doctrine of papal infallibility. I did not find their answers convincing. Even if those were problems with the Church, how could they be compared to murder? That is what I believed and continue to believe: the E.L.C.A. is an accomplice in the murder of unborn children. At least my friend Patricia agreed with me. When I asked her if she thought the abortion issue was reason enough to leave the E.L.C.A., her unwavering response was, "Of course it is." In the fall of 1996, she did just that and returned to the church of her childhood.

What was I to do now? Was the E.L.C.A.'s decision to fund abortions sufficient reason to leave? Colleagues suggested it was a negative reason for leaving and, therefore, not a good one. I should not become Catholic simply because I was disillusioned with the E.L.C.A. Instead, I should stay and struggle against the forces of evil within the Lutheran church. I was not so sure. John Paul II says in *Evangelium Vitae*, "Not only is the fact of the destruction of so many human lives still to be born or in their final stage extremely grave and disturbing, but no less grave and disturbing is the fact that conscience itself, darkened as it were by...widespread conditioning, is finding it increasingly difficult to distinguish between good and evil in what concerns the basic value of human life." I worried about my own conscience. Would I begin to lose my ability to distinguish between good and evil if I stayed in a church that had lost such powers of discernment? Was I spiritually and emotionally strong enough to wage a lifelong battle against the leadership of my church? Would it be good for my soul to do so? Scripture says we must, at some point, separate ourselves from evildoers. I was beginning to think I needed to do just that.

By this time, another person whom I deeply respect, the Lutheran patristics scholar Robert Wilken, had converted. In a letter he wrote to me about his experiences as a new Catholic, he said the difficulty with the Reformation was that it conceived of the Church's continuity with the past and its unity in terms of an idea (justification by grace through faith). By contrast, Catholicism thinks first of the concrete life of the Church—the life of a community with tangible links stretching back over the centuries. This observation made a profound impression upon me. Leonard Klein had written of the E.L.C.A.'s decision to fund abortions: "We need not doubt that faithful congregations and synods are still church, but in a most critical sense the wider fellowship to which they belong no longer deserves the credence which one would expect to give to 'the Church.'" In what sense are congregations and synods still church if the wider Church to which they belong is not Church? Klein seemed to be falling back on the minimalist definition of church found in the Augsburg Confession: "For it is sufficient for the true unity of the Christian church that the Gospel is preached in conformity with a pure understanding of it and that the sacraments be administered in accordance with the divine Word." I was finding this definition increasingly unsatisfactory. I had an image in my mind of congregations and synods floating around untethered in deep, dark space. I longed to experience those tangible links that connect Catholics to one another across time and space.

I was now questioning not only the actions of the E.L.C.A., but the foundations of Lutheranism's separate existence as a church. Was it possible that Lutheranism was misconceived from its inception? Was the E.L.C.A.'s funding of abortions a symptom of a more serious disease? My friend and fellow pastor convert, Jeff Finch, puts it this way: "The reformation had introduced two cancerous doctrines (*Sola Fide* and *Sola Scriptura*) which eventually metastasized and destroyed the very foundation of the faith as a whole, especially its accession to private judgment over the teaching authority of the Church." Shared societal standards had masked the problem for 500 years, but the antinomianism (lawlessness) inherent to Lutheranism exists virtually unbridled in the E.L.C.A. today. I was becoming increasingly convinced Christians cannot do without a Magisterium that interprets Scripture in light of the Great Tradition. My evangelical friends told me I did not take the authority of the Bible seriously enough. Several Lutherans recommended the conservative Lutheran Church Missouri Synod (the communion of my youth) as an alternative. However, history demonstrates that an insistence upon Scripture alone, no matter how much authority we grant it, leads to schism. If the teachings of Scripture are as self-evident as Luther argued, why do we have so many different Protestant groups all claiming their interpretation of Scripture is the right one?

As I mulled over these questions, I continued to read—papal encyclicals, Vatican II documents, the *Catechism of the Catholic Church*, theologians such as John Henry Newman, Louis Bouyer, Hans Urs von Balthasar, and Joseph Cardinal Ratzinger. I was struck again and again by the contrast between official Catholic Church documents and the statements emanating from the offices of the E.L.C.A. leadership. I wondered what would happen if we had to rely upon the leadership of the E.L.C.A. to preserve Christianity for future generations. The leaders of the E.L.C.A. had demonstrated a singular lack of courage in dealing with the defining issues of our time. Friends suggested I was seeking an authority in order to alleviate my own anxieties. I could not completely discount this notion though I wasn't exactly sure what was wrong with it. Perhaps my anxieties were pointing me toward the Truth. The unwavering leadership of the Magisterium in these times of cultural and moral turmoil suggested it was exactly what it claimed to be.

Protestants and the papacy

For theologically aware Protestants, the major stumbling block for considering Roman Catholicism a viable alternative is the authority of the Magisterium and especially the Pope. Even those who are not theologically inclined think papal tyranny made necessary the Reformation. Therefore, the papacy as an institution can never be trusted. When former Lutheran colleagues say Rome has problems too, they usually have in mind some form of perceived papal abuses. Better to live free, even if that freedom involves the risk of antinomianism. According to Lutheran theology, freedom from the law is at the heart of the Gospel which is the promise of justification by grace through faith (apart from works of the law). Lutherans are allergic to anything that could be possibly construed as a law one must follow in order to be saved. They believe the institution of the papacy is responsible for many such laws. They cannot forget the time of the Reformation and the specter of such abuses occurring again. So goes the Lutheran way of thinking. These are hard notions to dispel. Lutherans do not take kindly to being told there are things other than the Gospel message they are required to believe.

By contrast, for Catholics, servitude to the moral and ecclesial law leads to freedom; that is, freedom from sin, ergo freedom to be fully human. Ironically, Lutherans, who enthusiastically talk about our freedom in the Gospel, refuse to set men, women (and most importantly children) free from slavery to the sin of abortion because they are suspicious of any laws which bind the individual conscience. However, we do not need to be free from the law in order to love and serve others, as Luther claimed. Through the sacraments of the Church, God grants us the grace to fulfill the law. Though we shall always fall short of perfect fulfillment of the law, we are able with God's help to make progress. Our hearts expand more and more to the grace of God, and we become more loving, more Christ-like. Catholics believe Jesus not only laid down his life for us once and for all on the cross but makes present that Sacrifice at every Holy Mass. Each time the Eucharist is celebrated, we offer our own lives of sacrificing love in union with his Sacrifice. By entering into communion with Christ's Body, the Church, we embark on a pilgrimage of holiness. The moral and ecclesial law are the guideposts for this journey. Thus, the Church provides us with the means of grace and the moral guidance to grow in love for God and others.

Father Neuhaus has written: "For the ecclesial Christian, Christ the head and his body the Church are inseparable; faith in Christ and faith in the Church is one act of faith; the imperative of fidelity is to be in closest communion with the Church most fully and rightly ordered through time." In the end, belief that the Magisterium best orders the Church through time requires a leap of faith. All the arguments in the world for the necessity of the Magisterium will not change the minds of those who are determined not to believe; it is an act of faith. I can only credit the Holy Spirit with opening my eyes to the truth about the Magisterium. Once I passed through this door, nothing appeared the same to me.

A blessing in disguise

While intellectually I was bounding toward the Church, my personal and professional life was in a state of limbo. In the fall of 1996, I was not serving a parish. I had three small children and had decided to take a leave from parish work to care for them. I had left somewhat reluctantly, but the time off turned out to be a blessing because I could not have carried on with the kind of doubts I was experiencing. I was finding it increasingly difficult to simply attend a Lutheran church but could not yet bring myself to attend Mass. Though I had given my mind over to the Church, I had not as yet given my heart. It was perhaps the most spiritually arid time of my life. I was afraid to pray about my struggles because I did not want to receive an answer. When surveying the simple facts, the decision should have been a fairly easy one. In fact, former colleagues have suggested, with a certain amount of bitterness, that my conversion was a "cake walk," relatively speaking. They say that because I can afford not to work and because I am married to a Roman Catholic.

They are mostly right. I am indeed fortunate to be married to a lifelong Catholic. When I look over the course of my life, it now appears I have been on a path toward Rome the whole time. However, for most of our marriage I did not secretly yearn to be Roman Catholic. My husband comes from a devout Italian Roman Catholic family who strenuously objected to their eldest son marrying a Lutheran minister. It was a battle with winners and losers, and I had apparently

75

won. Though my husband remained a Catholic in name, in reality my ministry took him away from the Catholic Church. While I was in the parish, he attended my services and was active within the congregation. After we had children, I baptized them; and we always went to a Lutheran church. On a very personal level, I did not want to relinquish that for which I had fought so hard, namely my identity as a Lutheran minister.

My husband, who knew all this about me, did not try to persuade me either way. He understood that if I made a precipitous decision, I would regret it down the line. However, he did begin to talk about the need to be united in our faith for the sake of the children. Though he was trying to be helpful, this added to the pressure I already felt to make a decision. The boys were approaching first communion age. They were fond of their Lutheran church and Sunday School but had no real attachment to Lutheranism. It would have been a good time to make the transition. Yet, I could not bring myself to do it. We continued to worship at our Lutheran parish, and I became more and more disconnected from what was taking place on Sunday morning.

Shadow worship?

Louis Bouyer, in *Spirit and Forms of the Protestantism*, suggests Lutheran worship is a shadow or imitation of Roman Catholic worship—beautiful perhaps but without substance. This metaphor colored my perceptions as I went through the motions of attending Lutheran services and especially as I received Holy Communion. As a Lutheran, I believed in the bodily presence of Christ in the eucharistic elements; however, I also believed they remain bread and wine. Growing up, I was taught Christ is in, with and under the elements. As a child, I did not know what that meant, and I still do not as an adult. In seminary, I learned Lutherans do not agree on whether Christ remains present in the elements after the congregation finishes receiving Communion. Luther seemed to believe in a spatial, irreversible change; whereas Philip Melanchthon suggested Christ's presence is a temporal, that is, temporary event. Or so I was taught. In any case, the vast majority of Lutherans do not reserve the host, suggesting whatever takes place ceases to be after Communion is over. As a pastor, I did not reserve the host or finish the wine and was not bothered in the least. Now I found myself deeply troubled by what I was observing. Today's Lutherans are very fond of using baked bread for Communion. What this means is crumbs of all sizes invariably end up on the floor. These crumbs became the focus of my Communion experience. I knew the sexton would simply vacuum them up later in the day. I thought, if Lutherans treat the elements with such obvious irreverence, they cannot possibly believe they signify much of anything. If they believed the bread was Christ's body, they would not send it out with the trash. I began to doubt that anything was occurring during Lutheran Communion beyond a remembrance of Christ's death and resurrection.

As a Lutheran, I liked to point out the similarities in the Lutheran and Catholic understandings of the Eucharist. I even felt free to receive Communion at Catholic Mass because I believed in the Real Presence of Christ. (I am sorry to say several priests agreed with me and knowingly let me receive the host.) I now saw our agreement was illusory. The words we use to describe the Eucharist are similar, but the theological connotations are entirely different. According to Lutheran theology, the Holy Spirit, operating through the spoken words of institution, brings about whatever change takes place in the elements. In the end, it does not matter who speaks the words. Some Lutherans argue only ordained pastors should speak the words of institution for the sake of good order, if nothing else. However, I am personally familiar with circumstances in which bishops have given lay people permission to preside at Communion. The very fact there is disagreement over this issue demonstrates how ambiguous is the Lutheran theology of the Eucharist. For Roman Catholics, the identity of the speaker of the words of institution is the key to the sacrament's efficacy. The priest represents Christ at the sacrifice of the Eucharist, and only a man who has received the sacrament of ordination may preside. He is the conduit through which the Holy Spirit operates.

Questioning the validity of my ordination

I know this is a highly charged subject for Lutherans, especially among those who have been ordained, but I need to admit that as my contemplation of the Eucharist deepened, I began to question the validity of my own ordination. What do I mean by that? I do not mean I did no good as a Lutheran pastor. I do not mean I did not serve a valid function within the Lutheran church. In fact, that is exactly what I did: I served a function. I preached, I taught, I conducted marriages and funerals, and I visited the sick. I made a difference in some people's lives. I found it all profoundly rewarding. However, I had not received the special charism which would allow the Holy Spirit to work through me to change bread and wine into the body and blood of Christ. What is more, I could not have, not only because I had not received the sacrament of ordination but because I, as a woman, could not represent Jesus Christ at the Eucharist.

The women's ordination issue is a wrinkle many converts do not have to deal with directly. I had to, if for no other reason than because the first question almost everyone asked when I expressed an interest in converting was, "How can you become a member of a church body which does not ordain women?" Catholics asked it with the same frequency as Lutherans. Catholics who believe women should be ordained view me as a traitor to the cause. Better to stay in the E.L.C.A. and operate as one of the role models who might just persuade the hierarchy to relent on two millennia of tradition. In the opinion of these Catholics, I was taking a giant step backward. When my friend, Patricia Ireland, and I first started talking about converting, I immediately said I did not want to become "a poster child" for those who oppose women's ordination. That I could completely change my mind on the subject had not yet occurred to me. I knew some people who had converted to Catholicism and took their belief in women's ordination with them into the Church. I also knew I could never do that; I did not want to be a dissenting Roman Catholic.

I must confess I have never been an unmitigated believer in women's ordination. I always felt slightly odd in the role of being an ordained female. Even more telling, I never felt completely at ease at services conducted by female pastors. Somehow I figured it was different when I did them. In my experience, most ordained female pastors are theological liberals, and I reasoned that was the source of my discomfort. However, I also knew a few highly competent, orthodox female ministers. I was loosely associated with a group of female clergy who believed the Lutheran church had never adequately addressed the issue of women's ordination from a scriptural or confessional standpoint. I felt so strongly about this that I made an effort to present scriptural and confessional arguments for women's ordination in an article published by *Lutheran Forum* in 1993. For several years, I accepted my own reasoning.

I begin thinking with the Church

As I seriously contemplated becoming Roman Catholic, I began, on the advice of a fellow pastor convert, "to try to think with the Church." As a Lutheran, I knew well the Magisterium's arguments against women's ordination and had even started to sketch the outline for an article which would critique the Church's position. In retrospect, such ambitions seem like sheer arrogance, but *obsequium* is not a virtue highly valued among Lutherans. Out of deference and obedience to the Magisterium, I finally concluded others can and do know better than I on this issue. I do not intend to trivialize the issue when I say this or imply there is no room for the workings of individual conscience in the Catholic Church. However, for Catholics, to have faith is to be obedient to the faith, that is, to a body of teachings and doctrines that define one's faith. I cannot pick and choose areas where I recognize the authority of the Church—to be able to do so would make the Roman Catholic Church no different from mainline Protestant communities which elevate individual conscience over even commonsense understandings of God's law. In other words, I cannot decide I like the Church's position on abortion but reject it in the case of women's ordination. Over time, I have come to see the all male priesthood as essential to the faith of the Church, not only to her eucharistic theology, but to the Catholic understanding of creation and the inherent differences between men and women and their respective roles in life.

By the summer of 1997, I had made up my mind intellectually. I had arrived at the doorstep of *Lumen Gentium* 14: "Whosoever, therefore, knowing that the Catholic Church was made necessary by God through Jesus Christ, would refuse to enter or to remain in her could not be saved." Even if I was willing to take a chance with my own soul, I had my children to consider and that concentrates the mind. After years of relative silence on the issue, my husband was now open about his preference to return to the Church. My intense search for the truth served to confirm in his own mind that he needed to go home to Rome. That was now weighing heavily on my conscience as well. I had led a Roman Catholic away from the Church and possibly into apostasy. He would never have strayed if it were not for me. I was having all of these thoughts because I was really no longer an outsider but had entered the embrace of the Church.

Dealing with Mary

I found my thoughts turning increasingly toward Mary the Mother of God, typification of the Church. No convert can avoid the issue of Mary. After the Pope, she represents in most Protestants' minds the great divide between them and Catholics. In the parish, when I would tell my parishioners my husband was Catholic, the most common response was, "They believe in Mary, don't they?" The role of Mary is a stumbling block for the most sophisticated Protestant theologians as well. According to most Lutherans, Roman Catholics allow Mary to usurp the role of Christ as sole mediator between God and us. Moreover, the importance Catholics ascribe to Mary is simply unscriptural. One of the great contributions of Luther to the Church, they argue, was to take Mary down a notch or two and present a "biblical" view of her.

When I was Lutheran, I was drawn to Mary, but I never allowed myself to act on my feelings, with one exception. Once, I prayed directly to her and asked for her intercession during a particularly difficult time in my life. My prayer was answered. I never told anyone about this experience but kept it deep within my heart. Another strange episode in my life involved the stained glass windows of the first church to which I was called as a pastor. The church building, which dates from the early 1800s, has beautiful windows. I decided to put together a brochure with pictures of the windows and explanations of the symbols found on them. The only problem was I did not understand the window with the thing that looked like a M with Easter lilies protruding from it. I showed a picture of it to several colleagues, and one finally identified it as the symbol for Mary with the Easter lilies representing her virginity and Christ's resurrection. How could this be? My colleague and I concluded the maker of the windows must have been a Catholic. I have found no other Lutheran church with such a symbol in my area. I now believe Mary was pursuing me even then. To be able to openly believe in her intercession has come as a great relief. The claims the Church makes about her conception and assumption seem natural outgrowths of her role as *Theotokos* (God-bearer).

Though as a Lutheran, I believed Luther had corrected hundreds of years of misunderstanding about the proper role of Mary and the saints, I now saw it as one of the great losses to Protestantism. G. K. Chesterton once said, the Church is ever so much larger from the inside than from the outside. One of the effects of the Reformation was to shrink the Church. In the Catholic Church, I have discovered a fascinating and wonderful world populated by many different characters and encompassing a seemingly endless variety of traditions all held together by the invisible threads of a shared ecclesial communion spun like a web out of Rome. A friend of mine, Father Joseph Wilson, compares the Catholic Church to a vast Gothic cathedral, with many side chapels and intimate ways to experience God, but all opening onto the one Altar. As a Catholic, I never cease to be amazed by the astonishing diversity of private devotions, devotions surrounding saints, religious orders and movements all with distinctive patterns of discipleship, and rich schools of spirituality with writings inexhaustible in their depth. As Father Wilson says, "Real love finds a multitude of ways in which to express itself." Lutheranism is one dimensional, by comparison, and despite the fact some Lutherans now ordain women, starkly masculine. One result of the loss of the saints (though not the most pernicious) is a lack of women for Protestants to turn to for guidance. To be able to pray to women and reflect upon their lives has added a new and unexpected dimension to my spiritual life. Much to my surprise, I have felt a greater sense of affirmation as a woman in the Catholic Church than I ever had, even as a pastor, in the Lutheran church.

By the fall of 1998, I had entered a no man's land. I was still a rostered pastor, but I was no longer Lutheran in mind or spirit. I had begun to attend Mass with my family. I had hoped this would lead to a sort of spiritual awakening because I had felt dead inside for so long. It only made things worse. I found it much easier to be an intellectual Catholic than a practicing one. The longing which I felt to receive Holy Communion while studying Roman Catholicism disappeared when I began to attend Mass. Instead, I was an observer and a reluctant one at that. I was angry, and I took it out on my husband using phrases such as "you Catholics…" and "your church…." Catholic worship simply did not meet with my expectations. I was disappointed by the seeming lack of reverence for tradition, and I could not help but wonder if those leading and participating in worship really believed what they said they believed. I had actually hoped to participate in the ancient traditions and mysteries of the Church. Instead, I experienced modern music and liturgies that tend to secularize and trivialize the sacred order. The result is a mind-numbing uniformity in worship that is simply astonishing given the vastness of the Church's treasure of liturgical music and practices. At the same time, I missed the traditional Lutheran liturgy and music. I missed the sense of community that is a characteristic of most Protestant parishes. I missed hearing good preaching. Since I did not receive Communion, the truth is I often felt I got nothing out of Mass. Though I knew the purpose of Mass was not for me "to get something out of it," I still felt let down on a deeply personal level.

Leaving the E.L.C.A.

Around this time, I received notice from my Lutheran bishop that I needed to come speak to him about my future plans. I knew this was coming, but now I had to face it squarely. If I told him about my plans to convert, there was no turning back. Yet, I knew I must do just that — anything else would be dishonest. So, much to his great shock, I informed him of my intention to become Catholic. I took the opportunity to confront him on the abortion issue and the E.L.C.A. leadership's efforts to enlighten the laity on the topic of homosexuality. By this time, the E.L.C.A. had entered into altar and pulpit fellowship with the United Church of Christ, a denomination which ordains practicing homosexuals. I told my former bishop that I thought he should take a stand on these issues. He, in turn, was very "pastoral." He told me he would miss me but took joy in the fact that I had found a new church home where I would feel more comfortable. Whatever his true feelings may have been, he seemed unmoved by my assertions. He told me I had a right to my opinions, but the abortion issue, in particular, was not an issue about which the laity cared, as if that were the point. At least I left knowing I had made the right decision.

I just couldn't figure out why I didn't feel any better. Though I had announced to my bishop that I was becoming Roman Catholic, I took no real steps to do so. I did not look into RCIA classes; I did not speak to any priests. I was in conversation with some former Protestant pastors who had converted. They all seemed to know I needed time to work this out on my own. My conscience had driven me to this point, but my heart still lagged behind. C. S. Lewis once wrote of his conversion to Christianity: "The hardness of God is kinder than the softness of men, and His compulsion is our liberation." I hung onto these words because at the time I was experiencing the hardness of God.

I find Christ in the Eucharist

After several months of existing in this limbo of attending Mass and pretty much despising it but knowing there was no going back, Patricia Ireland insisted I go on a retreat with her for pro-life professional women at the Sisters of Life convent in New York. As a pastor, I had been on more retreats than I could count and was not a big fan of them. I often found them to be hokey and a little more touchy-feely than I care to be. I told her I was not interested; she continued to push. So I found myself on a wintry weekend in March traveling to New York proclaiming most of the way I was sure I would hate this.

Several things happened to me that weekend. I heard a theology of sanctification based upon the writings of St. Teresa of Avila that helped explain the spiritual desert through which I had passed. I now knew I had been through a dark night of the soul, and such experiences were often steps toward a deeper union with God—a preparation of sorts. This was just a taste of a spirituality about which I had previously known nothing. As a Lutheran, I felt I understood the essence of the Christian life as set out in the law/gospel dialect of Luther's theology. I could even be a bit smug about it. Now, I felt as if I had been deceived. No one ever told me about the lives of the saints, the writings of the spiritual giants, the incorruptibles, the truth about those who had received the stigmata, the appearances of Mary. I could go on and on. The point is, as a Lutheran, I knew nothing about these great gifts and, therefore, could not draw on them for strength in my own spiritual life.

At the Sisters of Life Convent, I participated, for the first time, in an adoration of the Eucharist and genuinely longed to receive the true body and blood of Christ with my heart as well as my mind. When I was Lutheran, I did not have a deeply personal relationship with Christ, which was a problem because the most faithful Protestants I knew had that one on one relationship with our Lord and Savior. I was drawn to Catholicism, in part, because I thought it would offer in the sacraments and sacramentals more props for my faith; that is, substitutes for a relationship with Christ. On the retreat, I realized I was completely mistaken about this. Those "props" do not substitute for my relationship with Christ and are not, as many Protestants maintain, barriers to a close relationship but are, rather, the means by which one is brought into an intimate relationship with him. There can be nothing more intimate than to receive into one's own body Christ's body and blood. The longer I am Catholic, the closer I draw to Jesus.

I also experienced the mystery, splendor and otherworldliness of the church in worship and in prayer at the convent. The sisters are a group of women unlike any I had ever met before. Though I had met individuals in my life whom I regarded as holy, I had never been in an environment such as this one. Holy people and places are not central to the Lutheran experience. While at the convent, I had an opportunity to step out of the madness of our world for a few precious days. Though the dwelling and chapel of the convent are as plain and unimpressive as can be, it is a holy place where those who enter its confines experience the love of Christ through the ministrations of the sisters.

After my experience at the Sisters of Life convent, I moved rapidly toward becoming Roman Catholic. I finally spoke with a local priest and told him of my difficulties in finding a parish where I could comfortably worship. After being initially surprised by my desire to convert, he recommended an inner-city Italian parish named Holy Rosary. I immediately went to find it. I walked into an unabashedly traditional sanctuary filled with statues and paintings of Jesus, Mary and Joseph. It was aglow with flickering votive candles positioned under statues of Mary holding pink rosary beads and of Joseph holding a plump baby Jesus. It was Lent and the organist was practicing "Oh Sacred Head Now Wounded." The following Sunday, I attended my first Mass at Holy Rosary. There I discovered a seemingly endless variety of Catholic devotions, including prayer hours, rosaries, Fatima devotions, Divine Mercy Masses, and nocturnal adoration. At Holy Rosary, I felt as if I had entered a world with endless layers of meaning with the mystery of Christ in the Eucharist at its center. On Corpus Christi Sunday of 1998, I was received into full communion with the Catholic Church and have never once looked back.

Jennifer Ferrara grew up on the campus of a Lutheran seminary where her father taught homiletics and literature courses. After attending Princeton Theology Seminary and the Lutheran Seminary in Philadelphia, she was ordained to the Ministry of Word and Sacrament in the Lutheran Church in America. She was a pastor for 11 years before converting to Catholicism in June, 1998. She resides in Pennsylvania with her husband, twin sons and daughter. She is a full-time mother and part-time writer, an activity she squeezes in between volunteer work at her church and children's school, sports events, music lessons, scouts, etc.

To Luther and Back

Patricia Sodano Ireland

My story begins long before I became a Lutheran, in my childhood recollections of life as a Catholic in the Church as yet unaffected by modernist cultural whims. I remember making my First Holy Communion at age six and how I loved to carry my never changing little missal with the English translations of the Latin Mass. I remember covering my head with a hat and, more to my liking, a long mantilla. I remember feeling awe in the presence of something so much greater than my little self every time I walked into the Church, and genuflecting until my knee touched the floor. I remember how my heart skipped a beat when I stepped into the holiest of holy places beyond the rail as I helped my mother change the altar linens beneath the tabernacle of the Lord. I recall memorizing the *Baltimore Catechism*, and staring wide-eyed at the holy pictures Sister Loretta Ann showed my class of Jesus' Sacred Heart and the Immaculate Heart of Mary, that we may know we were loved unconditionally. I recall frequent visits to the confessional, First Friday devotions, praying the rosary, weekly novenas, Stations of the Cross, and veneration of the crucifix on Good Friday afternoon. I remember meatless Fridays and three-hour- long, hunger producing, pre-communion fasts. I can picture the altar boy holding a bright shiny brass paten under my tongue when the priest gave me the Eucharist, that not a single crumb of Christ's broken body would fall to the floor.

These remembrances are not simply an excuse to wax nostalgic about a pristine Church in days gone by. The Church in every age is marred by sin of its members, but it was a time distinguished by its unabashed assertion of the transcendence of God. That all changed a few years after the close of Vatican II, when the *insertion* of the glorified self emerged in my little parish and parochial school in suburban New Jersey and elsewhere. Compliance, submission and a peaceful spirit are *not* among my strongest virtues. The birth of egocentrism and irreverence as badges of honor in the 1960s gave me the excuse I desired to follow my baser instincts. Mind you, the Catholic Church did not change its teaching; on the contrary, the Documents of Vatican II upheld and further clarified Catholic tradition and the authority of the Magisterium. Unfortunately, the Council occurred at the threshold of an era characterized by self-serving dissent in culture, politics, social mores, and religion. Capitulating to cultural trends, lay and clerical Catholics alike joined the ranks of dissenters. Professing conformity to a (false) "spirit of Vatican II," dissenters wreaked havoc with

Catholic theology, morality and liturgy.[13] The effects have been far reaching and damaging to generations of Catholics since. Relativism was in; Catholic distinction was out.

While still in parochial school, I experienced a completely different church than the one into which I had been baptized and received first communion. The nuns' habits were modified twice, and the familiar sight of the sisters pacing back and forth outside the church praying their daily *Office* disappeared. The Latin Missal was discarded in favor of solely English language disposable missalettes. The choirloft organ went into hibernation, and guitarists strumming sentimental folk ballads took front and center stage behind where the altar rails used to be. The tabernacle was shifted to the side to make room for the Presider's seat, front and center. Ironically, the statues of Mary, Joseph and the baby Jesus were removed from the sanctuary of my home parish, *Holy Family.* Women's bonnets disappeared, replaced by the new, preferred Sunday attire of blue jeans and sneakers. Meatless Fridays were dropped, and Saturday evening Mass was approved to accommodate convenience.

The change that made the biggest impression on me, however, was the religion curriculum of my parochial school. Doctrinal teaching was de-emphasized to make room for individual truth seeking. One course was called "Becoming a Person," and it encouraged a free range of irreverent expression, to which my argumentative self readily complied. I remember one particular occasion when I ranted and raved about a practice not to my liking in a church I had recently visited. My eighth grade teacher, Sister Maureen, let me go on and on, never once attempting a sound counter explanation. Romantic love as the vehicle for subjective "truths" was the catechetics of choice for my junior high years. My eighth grade graduation Mass served up the romantic and sexy "I Don't Know How to Love Him" from *Jesus Christ, Superstar,* which we belted out with all the heart-felt emotion star-struck teenagers could muster. Below is an excerpt (from memory, *emphases* added).

> I don't know how to love him...
> What to do --How he moves me
> He's a man--He's *just* a man!
> And I've had so many men before
> In very many ways--*He's just one more*
>
> Should I bring him down?
> Should I scream and shout?

---

[13] For an in-depth analysis of *What Went Wrong with Vatican II,* refer to Ralph McEnerny's book of the same name.

Should I speak of love?
Let my feelings out--I never thought I'd come to this
What's it all about?

What's it all about? It was about putting Jesus and me on a level playing field and pitching Catholic practice into the Christian pan-denominational heap. And to my discredit, I lapped up this pap.

I leave the Chuch

College theological studies at Boston College picked up where "Becoming a Person" left off. As an undergraduate theology major, I took five graduate courses, several in B.C.'s summer pastoral ministry program, to which I returned soon after graduation to receive a Master of Arts degree. Radical feminism and liberation theology were the name of the game. Oppression was the *credo* of women and minorities. The Boston Theological Institute (BTI), a consortium of graduate and theological schools, offered a veritable smorgasbord of modernist theologies. I took courses with, attended lectures, and read voraciously the works of dissenting Catholics and Protestants, such as Elizabeth Schussler Fiorenza, Rosemary Radford Reuther, Mary Daly, Gustavo Guiterrez, Hans Kung and Fr. Richard McBrien, to name a few. I gave up the Sunday pre-communion fast and going to confession. I skipped Mass whenever I felt like it, yet I played piano at folk Masses and received the Eucharist. I accepted the "culture of death," which was a staple of college life. I didn't flinch witnessing the abuse of drugs and alcohol around me. My friends' experiences of sexual relationships led me wholeheartedly to advocate birth control and pre-marital sex in the context of "love." I listened to stories of acquaintances' multiple abortions without offering a sobering word, for fear of hurting their feelings.

It was toward the end of my graduate pursuits in pastoral ministry at Boston College that I decided to leave the Catholic Church. For me, it became a *justice* issue, as it seemed all theology was reduced to justice in those days. I came to the *false* conclusion that the Catholic Church was one of the worst oppressors of women and the poor, and I was a victim, a marginal one, among the "*anawim*" described so eloquently in my liberation theology texts. My prayer life was dull. Catholic devotional life had long since given way to theological arguments. We used to joke in graduate school at Boston College, and later in seminary, that we were so busy talking *about* God, that we had no time left to talk *to* God.

Living inside my head became a sinful occupation. I made a conscious decision to leave the Catholic Church and chose Lutheranism, because its rich confessional and theological heritage stimulated my intellect, while its Catholic-like Eucharistic liturgy appealed to my senses. I began instruction with the interim pastor of a small Lutheran church in Newton Centre, Massachusetts. At the end of my course, the pastor, with tears in his eyes, asked me when he should write his letter to the (Lutheran) bishop recommending me to the ministry. Since I was completing my M.A. at Boston College, further education was not in my thoughts; however, I accepted my pastor's suggestion as a call from God. I met with the bishop, and a few months later found myself a Lutheran seminarian at Andover Newton Theological School.

Three memories stand out about this new life. The first was my difficulty in finding a rhythm of devotion. Weekday Mass, Hail Mary's and devotion to the saints had been part and parcel of my prayer life, dull as it had become; however, I felt to be a good Lutheran I had to give up those things. I made a mental note that it was *not* okay to invoke a saint. On the plus side, I began praying with the Bible, something my Catholic childhood did not stress. The second memory was my excitement at seeing an ordained female professor preside at Eucharist. It was like a taste of the forbidden fruit. I couldn't wait to do it, too. The third memory was of feeling like an outsider. Catholicism is a way of life. Add my robust Italian heritage to Catholic culture, and I felt as though I were giving up my identity. I never truly felt as though I belonged in the Lutheran Church, especially the first two New England congregations I served, which were ethnically German and Swedish. I quickly seized upon those uncomfortable (and guilty) feelings of leaving something important behind, and deemed them to be further evidence of my victimhood as woman and former Catholic. I embraced the feminist/womanist notion that being made to feel uncomfortable or an outsider in a male-dominated world is a good indication of one's victimization.

I soon discovered there was a benefit to being a victim: one's outsider or victim status was the entrance ticket into a whole new world of power and privilege in the Lutheran ministry. While a seminarian, I attended the fifteenth anniversary conference celebrating the ordination of women in the Lutheran Church. It was no celebration, but a lamentation orgy. Day after day was spent emoting angst over the suffering of female clergy at the hands of men. Here I was in a Church where women were ordained, and I couldn't find a satisfied woman among them. While many tales of inequitable compensation and prejudice rang true, the bigger the sob story, the greater the woman's popularity. It was like a secret club I longed to join. The "best victim" award went posthumously to one of the first women ordained in the Lutheran Church who, as I remember, was disabled. There wasn't a dry eye in the house, as the story of the prejudice she encountered in her pastorate unfolded, culminating in her death in a fiery blaze in her non-accessible apartment. I came to the crushing, albeit wrong, conclusion that the Lutheran Church was almost, but not quite, as unjust and oppressive as the Catholic Church.

By the time I was ordained in 1986, my *public* prayer life had become a political exercise. I spent more time in the liturgy listening for sexist language and changing it than I did praying. Yet, paradoxically, my *personal* prayer life deepened. Looking back, I see that the Holy Spirit was working a good in me, preparing me for my conversion. As a young pastor, I knew that to be effective I needed to develop a deep inner life. I devoted much more of each day to prayer. I still engaged in feminist activities, but they soon lost their luster. For instance, I always professed to be pro-life, yet I volunteered at Women's Way in Philadelphia, an organization that supports abortion and contributes funds to abortion clinics. I excused my involvement by saying that I worked only in the areas which had nothing to do with abortion. My volunteer days at Women's Way were numbered after my involvement at one of their conferences in which little pins were distributed, resembling what I think were embryos. Conference workers and attendees were expected to wear them as signs of their commitment to "choice." I couldn't do it. Seeing all those gleaming gold-toned pins on well over a thousand women made me sick. I felt ashamed to be there.

It was at that time, too, that the Lutheran Church seemed to be relinquishing much of its confessional, scriptural and moral identity. I found myself at odds with a church ever more silent on significant moral issues such as abortion, pre-marital sex and homosexuality. I began reading independent Lutheran publications, like *Lutheran Forum* and *Forum Letter* (the latter edited at that time by then Lutheran Richard John Neuhaus). I formed alliances with female and male clergy who struggled to assert traditional Lutheran teaching into modern discussions, most notably my friend and colleague, Jennifer Ferrara, who with her husband, Steve, helped me to discover the falsehood of the feminist agenda. Especially, I learned through my pastoral ministry that sin, forgiveness and salvation were at the heart of my parishioners' struggles. I felt *their* need for a deepened sacramental life. I openly lamented the fact that we Lutheran ministers could not offer sacramental absolution to penitents who confessed their sins. I hungered for the Eucharist, and for a time instituted a mid-week Eucharist at my parish. I found that modernist agendas only served to alienate the laity from the Church. The "I'm OK, You're OK" motto of the majority of my colleagues at the time frankly did not cut it with believers. With St. Paul, they admitted their frequent failure to do what they ought and their penchant for doing what they ought not.

Fathers do know best

In 1993, I entered a doctoral program in Historical Theology at Drew University, Madison, New Jersey. There I delved into the writings of the Church Fathers, and I was amazed at their richness and truth. Regretfully, I recalled the first time I read Augustine's *Confessions* in college when I was wrongly taught that Augustine was a repressed, guilt ridden man, obsessed with sex. The second time I read the *Confessions* was as a Lutheran seminarian. As any good

Lutheran, I believed Luther's understanding of justification to be more authentically Augustinian than Augustine, himself. The third time I read the *Confessions* was through the eyes of a faith wizened by life and pastoral experience, and was certain that I beheld Truth. I voraciously consumed as much Augustine as I could get my hands on. Then I delved into more Fathers and discovered the Catholicity of their teachings on faith and morals. A longing to be part of the Apostolic Church began to grow inside me. I accepted the authority of the Pope and the teaching Magisterium, the seven sacraments, redemptive suffering, the way of perfection, the intercession of the saints and purgatory. The absence of purgatory in the Lutheran Church was a source of great anxiety for me as a pastor, because there was no place in the Lutheran funeral service to storm heaven's gates on behalf of a poor sinful soul. My acceptance of purgatory, especially, meant I believed in a teaching untenable to Lutherans.

The more Catholic I became, the less confessionally and morally sound became the E.L.C.A. What came to be a semi-scrapped but well-publicized document on sexuality, audaciously pronounced that the nearly two thousand-year-old teaching on loving the sinner and hating the sin was passé. [14] The E.L.C.A.'s *Lutheran* magazine featured positive stories on alternative heterosexual and homosexual lifestyles and dubbed certain instances of abortion as a tragic *choice*. Worst of all was the E.L.C.A.'s insurance plan, which provided coverage for abortion. Ecclesiastically, the E.L.C.A. was forging ahead with inter-communion agreements between the Reformed traditions and the Episcopal Church, respectively.[15] One integral reason for my heretofore adherence to the Lutheran tradition was its high view of Christ's real, physical presence in the Eucharist. I believed that to grant inter-communion with denominations holding a low, spiritual or memorial view of the Eucharist was tantamount to exposing Lutheran sacramental practice as a sham. I wondered how the Lutheran Church could reconcile the differences, not only in its understanding of the Eucharist, but also in ordination practices. The Lutheran Church officially, although not always practically, required chastity from its clergy, while Reformed tradition's United Church of Christ ordained practicing homosexuals. There was also the intention of full communion with the Episcopal Church, which claims an historical episcopacy (invalid in the eyes of Rome). While many of my more "high-churchly inclined colleagues" in ministry lauded such an alliance as a step closer to Rome, I was appalled because of the Episcopal Church's self-admittedly loose view of normative doctrine and morals.

Thomas Reeves in the *Suicide of Liberal Protestantism*, speaks at length about the frenzied quest to form inter-denominational alliances within mainline

---

[14] A mildly toned down social statement on sexuality was released soon after.
[15] Both agreements have been passed and are in place.

Protestantism. In the vast majority of instances, these unions are sought to fortify weaknesses, rather than capitalize strengths. The E.L.C.A. seemed to be in a terrible commotion on all levels of its existence. I was certain that if the E.L.C.A. stood fast in its confessional identity through its adherence to the Augsburg Confession and the Creeds, it would *not* be making strange bedfellows with denominations radically different in their understanding of scripture, tradition, church teaching, sacraments and morals. I determined what the E.L.C.A. needed most was a teaching and authoritative Magisterium; however, at the time I did not venture so far as to think that it needed to be in *Rome*.

My deep concerns, misgivings and restlessness over the E.L.C.A.'s ecumenical intentions, as well as my growing attraction for the Church of the Fathers, occurred ironically over a period of years in which my spiritual, personal and professional life thrived. I returned to the Bible, not as I had earlier visited as something to be analyzed, changed and challenged, but to be embraced and lived. Additionally, I returned to Mary. The Church Fathers' devotion to the Blessed Virgin and the Church's teaching on Mary as *Theotokos* ("God-bearer") enkindled a new love for Jesus' mother, unfettered by feminist mistrust of her submissiveness. I started praying the Hail Mary, and I developed a keen interest in Mary's appearances and messages of personal and corporate conversion at Lourdes and Fatima. It was through Mary that I began to accept the beauty of faithful submission to God's will.

Embracing the culture of life

I became unabashedly pro-life in my preaching and personal associations. The more deeply I entered into the mystery of life, the more richly blessed was my ministry. Once I accepted the Catholic Church's radically incarnational teaching of Christ enfleshed in all humanity, my compassion for others deepened and thus my ability to minister to them, especially to those suffering from abortion. While there were a few radical pro-abortionists in my Lutheran congregations, many others sought me out to confess previous abortions and to seek help in unplanned pregnancies. I regretted, however, my inability to offer sacramental absolution to those in need, and I was saddened that I could not substantiate my own pro-life position with that of my denomination, a fact which my pro-choice protagonists consistently pointed out. I knew the Catholic Church alone denounced abortion since her inception. Years later, at about the same time I decided to return to Rome, E.L.C.A. pastor Leonard Klein wrote in *Lutheran Forum,* in reference to the denomination's tacit approval of abortion, that a church which condones abortion cannot be part of the one, holy, catholic and apostolic church.

Professionally, pastoral ministry fit me like a glove. I loved preaching and presiding at Eucharist, and the *Lutheran Book of Worship* provided beautiful settings for the Eucharistic liturgy and services of the Word. I enjoyed the challenge of ministering to troubled people, and after I left my team pastorate in a large Lutheran congregation, I accepted several interim pastoral positions in congregations divided by internal conflicts. I relished the challenge of fostering healing and growth, preparing parishioners for their next pastor. I was respected by my colleagues and acted as unofficial mentor to several new pastors. I taught Systematic Theology in the New Jersey Synod Diaconate program, preparing lay persons for professional ministry. I also liked being in a position of authority, and unlike many of my colleagues, I enjoyed the administrative duties of running a parish.

In the midst of this positive professional growth, however, a nagging doubt crept in. I wondered how long I could stay in a church that seemed to be abandoning its theological and sacramental foundation. I joined a society of confessional Lutherans, bound together by our strong desire to reform our denomination, theologically and morally. Most of us desired rapprochement with Rome, not as individuals, but as a Lutheran communion. For a time, this goal provided me with the momentum to continue my ministry. Then came the conversion of several prominent Lutherans. The occasion of their conversions increased my doubts about the viability of my little society's confessional endeavors.

I picked up Louis Bouyer's classic Catholic apologetics, The *Spirit and Forms of Protestantism*. Bouyer, a Lutheran convert to the faith more than half a century ago, provides evidence proving that Luther's great ninety five theses, the lynch-pin of confessional Lutheranism, were clearly stated centuries before in the Councils of the Church. This fact was not new to me, but hearing it again prompted me to re-visit my own justification for being a Lutheran. Boyer also instructs us not to be fooled by the beauty of some Protestant liturgies. Although they may surpass many Catholic Masses in liturgical music and style, they are, at bottom, a beautiful imitation. A Lutheran minister nearing conversion opined: "Once you've come to the conclusion that Luther's disobedience was wrong, you're a goner." When Luther left the Church, he left behind any attempt at reform and started something new, utterly *other* than the Roman Catholic Church. For me, this was the realization that Lutheran doctrine, orders, polity and social teaching were built on a *negation* of Catholic teaching. The early reformers did not foresee that once they negated the Holy See, they removed all positive authority, cohesion and controls from their new church.[16] The Lutheran doctrines of *Sola Fide* and *Sola Scriptura* (faith alone and scripture alone) necessarily placed private interpretation and judgment in a conflicted and

---

[16] See Louis Boyer's *Spirit and Forms of Protestantism* for a thorough discussion of the negative aspects of Protestant formation.

tendentious relationship with Catholic tradition. Unbridled by the reigns of an authoritative teaching office (i.e., the bishops), the church of Luther soon found itself fractionated. Luther himself complained about the grave errors of interpretation on the part of the laity, and he also was at odds with his own colleagues, eventually parting ways with some. It was only a matter of time before Protestants splintered into churches too great to number, each incorporation resulting from a negation of a rival denomination's understanding of faith and scripture. The Catholic Church alone offered the wisdom of two thousand years, positively expressed in the consistent teachings of the Apostles' successors.

Ironically, in the midst of my terrible spiritual torments, my personal life soared. I met my husband, Alec, at my congregation. He was a new parishioner when we fell in love and quickly married in 1990. Our first child was born nine months later, and our family rapidly grew larger. My husband enjoyed being a pastor's spouse. He was actively involved in the congregation I served, and we became a great team. He and the children loved to hear Mom preach, and the little ones would clamor to stand next to me after church to greet people and imitate me leading worship.

Prodigal daughter returns home

This relative familial calm would not last long. My professional and personal life changed dramatically in spring 1996, when I decided to return to the Catholic Church. My desire to be part of the apostolic Church and my refusal to accept the E.L.C.A.'s moral decline, especially its abortion policies, left me no alternative but to leave the E.L.C.A. Further, my rejection of Luther's disobedience meant that I believed all Lutheran orders were invalid and thus its Eucharist was invalid as well. I remembered a time not many years before when I claimed as my own Luther's sentiment: "Here I stand, I can do no other." I would reiterate those words when sharing my Lutheran "conversion" story with others. That sentence became the death knell of Lutheranism for me, as with difficulty I surveyed my years spent in sin apart from the Catholic faith. I felt utter sorrow and repentance over my dissenting Catholic years and my eventual break, yet I turned to God in hope of receiving his mercy.

My new zeal for Catholicism was tempered, however, by the continued presence of dissenting Catholics, sloppy liturgical practices and lackluster preaching in the Catholic Church. To my happy surprise, though, I found individuals and organizations dedicated to orthodox Catholicism, a proper reform of the liturgy and a return to Catholic devotions, like the rosary, novenas and Holy Hours. The Catholic Church was *ever* the Church, warts and all, a claim no other Christian church could make. I asked myself which church I would die for, and I immediately responded, the Catholic Church alone. I could not then deny the words of *Lumen Gentium* 14, which state unequivocally that once one knows the fullness of faith subsists in the Catholic Church, one must be *Catholic* to attain salvation. Augustine writes: "O God, from whom to be turned is to fall, to whom to be turned is to rise, and with whom to stand is to abide forever." Indeed, I was going home, painful as that road to reunion would be.

I had three major hurdles to cross before I could be admitted back into full communion with the Church. The first was telling my husband and dealing with the wide range of emotions that would accompany the news. The second was completing my commitment to the Lutheran congregation I served. The third was to have my husband obtain an annulment from a previous marriage.

Alec never thought I would leave the Lutheran Church. While I had spoken to him repeatedly about my desire to be part of the apostolic Church and my disillusionment with the E.L.C.A. over its confessional and moral decline, he listened to my words in the context of my reforming endeavors *within* Lutheranism. A life-long Lutheran married to clergy, Alec never concluded I would relinquish my ordination and vocation and disrupt our family life. He felt betrayed when I confessed my intention to return to the Roman Catholic Church. He said I wasn't the woman he married, and accused me of splitting the family apart. He thought I was crazy to throw away all I had worked so hard for. He couldn't imagine the situation in the E.L.C.A. was bad enough to leave, and he added that I managed to minister faithfully to the congregations I served with little interference from the church bureaucracy. I explained that I was returning to Rome because it is the right and only place to be, and I hoped I would have returned anyway, despite the deteriorating condition of the E.L.C.A. Those were very difficult words for him to swallow, for he was taught as a child that the Catholic Church was, in essence, the enemy. The Lutheran minister who prepared him for Confirmation warned him to "*never date a Catholic, for fear you might marry one*," and ticked off a shopping list of reasons why. Alec admitted he probably never would have considered marrying a Catholic. Those old tapes played in his head, along with his family's strong objection to my conversion. Rightly so, he sorrowed over the split in our immediate family caused by my conversion, as he foresaw the children becoming Catholic, too. The oldest ones are enrolled in Catholic parochial school, and with each child's first Holy Communion, his prediction is quickly coming true. Alec is slowly overcoming his initial anger, pain, resentment and sorrow over losing what once was, and has been very supportive. While he is still Lutheran, though now a conservative, pro-life Missouri Synod Lutheran, he has accepted my decision and the children's Catholicism. He attends Catholic Mass with us on occasion, listens to Catholic tapes and watches EWTN with me. But when Sunday morning arrives, we both feel sad when we depart for Church in two different directions. There are no easy fixes, just a trust in our love for and commitment to one another, God's providence, and the confidence that we are following his will and our consciences.

After my conversion in spring 1996, there was a long period of waiting before I could return to Rome. I was the vacancy pastor of a Lutheran Church in the process of calling a full-time minister. I had committed to serve the congregation until December 15, and taking their needs into consideration, I felt it was important to honor that commitment. Additionally, I was contributing to our family's income in a small but important way, so the wait provided needed time to seek another means of support, preferably in the Catholic Church. Arguably, the two most important features of this waiting period were (1) the time it afforded me to work through the difficulties my conversion had caused in my relationship with Alec, and (2) the suffering I experienced leading worship in the Lutheran Communion. It is to my personal suffering that I now turn.

The two most joyful and fulfilling aspects of my ordained ministry were preaching and presiding over the Eucharist. When I discovered the fullness of Truth resided in the Catholic Church, celebrating Word and especially Sacrament became a bitter pill to me. I felt as though my heart would break in two as I uttered the words of consecration and distributed Holy Communion to my Lutheran congregants who believed what I could not. My last pastoral act was preaching the sermon at the Installation Service of my childhood friend, Mary, and her husband, Steve, in their new congregation. Mary and I had gone to Catholic parochial school together. She went off to Notre Dame and I, Boston College, and then she joined me at B.C. to obtain an M.A. in pastoral ministry. I became a Lutheran a few years before she met and married a Lutheran pastor. It wasn't long after that she was ordained a Lutheran minister, too. What an irony: here she was commencing a team ministry with her husband, and I was leaving my ministry behind. I preached about the meaning of ordination and ministry. It was a very Catholic sermon, full of references to Pope John Paul II and St. Therese of Lisieux. When I was done, I was satisfied that I understood and lived out my ordination in the Lutheran Church, but I was grateful to God beyond words that he led me back home.

God showered me with his graces more abundantly than I could have imagined through my new ministry as part-time campus minister at Princeton University. For several years, I have been privileged to pray with students, teach Catholic theology, prepare converts, foster vocations and bring Catholic speakers to the campus. The students hunger for knowledge of the Catholic faith, and I never tire of sharing it with them.

I enter full communion with the Church
Telling Alec, completing my Lutheran ministry, and engaging in Catholic lay ministry are not the end of my story. It would be nearly three years after my

conversion until I would be granted *full* communion in the Catholic Church. My husband, Alec, had been briefly married several years before we met, and thankfully, that marriage produced no children. He willingly offered to seek an annulment that I might be received back into the sacramental life of the Church. The annulment process was arduous, painful, long and uncertain, but out of love for me, he underwent it. We had great pastoral support from Catholic friends and priests, which bolstered us along the way when time dragged on and things looked bleak. For me, it was a time of great spiritual growth, as trust in God's mercy was put to the test. Mass was both beautiful and painful. While I was ever thankful for the gift of witnessing Christ's body, blood, soul and divinity in the Eucharist, I could not partake of him, and there was no certainty that I ever could. Moreover, I had a seemingly endless laundry list of sins to confess since my last Confession as a young adult, the most serious being my rejection of Catholicism. I sorrowed over the knowledge that I had put my soul in peril and was unable to participate in the Church's offer of sacramental forgiveness. In my powerlessness, there was only one place to go, and that was to our Lord. I prayed that God would be merciful toward me, a sinner, and I prayed for the strength to accept whatever decision the Tribunal made. Shortly before my eldest son's first Holy Communion we received news that Alec's annulment was granted. Alec and I celebrated the sacramental union of our marriage. I received absolution for my sins, and for the first time in years, I received the Eucharist with my son, Patrick.

Since my conversion, I have received calls and letters from former colleagues in the Lutheran Church who long to be Catholic. Most do not become Catholic for a variety of reasons; however, there are two reasons which stand out. The first is the fear of an uncertain professional future for ordained Protestant men and women. Clergymen who would like to be re-ordained know the process is long, re-ordination is not guaranteed, and the types of ministry available to a married priest are limited. Clergy women are well aware that re-ordination is not a possibility, often a prospect too painful to consider. The second reason is the Catholic Church's beautiful, steadfast position on the indissolubility of marriage. I have shared my experiences with divorced and remarried clergy and laity, encouraging them to take a leap of faith, unite *imperfectly* with the Church, and trust in God's providence. The wrenching process of applying for an annulment, knowing that it may not be granted, is often too much to bear; thus it is easier to stay away. Becoming Catholic and *being* Catholic is not easy, for the Church requires much. Indeed, to those who have been given much, much is required. We have been given a gift beyond measure in the body, blood, soul and divinity of our Lord and Savior every moment of every day in the Eucharist. With God, nothing is impossible.

God has also given us great *company*. St. Augustine thanks the Lord for those who led him to the Church: his mother (St. Monica), his teachers and friends. Faithful disciples have walked with me along my journey, too, from my first utterances of doubt about the veracity of Lutheranism, to my longings to be part of the apostolic church, to my conversion, and beyond. My long-time friend, Jennifer Ferrara, and I spent countless hours burning up the phone lines, discussing the decline of the Lutheran Church and searching for Truth in the Catholic Church. Throughout our crisis, we made many trips to conferences and to seek advice from respected colleagues. A fellow convert and student at Drew University, Jeff Finch, gave me the push I needed to make the final decision to reclaim my Catholicism. He phoned and said, "I hear you're thinking of crossing the Tiber." Then he introduced me to a group of converting clergy who met regularly for support. The late Father Joseph Procaccini took our little convert group, Alec and me under his wing and provided continual pastoral support. Throughout the years, faithful and concerned Catholic family and friends prayed to God for my conversion. The company I share is ever growing, and God has allowed me to be company to others. A convert to the Church and former Episcopal priest, Linda Poindexter, recently wrote: "I thank God every day that I am a Catholic." Amen!

Patricia Ireland and her husband Alec are parents to four young children, Patrick, Aidan, Maria Christiana, and Caroline. She received her Bachelor of Arts and Master's Degree from Boston College, her Master of Divinity from Andover Newton Theological School, her Master of Philosophy from Drew University and is a Ph.D. candidate. She spent 10 years as Lutheran pastor in the New Jersey Synod. For the past four years she has served part-time as the Catholic Campus Minister at Princeton University.

The Road from Wisconsin to Rome

Marie Hosdil

In my Junior year in a Lutheran high school I overheard a conversation between a few of my classmates and the pastor who taught our religion class. They were discussing how vile Catholicism really is, and to what extent Lutherans should go to distance themselves from its errors and its adherents. My classmates seemed to be trying to persuade our teacher towards a more "live and let live" attitude.

"But Pastor, what would you do if your daughter married a Catholic?" Without batting an eye Pastor seized the teachable moment. "Out of love I would have to disown her."

I don't know what effect this had on my classmates, but for me it was a teachable moment indeed. I already knew that practically everything Catholics believed was false, and that the very foundation of Lutheranism was its opposition to Catholicism. However, this deep, personal and self-sacrificial anti-Catholic conviction expressed by my teacher shocked me for a moment as taking things a step too far. But after mulling his comment over in my heart in the days and years following, I concluded my teacher had been essentially right. Catholicism is evil; God hates evil. I love God; therefore I ought to hate Catholics.

Turned on to Luther

When this episode took place, I had already been nurturing my commitment to follow Jesus for several years. As I grew up, my mother took my brother and I to Sunday School and services at our Wisconsin Synod church regularly. When I was very young, this routine bored me and I did what I could to avoid it when possible. But around age 9 or 10 I began pondering heavy the questions about the meaning life. It was then that a special Sunday School teacher sparked my interest in learning about God, the source of life's answers. This teacher taught us with personal concern and respect, and shared how God was present in her own life. She had my attention.

It was she who first taught me about my Lutheran heritage. For several months she began class with some fascinating vignette or other from Luther's life. I learned how Luther went from being a superstitious and fearful works-righteous monk, to the servant of the truth who rediscovered the gospel. I learned to admire Luther as the hero of the true Christian faith.

First Conversion

Before my "first conversion" which occurred in March of 1978, I held Christianity to be a body of true information. I didn't completely understand why we all had to come to church on Sunday; the pastor said it was because we needed to hear the gospel again and again. The gospel as I understood it was this: We are sinners and deserve to go to hell. We cannot earn our salvation and we cannot do a single thing that is good, since "all of our righteous acts are as filthy rags." We cannot choose to believe in Christ, but we can cease striving against His will. Since no one can save himself, Jesus saved us by dying on the cross. This shows us God's love. God gives us the gift of faith, and it is our place to love and thank Him for all Jesus did for to save us and take us to heaven when we die.

The conversion I experienced changed the pronouns in my understanding of the gospel from "we" to "I." Students from the same Lutheran high school I later attended gave a slide presentation at our evening Lenten service about their missions trip to Jamaica. The simple verse which I had already memorized lit up with new meaning: "For God so loved the world that He gave His only begotten Son, that whosoever believeth in Him should not perish but have everlasting life." In that graced moment I saw the key difference between knowing true information and being a Christian -- I had to come to be one of the whosoevers! I had to believe in Christ!

By the time I was 12, I realized the dramatic difference that evening had made in my life. I had a zeal for evangelizing, began reading Scripture and stumbled into the beginnings of a personal prayer life. I was truly excited about going to church, and if I ever found any sort of Lutheran religious book, I ate it up.

W.E.L.S. Beliefs

My home church was the Wisconsin Evangelical Lutheran Synod, or the W.E.L.S. It is predominantly German in ethnicity and Midwestern in locality. One of the smallest of Lutheran synods, some define it as "ultra-conservative" Lutheranism. We considered ourselves to be the truest interpreters of the truths Luther taught. Even the Missouri Synod (L.C.M.S.) seemed liberal on many points to us, and the joke went around about how "A.L.C." and "L.C.A." (in the days before the E.L.C.A. merger) stood for the "Almost Lutheran Church" and the "Lutheran Church Almost."

The W.E.L.S. is distinguished from other Lutherans by their strict adherence to belief in the verbal inspiration of Scripture and their rejection of scholars who hold certain parts of Scripture to be historically inaccurate. It holds an unswerving creationist view of natural origins, and strongly disapproves of preaching a "social gospel" message that focuses on humanitarian or political agendas. The W.E.L.S. is also noted for very rigorous fellowship practices. Joining in a prayer or a worship service led by a non-W.E.L.S. Lutheran is rejected as sin, as is intercommunion with other Lutherans or other Christians.

I once asked my pastor in confirmation class whether it was true that the W.E.L.S. was truly the only correct church on the face of the earth. He seemed a bit uncomfortable with the question, but he affirmed that we and those officially in fellowship with us (the Evangelical Lutheran , or "Norwegian," Synod and a few international missions) were "it" in terms of doctrinal purity. He stressed that other Christians could be saved because the Word of God was preached in their churches, too. But they faced the danger that false doctrine would lead them away from trusting in Christ's free gift of salvation.

This encouraged me to take my denominational identity very seriously. I came to view false doctrine as a dreaded enemy, as Satan's most heinous weapon. But I couldn't purge one skeptical thought from my mind. How convenient that the only true church in the world exists primarily in Wisconsin, and that I happened to be born into it.

The security Lutheranism gave me received its first gentle poke when as a pre-teen I was paging through the religion section of the World Almanac. I read down the list of what made up the basis of beliefs for various denominations, shaking my head that almost all of them listed Scripture plus something, like human reason or a catechism. I knew that we W.E.L.S. Lutherans believed that the Bible alone was true; we rejected man-made rules and traditions that others (especially Catholics) believed in. As I came to the Lutheran entry, there it was in black and white -- Lutherans claimed not Scripture alone but Scripture and the Lutheran confessions as the basis of belief! I was shocked at this beschmerching of Lutheranism's good name, but I assured myself that they had probably gotten this information from a liberal.

Seeking Fellowship

Vibrant Christian fellowship was a lack I felt more and more deeply as I grew older. In all fairness, I contributed significantly to my own sense of isolation. Solitary and ponderous by temperament, intellectual pursuits came more easily to me than social interaction. Yet I longed for fellowship with other Christians, though I didn't even know what to call this desire. As a teen I used Christian radio and Contemporary Christian music to fill this void. The fact that these were non-W.E.L.S. sources was not as important to me as the love and excitement for Jesus I heard expressed in the music and teaching programs. And I was drawn to the exhortation and encouragement to live a holy life, seeking to serve and please the Lord in all things. In my own church, it seemed I heard more about my sinfulness and Christ's sufficiency to cover my sin than about how I should seek to live in Him, now that I had been saved.

Even in my first years of reading Scripture I encountered difficulties rectifying the relationship between faith and works. I understood my role in salvation to be completely passive. My pastors emphasized verses like Eph. 2:8-9, "For by grace are ye saved through faith. It is the gift of God, not of works, lest any man should boast" which, they said, taught that our works played no part in our being saved. But then I would read verses like Is. 45:22 where God exhorts "Turn to me and be saved," or verses like "believe on the Lord Jesus Christ and you will be saved," that indicated some necessary action, or at least disposition, on man's part. I knew we believed that good works were to be our response of love to God. Yet the subtle message I gleaned was that we Lutherans feared more than anything falling into the "Catholic trap." Catholics, remember, worried constantly about whether they were doing enough good works to be saved. We knew we were saved -- so why should we worry whether we did enough good or not?

Doctrinal Questions

This tension between faith and works and the place of each was a silent irritant in my conscience for years. Then one day a radio preacher firmly planted a seed of suspicion in my mind. He asserted that infant baptism was a Satanic deception because it posited that salvation could be put on a person from outside, circumventing the surrender of his own will to Christ, which was the true beginning of saving faith. My own experiences seemed to confirm his words. I began putting Lutheranism on trial to prove itself.

In my high school religion classes I tried hard to articulate to myself both my doctrinal doubts and Lutheran orthodoxy, without seriously compromising either. When I started Theology classes at Wisconsin Lutheran College in Milwaukee, however, being a Christian was far more important to me than being a Lutheran. While I accepted that Lutheranism was best show in town (albeit by default), I lamented the fact that what we really needed was a new Luther who would reform the whole church all over again. I had grown to hate the doctrine of infant baptism and I struggled to burst out of the passive paradigm it represented to me. I thought of myself as a radical Lutheran who wanted nothing more than to upset comfortable Lutheran religiosity.

Having learned enough of the elemental building blocks of Lutheran doctrine, I began flexing my intellectual muscle and asking pointed questions of myself, and occasionally of my instructors as well. I had learned the Lutheran definition of a sacrament: "a sacred act, instituted by Christ, whereby He through earthly elements connected with God's Word offers, gives, and seals unto us forgiveness of sins, life, and salvation."1 But now I wondered -- why is that the definition of a sacrament? I didn't see sacraments defined as such in Scripture. I remembered that fateful encounter with the World Almanac, and began to think that Lutherans were not such pure *Sola Scriptura* believers after all.

I questioned a seminarian who lived on campus about why we all swore to uphold the Lutheran confessions when we were confirmed, and why we didn't simply swear that we believed in Scripture. He asserted with nonchalance that we couldn't "just believe in Scripture" since everyone who claims this belief interprets Scripture differently. He said Luther had done the best job of anyone at teaching what Scripture truly means, and so even though he's not divine and the confessions aren't inspired, they are as strong an authority as we can hope to have, this side of heaven.

I saw his point and accepted his explanation, though it stirred me to malcontent. In my heart, the whole matter smacked of human tradition -- of Roman Catholicism. We had just substituted the Pope with Luther! Yet in my head I couldn't bring myself to seriously assert anyone else's doctrinal reasoning as superior to Dr. Luther's (though I was itching to simply take the job upon myself). I admired the Reformed and Evangelical Christians, but I knew they were wrong in believing the Lord's Supper to be only symbolic. I tried to set my dissatisfaction with Lutheranism on the back burner and focus instead on spending my energy on serving God in whatever way I could.

We See But Darkly

Music ministry was my passion and my dream in college. I spent hours on end in our chapel playing guitar and singing songs I'd written, pouring out my heart to God. Sometimes I took my guitar when I taught Bible lessons to teens at the county mental health complex, and occasionally I played and sang for chapel services at school. I dreamed of becoming a singing evangelist, using my music to bring others to deeper faith in Christ.

Music also gave me a safe place to air the feelings of despondency that had crept into my relationship with God. The stuff of my intellectual struggle regarding passivity and salvation was bearing bad fruit in my heart and life. One particularly despondent day when I was 19, the phrase from 1 Cor. 13 ran through my mind repeatedly: "we see but darkly." I took this as an invitation to tell God in song just how dark life seemed. "We See But Darkly" became the song's title. In it I asked: "If Jesus is my Lord and God my Father/Why should I have to even bother with this earthly life?/Why can't I just go to heaven now?/What difference would it make anyhow?" If salvation was our ultimate goal, and none of our grand accomplishments moved us toward that goal, I struggled to see what meaning or dignity lay in doing or attempting anything. Even our attempts to please God are riddled with sin and weakness. Ultimately, only Jesus had pleased God, and God loves us on His account, in spite of ourselves. I was certainly glad for that love, and yet my heart still ached for a love somehow more personal, more specific to me. A love that would do more than excuse my earthly existence. Vaguely I had hope that beyond that murky moment, God would show me a better answer.

The Lord wasted no time in setting the stage to respond to my cry. Within days of writing that song, the Holy Spirit set my life on a completely different course. Until then it was as if I had been waiting in line to board a roller coaster. Now I was in, and the thing took off.

It began when, through a wrong phone number, I was introduced to man who had spent most of his life on the wrong side of the law. He claimed he was turning to God in earnest now, and was requesting help to do so. The fright of suddenly being thrust into this very weird situation drove me to my knees in prayer and to my church to find someone, anyone, who would pray with me. I found Betty, who hosted an occasional prayer gathering of women from the church in her home. Finding that these meetings had sprung up since I'd been away at college added to my sense of joyful shock at how life was unfolding before me.

I was gripped by an intense need to pray as if I had never prayed before. I enlisted my best friend Gail to pray with me, too. We'd been friends since 5th grade. Gail had been raised as a Buddhist and was baptized in 1987 in the A.L.C. I had always had her companionship, but now she was my sister in the Lord. I shared with her as well as with Betty what the Lord was doing in my life.

Six weeks into this wild summer, Betty questioned me about my attitude towards the charismatic movement. "It might be true, or it might be false," I told her. In light of the W.E.L.S.' definite anti-charismatic stance, my hesitation to commit to a verdict bespoke some openness. I later discovered that both Betty and the friends of my convict-friend had all experienced what they called the "baptism in the Holy Spirit." After listening to their testimonies and studying what Scripture said about this, I was convinced that God had intended to give charismatic gifts in every age. My conviction was only intellectual assent, though, until one of my new friends experienced this "baptism" herself. Selfishly, I didn't understand why God was favoring her with this gift, but not me. In prayer God showed me that true faith acted. I needed to cooperate with His grace, to use my will and to ask in faith for what He promised. And as soon as I got over whining and got around to asking; I too received the Baptism in the Holy Spirit.

You Will Receive Power

This powerful experience set my life on fire. Scripture came alive as if it were written just for me. Singing praises to God filled my heart with a joy that energized me and dispersed my gloom. Even the bricks in the walls of the chapel seemed to be singing the praises of God's creative power. I began to realize that people around me needed Jesus' love as much as I did, and this called me to action. I began reaching out to my friends to share my joy, though as a newbie in doing so, I usually came off with heavy-handed arrogance. I was giddy, almost drunk with a new spiritual high.

After sometime of getting used to this new dynamism in my life, going to church on Sundays began to feel like putting on shackles. Back in my hometown I had my small enclave of charismatic friends, but in college, it was only church as usual. In time the confidence that God's power was real in my life dwarfed my loyalty to Lutheranism to such a degree that without a qualm I stopped going the W.E.L.S. church and began attending a charismatic fellowship. By the time I graduated from college I had officially resigned my W.E.L.S. membership, and was re-baptized as a member of my new fellowship.

When I was firmly planted in my new church home but still in my last year of college, I took a challenging class in Medieval and Renaissance Philosophy. Facing the need to choose a research topic for a paper that would count for 50 percent of my grade, I anxiously paced the library stacks. "Abba," I prayed, "please show me what I should write about." The answer came clearly. "Mysticism." "OK, Lord," I responded happily. "But what's that?"

I discovered a bit of what it was as I read the works of Hugh of St. Victor, St. Bernard of Clairvaux, St. Theresa of Avila and St. John of the Cross. My heart burned within me as I read of the power of God's love that filled these mystics with an exulted vision of God that surpassed all telling. They struck me as the charismatics of centuries gone by. I wasn't greatly disturbed that they were all Roman Catholics. After all, most of them lived before the Reformation and I was sure they would have become Protestants if history had given them the chance. I lamented that the modern Catholic Church had so completely lost sight of these saints of old, and that this spirituality only existed in the pages of dusty old library books. As I discovered these riches I prayed earnestly, "Lord, if there is anyone left on the face of this earth who believes and lives like this, those are the people I want to be with."

Non-Denominational Days

I spent five years in the fellowship I joined in college. In these years I abandoned myself, heart and soul, in surrender to God as deeply as I knew how. I was also active in many different ministries. I taught Sunday school, did door-to-door evangelism, participated in Home Fellowship groups, and led worship as a music ministry member. The fellowship was like family to me, and I drank it in.

I experienced much true healing, especially through the praise and worship while in this fellowship. However, I also amplified and exaggerated tendencies I already had towards a sort of anti-incarnational, super-spiritual approach to my relationship with God. I lived for Bible study, spiritual reading and edifying worship almost to the point of feeling like an addict. I started feeling jittery and insecure when I felt I wasn't doing enough spiritual things, or when my spiritual pursuits felt less than satisfactory. Even though I felt like I was progressing in building a spiritual fortress for myself, little fruit was leaking over into my relationships. Even the joy of worship I experienced mostly as a isolated individual, despite the comfort I felt with my fellow church members. Brothers and sisters in Christ to me meant others who shared this same "me and Jesus" mentality.

My fellow church members and I didn't trouble ourselves with doctrinal matters to much extent. But even so, it was important to me that my conscience was at peace with our monthly communion service. Though I had rejected the notion of sacraments I still embraced from Scripture that we receive the true presence of Jesus, not a symbol, in communion. My pastor was very careful to refrain from interpretive comment and simply read 1 Cor. 11:23-32 at these services, encouraging us to repent before receiving the body and blood of the Lord.

In 1989, my best friend Gail married Keith Massey, an E.L.C.A. seminarian. Early the following year, she began to tell me that Keith was expressing strong sentiments in favor of the Catholic Church. My response was unhesitating: "He's being beset by evil spirits. We've gotta pray!" It was preposterous to me to even consider Keith's claim that God was leading him out of Lutheranism into Catholicism. That false religion? Though I had become quite mellow regarding issues of doctrine, I felt confident that I knew a trick of Satan when I saw one.

After several months of asserting the evils of Catholicism to Gail, a friend from my home fellowship group, John, completely stunned me with the announcement that he was leaving our church and returning to the Catholic Church he'd left years before. Since meeting him, I had considered John the most intellectually and doctrinally balanced member of the fellowship. His news, in light of my respect for the integrity of his faith and my other friends' flirtations with Catholicism, hit me like a bombshell and brought me to my knees. I nervously reasoned with God: "Lord, Catholicism is plainly contrary to your Word. It's evil, and You hate evil. I love you, and I want to hate what you hate. But Lord, hating my friends.... I just can't imagine that's your will. And still, I can't believe it's not wrong for me to hate Catholicism for the blatant evil it teaches. Lord, help! If it's not right for me to hate Catholicism and reject Catholics, You have to show me why not!"

Shortly after I prayed this prayer, in the Lord's great sense of humor, I was assigned a task at my job that required me to call every Catholic parish in the Milwaukee area! I fumed over this task and found myself filled with ridicule for everything from Marian titles for churches to the way people answered the phone. Deep inside my heart, a monster of prejudice reared its ugly head. All the images of Luther's anger against the Church came back to me in a flood. I felt anything but charitable and "in the Spirit."

Slowly I admitted my disgust with myself and began handing my attitudes to the Lord in prayer. But I struggled to believe that any Catholic was really a Christian (though I made an exception for John Michael Talbot, whose music I greatly admired). I blamed Catholics for being too ignorant and lazy to combat the unscriptural teachings of their church. But as the Lord dealt with me about my uncharitable heart, I was able to quiet these thoughts for a brief moment. I considered the possibility that Catholics use a different paradigm that resulted in these unusual beliefs. Of course, I presumed this Catholic paradigm, whatever it was, was wrong. But at least it would explain how so many could be so far off. Eventually I realized that I didn't really know how Catholics defend their own beliefs, and I admitted to myself that I'd never read or heard anything about Catholicism from a Catholic perspective. That was soon to change.

My friend John, now a practicing Catholic, still attended our Home Fellowship meetings. After about two months my stomach stopped turning when he'd pull out his Catholic Bible with its big metal crucifix bookmark. I was able to bring myself to speak to him again. One evening after the study I asked him a few questions about his new faith. I was impressed with his answers and was secretly relieved that he still sounded Christian. My relief somehow loosened a question from the back of my mind, planted in my college philosophy days. "You know St. Theresa of Avila and St. John of the Cross? Does anyone in the Catholic Church really believe that kind of stuff anymore? Like mysticism -- the firey, transforming love of God -- that kind of stuff?"

He assured me Catholics did indeed believe "that stuff," and the next week he handed me the proof of his affirmative answer: a book on St. Theresa's rule of prayer. He'd gotten it from the Carmelite motherhouse some 40 miles away in Hubertus, WI. I was thrilled with this book, but I figured that God would meet anyone who prayed, even if they happened to be nuns. John also lent me an apologetics booklet that I examined critically. Later as I tried to argue my points with John, he simply exhorted me to keep seeking the truth. Shortly thereafter he left Milwaukee and entered a seminary overseas.

I was reading about Catholic doctrine on my own then, and little by little I realized that what I had been taught about Catholicism by Protestants was simply not what the Catholic Church taught. I was willing to grant that it was possible to be both a Catholic and a Christian, but I was by no means convinced that many Catholics were actually committed to Christ. But I read the documents of Vatican II, which to my amazement dispelled my image of Catholics as "idol worshipping heathen." Rather, I saw a Church that emphasized the importance of Scripture, commitment to Christ, and a life of continual conversion and discipleship.

In the fall of 1991 my friends the Masseys decided to become Catholics. At our get-togethers, conversation gravitated towards apologetics, and Keith was ready with an answer to all of my doctrinal arguments. A significant crack in the wall between Catholicism and me occurred when he reasoned with me about the relationship between the Church and Scripture. "Which came first, the Church or the Bible?" he asked. I believed the Bible had the right to define the concept of Church. But Keith pointed out that the Church came into being before the New Testament was even written. And that the Church existed for centuries before it defined the canon of Scripture. Luther had no more apostolic authority to re-write Scripture than Keith or I would. For Christ, Keith concluded, had given a charism of authority not to every individual Christian, but to His apostles, to supernaturally provide the means for unity in the church.

Charism? I already accepted that God acted in His church through the means of charisms, which clearly meant His channels of power were broader than Scripture alone. The Catholic paradigm began to dawn on me. What if God had given the Church a charism of leadership through Peter? And what if it wasn't meant only for that time, but for all times? And what if God had given Scripture to the Church, and therefore this leader who exists by God's charism is entrusted by God with the responsibility for correctly interpreting Scripture. That would have to mean... the authority of the Catholic Church is ... from God!

For the moment, this was almost too scary to be anything more than a very interesting intellectual possibility. But only for the moment.

Jesus Calls

John was home from seminary for the Christmas holiday a few months later, and my grandmother's death was to postpone our family Christmas gathering until after her Dec. 27th funeral. This left me in Milwaukee on Christmas Eve. John invited me to go to Midnight Mass with him and some of his friends, and I agreed, figuring it was about time I bite the bullet and go to a Mass. I had never really attended one except for social reasons. Even though I went willingly that evening, I couldn't hide my residual discomfort with the unfamiliar Catholic trappings.

The parish was named for St. Anthony of Padua, and in the entryway a statue of this saint greeted us. "Who is that?" I asked tensely, as if my question would make this uncomfortable sight go away. John calmly explained about St. Anthony as we were seated in the sanctuary. My eyes darted around the altar area, looking for anything else for which I might need to absolve the Catholics. I spotted a second statue mounted on the wall -- some other Catholic guy I didn't recognize. "And who is that?" I asked, condescension oozing. My high horse jostled a bit with John's slightly less patient response. "That's Jesus!"

106

"Oh..." I mumbled. A bit embarrassed, I quieted down and waited for the Mass to begin.

During the Mass, two lightening bolts of grace brought me right where God wanted me. The first came during the penitential rite. The priest led the congregation in asking for mercy. As I saw it, he was talking about his people -- the Catholics. "Lord, have mercy on us, forgive us our sins." But my heart was rent open. My life-long animosity, prejudice, and ridicule of Catholics -- suddenly I saw all of it for what it was -- sin. "Lord," my heart cried out under the humbling power of God's grace, "it's not these people that need to ask your forgiveness. It's me! I've been filled with nasty thoughts and said nasty things about them, accusing them of horrible things, all my life."

If the penitential rite brought me, as it were, to my knees, the Eucharist brought me face down and prostrated before my Lord. As my companions went forward to receive, I was overcome with the realization of truly meeting Christ's Eucharistic Real Presence for the first time. That's Jesus! my heart screamed. What is Jesus doing in a Catholic Church!?

My state of spiritual shock following the Mass lasted until the evening of Dec. 26. The intervening hours were one long wrestling match during which I got very little sleep. I felt the Lord tapping at my shoulder, tugging at my sleeve, wanting me to turn and acknowledge Him. I resisting facing the Lord. I tried to pray on my own terms, but knew only more turmoil. I made a big mistake in trying to calm myself with a John Michael Talbot tape! I had to turn it off, but not before I yelled over his placid voice, "I'm the Protestant here! I'm the one whose right, and I'm supposed to be the one with all the peace!" Finally, fearing that I couldn't physically endure my tormented conscience much longer, I turned my heart to the Lord in prayer, of sorts. "OK, Lord," I barked. "What do you want?!"

In a moment I saw a picture in my mind, a sort of mental vision. At first I saw a path. It was long, open, devoid of obstacles, and somehow I recognized this as representing the path in life I was following. I realized that God was offering me the choice to continue going that way. Then I saw that I was near a fork in the path, near another road. It too was long and open, but a short way down the path stood a huge cross. Immediately I knew three things: the cross showed me where Jesus was; the cross was the Catholic Church; and I was about to choose to go that way.

I knelt beside the couch in my room. "Oh God," I prayed, with a touch of melodrama, "I'll do anything you want, anything. Even if it means... becoming a ... Catholic." God spoke to my heart as plain as day: "I don't want you to say it, I want you to sing it! Sing 'I Have Decided to Become a Catholic.'" I sprang up on my feet. You've got to be kidding, Lord. This is no time for a joke. I felt like a fool. I quickly flipped through my Bible to find a verse Keith had shown me about saint intercession. "Now, Lord, if I could just find that one verse, I'd be willing to concede on that point for now..." My conscience cleared its throat again. It wasn't time for a joke, but neither was it time for hiding in my intellectual refuge. It was time for joyful obedience. I went back to kneeling, opened my mouth, and warbled out the most pitiful rendition imaginable of this new ditty:

> I have decided to become a Catholic
> I have decided to become a Catholic
> I have decided to become a Catholic
> No turning back, no turning back.

I didn't jump for joy, but I did peacefully go to sleep.

Finding Home

The next morning I had a spare hour before leaving town for my grandmother's funeral. I had heard that there was a thing called a breviary by which Catholics the world over could pray together. So I stopped off in the Catholic bookstore buy myself one. I found myself drawn to the section filled with saint statues and medals and books. On Christmas Eve, John's friends were stumped to remember which saint day fell on my birthday, November 22. I paged through a book and found the answer -- St. Cecilia, patroness of church musicians! My heart in my throat, tears gathered in my eyes. It was as if I were being greeted by all the siblings I'd been estranged from, beginning with this woman whose ministry was so close to my own heart!

Within a very short time I went from being frustrated with Catholics for believing as they did, to being frustrated with Catholics for not letting me join them fast enough. One of the first homilies I heard when I began going to Sunday Mass (the earliest Mass possible, so I could still attend my fellowship as well) was about the miraculous catch of fish after the Resurrection. The priest spoke eloquently about how Catholics were to reach out to evangelize those outside Peter's Barque. Strange, then, that I felt more like a fish who was trying her hardest to throw herself into the boat, or get herself caught in the Church's net, only to be deflected or thrown out at every turn. Some Catholics who I told of my desire to convert assured me that I didn't have to convert, that Catholics accepted that Protestants were Christians! After two or three tries of leaving messages at the local parish to discuss my desire with a priest, I finally talked with a secretary. I told her I wanted to become a Catholic. "Why," she asked, "are you getting married?" And when I finally met with the priest he informed me that about one year hence I could begin instructions for Confirmation.

That year and a half between accepting Catholicism and entering the Church was filled with extraordinary graces from God and many (deeply needed) humbling moments. I struggled with the reactions of my church friends, some of whom offered to pray with me to cast out the demons who were besetting me. When I finally stopped attending there, I felt like I was jumping off a cliff into the dark, hoping that God was there, ready to catch me.

It was hard to go to Mass when I didn't know a soul in the huge parish I'd picked. At each Sunday or daily Mass I watched the entire congregation go to receive the Lord in the Eucharist. Habitually I sat on the outer end of the pew for the inevitable routine of letting others go by so they didn't have to crawl over me. Occasionally I caught myself muttering "I love God more than all these people here put together, and look -- they're not even thinking about Jesus who they're receiving." I had much to learn about honoring my brothers and sisters and, as Luther had taught, putting the "best construction on everything."

April 18, 1993 -- I was finally received into the Church with Gail as my sponsor. A Catholic co-worker who attended the Mass told me she had seen many a bride not beam as brightly on her wedding day as I did then.

A few weeks after entering the Church, I had a powerful and formative healing of sorts which burned into my memory God's commission and His "marching orders" for me in this new life.

In May of 1993 I went to the Holy Land on pilgrimage. It was the first chance I'd had to spend so much time with other Catholics. Before long I was feeling "Catholic culture shock" much more acutely than the shock of my physical foreign location. It seemed everywhere we went, people were obsessed with touching the "holy spots," blessing themselves, dragging rosaries and saint medals through holy water and other bizarre practices. Not even the Protestants among us seemed to think this was strange, however. I on the other hand was lonely for the invisible spiritual world that had nothing to do with objects and places and blessings. Suddenly I was supposed to live in this new life and I didn't know how. I feared that these sacramentals (holy places, holy objects) spelled spiritual deadness and superstition. I feared I was stuck in a spiritually dead church full of non-sensical trappings. I feared that being a Catholic would kill me, spiritually. I feared I would spend my life swimming upstream alone in search of the spiritual treasures I knew Catholicism was hiding -- somewhere. In the church in the Garden of Gethsemane I cried out to God, "Lord, I don't want to touch rocks and buildings. I want to touch you!"

Back in the bus, a companion tried to explain the notion that holy places can have special and particular graces attached to them. Not so gently, I reminded her I was just a brand new Catholic. "I'm having a little trouble believing that right now!" I said through gritted teeth.

The next morning during some private prayer time on the Mount of Olives I brought my frustration to the Lord. I decided an "atheist's prayer" about this nonsense was the most fitting route. I prayed, "Lord, I don't believe any of this stuff about holy places having special graces. Period. But if any of this is true, you can go ahead and convince me of it."

Later in the day our group had a private Mass in the church of the tomb of Lazarus. The priest used the gospel and the prayers proper to the church, about Lazarus' resurrection. During the Eucharistic prayer I was suddenly and terrifying overwhelmed by the power of God. I wept uncontrollably as this power enveloped me and pushed every thought from my mind. As I went forward to receive Him in communion, I could hardly walk. He, the Master of all things and Lord of the Universe, called me, a tiny speck of creation, to receive His resurrection power into my body, into my heart, into my life. The words of the Gospel were thundering through my heart "He who lives and believes in me THOUGH HE WERE DEAD, YET... SHALL... HE... LIVE."

As I continued to sob after communion, God's message to me was more than clear. I created you for a purpose, and I redeemed you for a purpose. I call you to share my very own life. It is yours! Now, wherever you go and in whatever you do, bear my life to others. Are you concerned about the deadness in your own heart? You will live in Me, I promise you. Are you concerned in the deadness you perceive in the Church? It too will live in Me, I promise you. You, go, and bear the life I give you to all.

After Mass concluded and my eyes were running dry, a question danced through my mind. "By the way, Marie, where are you?" "Lord, I'm, uh ... I'm in the church of the tomb of Lazarus, the "dead" man who was um, brought back to life. OK, Lord, I hear ya! Holy places sure do have special graces!"

The love of God has slowly, surely, melted my heart and transformed the way I live. I have had the great opportunity to study Theology at Franciscan University of Steubenville and to work for Scott and Kimberly Hahn and share one-on-one with hundreds of individuals about the beautiful truths of the Catholic Church.

Thanks be to God for His indescribable gift!

Marie Hosdil is a native of Madison, WI, but currently resides in Steubenville, Ohio, with her husband Erol. She works for Dr. Scott Hahn in the Institute of Applied Biblical Studies at Franciscan University of Steubenville. A lover of genealogy, Marie has yet to discover another Catholic in her ancestry within 15 generations!

We Do Not Stand Alone

Todd von Kampen

Well, this is going to be a great story, I thought.
I was in Denver's Mile High Stadium, and it was August 12, 1993. Ninety thousand young people from all across the globe, worked up to a fever pitch, erupted with thunderous cheers as they first spotted their hero: Pope John Paul II, just arrived to officially open World Youth Day.

My wife, Joan, was nearby with a group of Catholic young people from Scottsbluff and Gering, Nebraska, where we lived and worked at the daily newspaper. She was there as a participant, a cradle Catholic taking advantage of a once-in-a-lifetime opportunity to see her spiritual leader. I was plying my trade.

I jotted down impressions in my notebook as John Paul toured the stadium, then began his greetings to the numerous nations represented in Denver. Nothing unexpected for a world leader, I thought, as the pope began greeting the non-Catholic Christians in the audience.

"Most of you are members of the Catholic Church, but others are from other Christian Churches and Communities, and I greet each one with sincere friendship," he said. "In spite of divisions among Christians, *'all those justified by faith through baptism are incorporated into Christ ... brothers and sisters in the Lord.'* "

I doubt the Holy Father knows how much he shook up my life in that moment. And it may be difficult to understand why ... unless you've grown up Lutheran.

I had just heard a statement echoing the key battle cry of the Reformation, the one cited by Martin Luther and all Lutherans after him as the doctrine on which the Church stands or falls: "For it is by grace you have been saved, through faith – and this not from yourselves, it is the gift of God – not by works, so that no one can boast" (Ephesians 2:8-9, NIV).

And it had come from the *pope* – the successor of the man who excommunicated Luther nearly 500 years before. Well-versed Catholics will recognize that John Paul merely quoted *Unitatis Redintegratio,* the Decree on Ecumenism from Vatican II. But I didn't know that. It was one of many things I didn't know – one of many things I wouldn't have believed only a few years before.

My mind raced back nearly six years to the day, back to the rectory at St. Agnes Catholic Church in Scottsbluff. I thought I wanted to marry Joan, but I had to be sure. I asked my most burning question point-blank to her pastor, Fr. Robert Karnish: "What is the way salvation is obtained?"

Without hesitation, Father Bob answered: "Faith in Jesus Christ, which is totally unmerited by us."

His answer backed up what Joan had been telling me – that she believed what I did when it came to justification. Because he answered that way, I stood before him to marry Joan a few months later.

And because the Holy Father said what he said at that moment in Denver, God eventually led me into the Catholic Church.

Scenes From a Journey

Every life's journey has its key scenes, its watershed events that set the course for all that follow them. Mine are placed roughly at five-year intervals from my confirmation in my native denomination, The Lutheran Church-Missouri Synod (L.C.M.S.), on April 2, 1978, to my reconciliation with Rome on March 29, 1998.

These scenes hardly seem enough to tell the story. My heart and mind are full of thoughts, my bookcase bulging with books and magazine articles that multiplied as the journey went on. I could easily fill a special newspaper section – if not a full-length book – with the things that seem absolutely essential to understand how this born, bred and convicted conservative Lutheran ended up in the Roman Catholic Church!

But throughout these five scenes, the issue of justification was there all the time. If you grow up in the L.C.M.S. and really believe what it teaches, it can't be otherwise. Of all the thousands of Protestant denominations, few are more dedicated than the Missouri Synod to preserving the original arguments with Rome – especially when it comes to justification, the article on which Luther said the church stands or falls.

To Catholics then and now, the key issue in the Reformation is authority – Luther's rejection of the doctrinal authority of the pope and the Magisterium of the Church. And, indeed, the continuing rejection of that authority is very important to Lutherans. But it's not the first issue they talk about.

Justification comes first – for Luther and the Reformers couched every disagreement in terms of their conviction that the Catholic Church doesn't believe that salvation comes through Christ's free gift, but from performing this sacrament, that rite, this prayer to Mary, that indulgence.

Almost any spiritual journey from Wittenberg to Rome – especially if it detours through Missouri – hinges totally on that conviction. Unless Lutherans perceive common ground with Catholics on justification, Catholics can't hope to get Lutherans to listen to the Church's views on authority, Mary and the saints, purgatory and indulgences and the sacraments, especially the Eucharist.

Unless the cornerstone of Lutherans' mighty fortress against Rome is removed, the rest of the wall won't fall.

Let's go back to the place where my fortress was built.

Scene 1, 1978: "We Knew What Was Right"

I was in a classroom in a Lutheran school in western Nebraska, not too long before my confirmation. My pastor drew a diagram on a chalkboard to outline the differing beliefs on what happens when the Words of Institution are spoken in the Eucharist.

The Catholic section of the diagram said only "body" and "blood"; the Protestant section, "bread" and "wine." The Lutheran one linked "bread" to "body" and "wine" to "blood," showing Luther's belief in Christ's Real Presence "in, with and under" the bread and wine. Catholics believe in transubstantiation, Pastor said; Protestants believe the Eucharist is only a symbol. Both were wrong; Luther was right. This is where our Synod stands.

Missouri's big on taking stands. The Synod's founders were Saxon Germans who emigrated to America in 1839 rather than submit to the forced union of Germany's Lutheran and Reformed (Calvinist) state churches. Their spiritual leader, the Rev. C.F.W. Walther, firmly believed in the doctrines espoused by Luther and his fellow German Reformers, especially as expressed in the Lutheran Confessions – the doctrinal statements adopted by Lutherans in the 1580 *Book of Concord.*

Walther's beliefs have been enshrined in the Missouri Synod since its founding in 1847. Article II of the L.C.M.S. Constitution makes it crystal-clear what every member congregation must uphold: "the Scriptures of the Old and the New Testament as the written Word of God and *the only rule and norm of faith and of practice"* and the Lutheran Confessions *"as a true and unadulterated statement and exposition of the Word of God."*

That constrains Missouri's members to stand firm against all who believe otherwise – even if they're in another Lutheran church body, even if they're part of the L.C.M.S. itself. During my childhood (though I knew nothing of this before college), most of the faculty and students of the Synod's main seminary in St. Louis walked out after a majority of delegates to the L.C.M.S. convention declared they were drifting too far from that course and too close to liberal theology and its denial of Scriptural authority. (A number of congregations followed them out and eventually joined two larger church bodies in the 1988 formation of the Evangelical Lutheran Church in America.)

These beliefs also commits the L.C.M.S. to the historic litany of objections to the Catholic Church's teachings: Catholics believe salvation depends on your works; they place the pope above the Bible; they pray to Mary and the saints;

they believe in purgatory; they accept seven sacraments, not two; and, of course, they insist on this magic show called transubstantiation.

I absorbed all the objections, along with the absolute emphasis on justification by grace through faith as the chief cornerstone of Christianity. Christ died on the cross to save us from our sins. We're born sinful; there's nothing we can do to earn salvation. We are saved only through God's free gift of faith through Christ's sacrifice on the cross. And we need that free gift throughout our lives, for the Christian is both saint and sinner – always prone to fall into the trap of believing he or she can make it to heaven without God's help.

There was no doubt whatever in my mind about it – indeed, no one in our family doubted it. My maternal grandmother summarized it best when recalling her own childhood a century ago: "We knew what was right, and it never occurred to us to do otherwise."

Which only more strongly poses the question: Given my background, how on earth could I end up Catholic?

On one level, the answer is easy: It was God's grace. More to the point, I apparently missed something in my Lutheran education. For if you believe the Confessions are drawn from God's Word, you also commit yourself to believing "the Pope of Rome and his dominion" (to quote a 1932 L.C.M.S. document) are the Antichrist – Luther's incendiary charge against those who threw him out of the Church.

That simply wasn't part of my training. Young Lutherans aren't taught the entire content of the Lutheran Confessions. They are expected to read and master Luther's Small Catechism, which certainly includes the key elements of Lutheranism – the stress on justification, the views on the Real Presence. But you won't find the word "Antichrist" – or any anti-Catholic polemics – anywhere in it.

Though my pastor taught the theological differences with Rome, he didn't teach the polemics, and I don't recall him teaching the Antichrist. And the standard L.C.M.S. confirmation vow requires a new member to confess belief in Lutheran teachings "as you have learned to know it in the Small Catechism" – not the Confessions as a whole.

So I didn't carry all the anti-Catholic baggage into life as an adult Lutheran. But I believed the Missouri Synod's take on Rome's beliefs as firmly as Luther ever did.

Scene 2, 1983: Once Saved, Always Saved?

Fast-forward a few years. I was in a hotel room in Germany on the Fourth of July, the last day of a five-week tour with my L.C.M.S. college choir in honor of Martin Luther's 500th birthday. I was paging through my Bible, writing

114

in my diary, looking for answers to reconcile what I believed about justification with what I'd witnessed among our group.

I had entered that school a year before with the intention of becoming a music teacher in L.C.M.S. high schools. The European tour changed my life. We sang in beautiful cathedrals, drank in the sights of our ancestral land and even sang a surreptitiously scheduled concert behind the Iron Curtain in a tiny, embattled church in Leipzig in what was then East Germany.

Those were the high points. They weren't why I was in that room.

Several of our members – people planning to be pastors, teachers, church musicians – largely abandoned the pretense of consistently living their faith while they were so far from home. Some of them drank to excess, which didn't help. But they also ridiculed those who suggested they weren't setting a good example.

And the leadership of the choir, all too often, sided with them.

It shattered my beliefs about who we were and what we were supposed to be doing. It wasn't that I expected people not to sin; I learned my confirmation lessons too well for that. But these ministers-in-training not only were sinning ... they didn't seem to care.

So there I was, trying to make sense of what had happened, asking myself: Was I wrong? I found myself in Paul's letter to the Romans, the epistle Luther used more than any other in building his theology of justification.

"What shall we say, then?" Paul wrote in Romans 6:1-2 (NIV). "Shall we go on sinning so that grace may increase? By no means! *We died to sin; how can we live in it any longer?*" He emphasizes and expands on the point in Romans 8:9: "You, however, are controlled not by the sinful nature but by the Spirit, *if the Spirit of God lives in you.* And if anyone does not have the Spirit of Christ, he does not belong to Christ."

Then, in Romans 8:12-14, Paul lays it on the table for Christians who are tempted not to live the life to which Christ has called them:

> Therefore, brothers, we have an obligation – but it is not to the sinful nature, to live according to it. For if you live according to the sinful nature, you will die, but if by the Spirit you put to death the misdeeds of the body, you will live, because those who are led by the Spirit of God are sons of God.

I wasn't wrong. Here was the proof in the Scriptures. We can't sin without consequences, even after we've been justified by grace through faith. God expects His people to shine their lights all the time, not just during the concert – to live their faith at all times, not put it away when it's time to have fun. To do otherwise – to sin and not care – is to throw away that undeserved gift of grace through faith in Christ.

At the time, that discovery saved me from total disillusionment in my Lutheran faith. It also started me down the road toward the Catholic Church – though it would be years before I understood how important, both personally and theologically, that moment would be.

I came home deeply conflicted about God's plan for me. I didn't think I could function in a ministry that appeared to tolerate such a gap between belief and practice. Then, quite unexpectedly, I got a call from the publisher of my hometown newspaper, for which I had written a column on high school activities. He wanted me to fill in for the rest of the summer for a sports editor who had suddenly quit.

I enjoyed it and found my niche. And after I returned to college that fall, opportunities in journalism kept coming my way without my asking for them. After a month, I decided God was giving me a different mission. I transferred at semester's end to the University of Nebraska-Lincoln, home to one of the nation's best journalism programs. I've been a journalist ever since.

Scene 3, 1988: That All May Be One

Less than five years later, on May 28, 1988, I stood before a Catholic altar on my wedding day. Not only had God yanked my professional life in a different direction – He had sent me my life's partner from the most unexpected of directions.

My three years at UNL had been everything I hoped for – in every area but one. I was fortunate to land in an L.C.M.S. campus ministry full of young people who lived their faith amid the admittedly more hostile atmosphere of a secular university. I wrote for and eventually edited the monthly newsletter when I wasn't studying or writing for the main UNL campus newspaper, the *Daily Nebraskan*.

But I had hoped for, tried for, and frankly embarrassed myself in the quest to find a woman to share my life. Simply put, I crashed and burned. My last hope among the girls I met at UNL faded for good soon after I left for my first job in North Platte, Nebraska.

Or so I thought.

Quite unexpectedly, a friendship with my copy desk chief at the campus newspaper, the *Daily Nebraskan* – Joan Rezac – began to blossom. I nearly missed the signals when she started hinting she was interested in something more – but I came to my senses just in time. On April 5, 1987, I asked her on the phone: "Are we moving beyond a friendship?"

"I'm glad you called," she said. "The thought had crossed my mind!"

116

Right then, I knew – absolutely *knew* – the search was over. I can't explain why, and I didn't tell Joan until much later. But the phone calls and trips back to Lincoln for dates proved it. Here was a fellow journalist who loved music and seemed to understand me better than anyone ever had.

I can't do justice in this short space to how perfectly Joan fit into my life – other than to say I've never doubted in the years since that phone call that she was, and is, God's precious gift to me.

But she was Catholic. *Catholic.* Why, God – why did you send me a CATHOLIC? This surely can't work – can it?

We started working on the answer only a few weeks into our relationship. I gave her a copy of Luther's Small Catechism, while she gave me a U.S. Catholic catechism she had studied from in her confirmation class. Naturally, as a good Missouri Synod Lutheran who knew Catholics were wrong, I figured I had the tools to wake Joan up. If we were to have a future as a couple, I had to.

And I tried hard and long during those first few months. There was only one problem: It made her a stronger Catholic. And I was the one who had to adjust.

I attended church with her occasionally, heard the Mass in the vernacular, saw Communion under both kinds. She told me how Vatican II had changed the Church's approach to other faiths. I read a passage in her catechism that said Catholics were finding Luther's teachings weren't as un-Catholic as they had thought. And on justification? Joan said she believed that works, while they don't save you, let our faith shine through.

In other words, this Catholic Church was ... so to speak ... more Lutheran than I imagined. It was my first clue that I had been viewing Rome through a distorted mirror – the one held up by my confirmation instruction. Though Vatican II had happened a decade before that, the Rome that I was taught as a young Lutheran was the Rome of 1517 – at least in the way Rome presented itself at that time. Something was different.

I couldn't escape that fact as Joan and I debated the spiritual issues that summer of 1987. It wasn't an easy ride, to be sure. Sometimes it seemed that Joan and I were speaking different languages. I certainly didn't believe all that stuff about Mary, the saints, purgatory and the sacrifice of the Mass, though I was hearing things here and there that gave me pause.

But we came through that time closer than ever. And Father Karnish's straight answer to my straight question about justification helped convince me that Joan and I could function as a Christian couple. If the priest who helped form Joan's faith was saying the same thing she was, we could grow in faith together as husband and wife.

But finding some points of agreement with Catholics wasn't enough for me to become one – though we did get married at St. Agnes. We resolved to attend each other's churches regularly, minister together where we could and let God tell us whether he wanted us to join one or the other or remain in both. I needed more proof that the Catholic Church I was hearing about from Joan and Fr. Karnish was the Church that really existed.

It took me 10 years to be convinced.

Scene 4, 1993: The Surprising Pope from Poland

The moment in Denver when I heard those astonishing words from the pope happened almost halfway in between. It came at a time when our marriage was full of spiritual blessings and professional challenges – but it seemed that we were destined to be a two-faith couple.

Joan had taken Lutheran confirmation classes in Des Moines, where we moved after our marriage. But she just wasn't inspired to join. Something would be missing, she said – something she couldn't put into words. So after we moved to Scottsbluff in 1991, I entered an RCIA class at St. Agnes, intending to stop before the point that I would have to commit myself to join.

Again, I was surprised at the level of agreement I was finding between the two faiths. I remember thinking that I could be comfortable at St. Agnes – but something kept gnawing at me. You see, I had started RCIA instruction in Des Moines, but left after two weeks. That priest seemed to doubt the essence of Christian faith – Catholic, Lutheran or otherwise.

So I asked St. Agnes' new pastor, the Rev. Charles Torpey: Could he guarantee me that I would hear the same message about Catholicism in another parish or another diocese?

No, he said.

He was merely reflecting the variety of interpretations of Vatican II that have plagued the Church for most of the 35 years since the Council. But for me, at that time, Father Torpey's answer stopped me cold. I was comfortable with what Joan believed, her family believed and her parish believed. But they must be aberrations, I thought. It doesn't mean the Catholic Church as a whole believes them.

A year later, John Paul II shook up that assumption in Denver.

As we had our second child and then moved back to North Platte, the pope kept doing things I couldn't ignore. The year after World Youth Day, the Vatican released the English translation of the *Catechism of the Catholic Church*. While I didn't read it cover to cover until after I joined the Church, its release was a profound event – the beginning of order from the chaos of interpretation of Vatican II.

Then John Paul issued *Ut unum sint*, the great 1995 encyclical on ecumenism in which he urged Protestants and Orthodox alike to join Catholics in restoring the Church's unity. A year later, the Holy Father went to Paderborn, Germany, and directly urged Lutherans and Catholics to look at the complete picture of Luther and the Reformation and approach their 500-year feud in a different way:

> Luther's thinking was characterized by considerable emphasis on the individual, which meant that the awareness of the requirements of society became weaker. Luther's original intention in his call for reform in the Church was a call to repentance and renewal to begin in the life of every individual.
>
> There are many reasons why these beginnings nevertheless led to division. *One is the failure of the Catholic Church* ... and the intrusion of political and economic interest, *as well as Luther's own passion,* which drove him far beyond what he originally intended into radical criticism of the Catholic Church, of its way of teaching.
>
> *We all bear the guilt. That is why we are called upon to repent and must all allow the Lord to cleanse us over and over.*

After nearly a decade of study and close observation of Catholicism, I could take the Pope's words and sentiment for what they were. The messages I first heard in 1987 had been confirmed week in and week out from Catholic pulpits. I had absorbed the wonderful liturgical music coming from Catholic Church musicians like John Michael Talbot, David Haas and Marty Haugen (himself a Lutheran writing for Catholics!) I prayed for unity in God's Church more strongly than ever.

And yet ... I remained confirmed in my Lutheran thinking. When it came to Mary, the saints, purgatory and so on, I had searched in vain for a response to Luther's ancient challenge: Prove it to me from Scripture!

In mid-1997, we moved to Omaha. As always, I started looking for an L.C.M.S. congregation to join. I found one I thought I liked − one that did contemporary music, one that had people I had known from other parts of Nebraska. But something wasn't right. Something kept gnawing at me, preventing me from becoming an official member of the congregation. I didn't know what it was.

At Christmas, we got a gift from Sister Mariette Melmer, a double cousin of Joan's mother and a Notre Dame Sister based not far from our new home. She told Joan she thought we would find it interesting. Joan read it, then passed it on to me. It's a familiar title to people in the Coming Home Network: *Rome Sweet Home,* Scott and Kimberly Hahn's story of their journeys from Presbyterianism into the Catholic Church.

It wasn't a perfect fit; I was a Lutheran reading an ex-Calvinist's conception of what Luther believed. And yet ... here were all these Scripture passages Scott Hahn was throwing out at me on the points of difference between Lutherans and Catholics. After all these years, a Catholic was meeting Luther's challenge. He was pointing to Scripture. And he was making sense – for instance, his connection of purgatory to passages in 1 Corinthians 3 that I never had paid attention to before!

As so many ex-Protestant converts have said ... I knew I was in trouble. It was time to answer the questions once and for all. I was driven by something the Pope had written in *Ut unum sint:*

> In the first place, with regard to doctrinal formulations which differ from those normally in use in the community to which one belongs, *it is certainly right to determine whether the words involved say the same thing. ...*
>
> In this regard, ecumenical dialogue, which prompts the parties involved to question each other, to understand each other and to explain their positions to each other, makes surprising discoveries possible. *Intolerant polemics and controversies have made incompatible assertions out of what was really the result of two different ways of looking at the same reality.*

I couldn't pass up that challenge. It called on skills I use all the time as a journalist – the translation of the jargon of doctors, lawyers, school administrators, etc., into language common people can use. After 10 years of virtual dual membership in the Catholic Church and the L.C.M.S., I believed I knew both sides' theological languages well enough to test it.

The 20-year journey was entering its final phase.

Scene 5, 1998 – Amid the Crumbled Fortress

Just over a month later, on Feb. 1, I stood over the dishes, looking out at the winter night. The tears kept coming. I knew I had run out of arguments. The walls of my mighty Lutheran fortress lay in ruins around my feet. I knew I had to become Catholic.

I was nearing the end of the second draft of what became a 40-page paper, a conversation with myself about my journey. I had pored through Internet pages, haunted the libraries of our city and a nearby Catholic university and raided bookstores in my quest.

For the most part, the pope had been right. It had been less a matter of giving up Lutheran beliefs than coming to understand how Catholic so many of them really were.

Naturally, justification was the first issue. As I sorted through a decade's worth of evidence, I found I had no doubts left: On this most important issue,

120

Lutherans and Catholics were arguing over style – not substance. And after 500 years of diatribes by both sides, both faith traditions are beginning to understand that at last!

Over time, I had come to understand that two questions govern our lives as Christian believers: "How are you saved?" and "OK, you're saved – now what?" The first refers to the moment and means of salvation; the second, to our spiritual journey from the moment of salvation until death. Just as Paul did throughout Romans, we must ask and answer *both* questions together to understand the entire picture of salvation.

Lutheran sermons typically focus on the first question, while Catholics concentrate on the second. Consequently, each thinks the other doesn't answer the key question. Lutherans assume Catholics believe our totally undeserved gift of God's grace is *not* the *sole* means of our salvation – but the very beginning of the Council of Trent's Decree on Justification freely confesses our utter dependence on God:

> If anyone shall say that man can be justified before God by his own works which are done either by his own natural powers, or through the teaching of the Law, and without divine grace through Christ Jesus: let him be anathema. (Canon 1)

> If anyone shall say that without the anticipatory inspiration of the Holy Spirit and without His assistance man can believe, hope and love or be repentant, as he ought, so that the grace of justification may be conferred upon him: let him be anathema. (Canon 3)

For their part, Catholics assume that "faith alone" means that Lutherans believe that "once saved, always saved." Paul didn't believe that, as we have seen. Christ didn't believe it, either, as we see in Matthew 7:21: "Not everyone who says to me, 'Lord, Lord,' will enter the kingdom of heaven, but only he who does the will of my Father who is in heaven."

We *are* totally dependent on God for our salvation, Catholics teach, but we *can* throw it away. How? By willfully returning to a life of sin and assuming we're saved anyway! Thus the *Catechism of the Catholic Church* teaches: "Mortal sin ... results in the loss of charity and the privation of sanctifying grace, that is, of the state of grace. If it is not redeemed by repentance and God's forgiveness, it causes exclusion from Christ's kingdom and the eternal death of hell" (CCC, No. 1861).

So ... do Lutherans believe you can throw your salvation away? The Lutheran Confessions say: *Yes!* One of the most unequivocal statements to that effect can be found in the Apology of the Augsburg Confession, where Luther's right-hand man, Philip Melanchthon, writes about Paul's statement that "if I have a faith that can move mountains, but have not love, I am nothing" (1 Corinthians 13:2):

> In this text Paul requires love. *We require it, too.* We have said above that we should be renewed and begin to keep the law, according to the statement (Jeremiah 31:33), "I will put my law within their hearts." *Whoever casts away love will not keep his faith, be it ever so great, because he will not keep the Holy Spirit.* (Apology, IV, 219)

Now we've reached the common ground. Recall that many English translations render the "love" of 1 Corinthians 13:13 ("And now these three remain: faith, hope and love. But the greatest of these is love") as "charity" (in Greek, *agape;* in Latin, *caritas*). Charity is an *active* love of both God above all things and our neighbor as ourselves; as such, it's considered by Catholics as the greatest of the "theological virtues" (which also include faith and hope). It's what following through on our faith – the Catholic concept, much maligned by Lutherans, of "faith fashioned by love" – is all about.

Lutherans speak of these issues under another name: the "third use of the Law," as found in the 1580 Formula of Concord:

> The law has been given to men for three reasons: (1) to maintain external discipline against unruly and disobedient men, (2) to lead men to a knowledge of their sin, (3) *after they are reborn, and although the flesh still inheres in them, to give them on that account a definite rule according to which they should pattern and regulate their entire life. ...*
>
> We believe, teach and confess that the preaching of the law is to be diligently applied not only to unbelievers and the impenitent but also to people who are genuinely believing, truly converted, regenerated, and justified through faith.
>
> *For although they are indeed reborn and have been renewed in the spirit of their mind, such regeneration and renewal is incomplete in this world. In fact, it has only begun,* and in the spirit of their mind the believers are in a constant war against their flesh (that is, their corrupt nature and kind), which clings to them until death. (Formula of Concord, Epitome, VI, 1, 3-4a)

Put another way: The Law – loving God with all your heart, soul and mind and your neighbor as yourself – doesn't cease to apply to you once you're saved. The commandments of the Law tell believers what they ought to be doing *as a matter of course*. If Christians aren't doing good works and don't care, how can anyone tell they are saved? Indeed, how can they themselves expect to see heaven with such an attitude?

That's what James was getting at when he wrote that "faith without works is dead" (James 2:26). But it's also what Catholics mean when they speak of justification as a process – one that lasts until God calls us home. If we freely sin and don't care, we fall into the category of those who "have shipwrecked their faith" (1 Timothy 1:19). But we have the sure promise in 2 Timothy 2:11-13 that "if we endure, we will also reign with Him" and that "if we are faithless, He will remain faithful, for He cannot disown Himself"!

This is the common ground of the Joint Declaration on the Doctrine of Justification, the breakthrough agreement between Catholics and many Lutherans (though not the Missouri Synod) signed in Augsburg, Germany, on Reformation Day 1999.

Its key passage answers both of our key questions of the Christian life: *"Together we confess: By grace alone, in faith in Christ's saving work and not because of any merit on our part, we are accepted by God and receive the Holy Spirit, who renews our hearts while equipping and calling us to good works"* (Joint Declaration on the Doctrine of Justification, No. 15).

Does that seem familiar? It should. It's anchored not only in Ephesians 2:8-9 – the "justification in a nutshell" passage that Lutherans cite so often – but also verses 10 and 11, which Catholics insist must not be forgotten: "For it is by grace you have been saved, through faith – and this not from yourselves, it is the gift of God – not by works, so that no one can boast. *For we are God's workmanship, created in Christ Jesus to do good works, which God prepared in advance for us to do."*

The Joint Declaration doesn't cover everything. The two faith traditions are still seeking common ground on *how* we live out our faith, *how* we know what God expects us to do and *how* He gives us the grace to do it through Word and Sacrament. But it's clear that Catholics and Lutherans – in two different ways, just as John Paul II perceived – agree on what one might call "the circle of eternal life," one that begins and ends with God.

In a nutshell: God, through Christ's death for our sins, alone makes our salvation possible – but we have to accept His gift of faith, and we absolutely *must* live that faith by following God's commands, lest we lose the Holy Spirit and the salvation that Christ earned for us. ***But* ...** we *cannot* follow through and we *cannot* accept the gift of faith – or, put in the passive form that Lutherans prefer, the reception of faith by us cannot take place – unless God alone gives us the ability to do so. So, in the end, ***we are totally dependent on God!***

The belief that Catholics and Lutherans somehow disagreed on that was, and is, the cornerstone of the typical Lutheran's mighty fortress against Rome. Once the cornerstone was removed from my wall, the other bricks began to collapse.

I began to perceive other similarities between Catholics and Lutherans that hadn't occurred to me before – most notably on the two key ingredients of the Church's authority: the relationship between Scripture and Tradition and the question of infallibility.

Luther, of course, set the tone for Protestants everywhere with his emphasis on *Sola Scriptura* – the Bible as the sole authority. But John Paul changed the tone of the debate in *Ut unum sint*, defining the question in dispute as "the relationship between Sacred Scripture, *as the highest authority in matters of faith*, and Sacred Tradition, *as indispensable to the interpretation of the Word of God.*"

Compare that to Article II of the L.C.M.S. Constitution. It's the same order of primacy! Catholics indeed look first to the Scriptures – but they interpret those Scriptures in the light of the teaching they uphold as directly passed on from the apostles, the Church Fathers, and the ecumenical councils. And in Missouri's universe, at any rate, the Lutheran Confessions have the same relationship to Scripture. They define how the L.C.M.S. reads and lives its faith.

That harmonizes well with Notre Dame theology professor Fr. Richard McBrien's simple definition of Tradition: "the living and lived faith of the Church." In other words: *Sola Scriptura* is nothing more than a phrase or slogan. It can't be anything else as long as a group of Christians follows a particular set of teachings, whether it comes from Luther, John Calvin, John Knox or John Wesley.

In that case ... which side has the better case for its Tradition? Lutherans – who kept much of the Catholic Tradition, but based the rest of their teachings on the interpretations of a handful of 16th-century men? Or the Catholic Church, which can do what Luther cannot – cite the Scriptures in defense of its authority to pass on and interpret the faith?

It isn't that the L.C.M.S. *in practice* denies the connection between Scripture and Tradition. It's a question of *which* Tradition it accepts. The issue of infallibility is much the same. The L.C.M.S. believes the Holy Spirit guides its officers and pastors (its Magisterium, if you will) and its triennial conventions (its ecumenical councils) in deciding doctrinal issues. Again, which has the better Scriptural case for its authority?

There were other areas in which it appeared that Lutheran practice mimicked Catholic reality. Luther may have reduced seven sacraments to two by his own definition – and yet Lutherans hold confirmation, marriage, ordination, confession and absolution (in the corporate sense, anyway) and pastoral care of the sick (parallel to Anointing of the Sick) in high esteem. In each, they believe God blesses His people as the pastor proclaims God's Word. And isn't that the essence of the "means of grace" that explains the basic act of both baptism and the Eucharist – the application of God's Word to visible elements to impart His grace? Coupled with my new Scriptural proofs and my conclusions on Catholic authority, the sacraments proved easier to deal with than I thought.

I didn't expect the issues of Mary and the saints to fall as easily as they did. But both are linked to one question: Do Lutherans believe the "communion of saints" unites the saints in heaven and on earth in one body of Christ? If that's so, one cannot ignore Paul's observation that "the eye cannot say to the hand, 'I don't need you!' " (1 Corinthians 12:21a, NIV). We ask our fellow living Christians to pray for us in time of trouble. Why not then the Christians who have gone before?

As for Mary, I found the case for Catholic dogma bolstered by a most unexpected source: Luther himself. Evidence can be found in his writings that he believed Mary was Mother of God, was perpetually a virgin, even that she was immaculately conceived. (There also is evidence that he believed in the Assumption, though it's more scanty.) Most astonishingly, the founder of this church that disdains praying to Mary invokes her intercession at the beginning and the end of his 1521 commentary on the Magnificat!

It's quite another thing to equate Mary or the saints with God or to expect them to accomplish specific *things* for you. Luther was adamant in opposing that thinking – but so is the Catholic Church. Pope Paul VI clarified the point for Catholics when he cautioned that veneration of Mary and the saints must be done within the context of "a rightly ordered faith" – one that looks to Christ as the sole Source of salvation and grace.

Ultimately, it came down to the Eucharist. The dispute over the sacrifice of the Mass wasn't the obstacle I expected it to be. Catholics today don't speak of it as a necessary repetition of Christ's sacrifice – as Luther and the Reformers perceived their position – but as the *one single sacrifice* presented again to us, a re-enactment of Calvary every time we "do this in remembrance of Me." (I later found a quote from the late L.C.M.S. theology professor Arthur Carl Piepkorn that used virtually the same language.)

One obstacle remained – the transubstantiation issue, the fate of the bread and wine after the Words of Institution. I had come a long way by following the pope's advice. I had had to give up very little of my Lutheran way of thinking. But transubstantiation couldn't be resolved as two different approaches to a common belief. I was back to the diagram Pastor had put on the chalkboard 20 years before: Either the bread and wine are still there – or they aren't.

So I went to Luther's 1520 treatise *The Babylonian Captivity of the Church,* the work that defined his views on transubstantiation and redefined the sacraments. I had been struck by an oddity: Catholics and Lutherans appealed to the same Scripture passages and emphasized a plain, literal reading of the text. There must be something more to Luther's position.

There was. Luther wrote:

> Does not Christ appear to have anticipated this curiosity admirably by saying of the wine, not *Hoc est sanguis meus,* but *Hic est sanguis meus?* ... That the pronoun "this," in both Greek and Latin, is referred to "body," is due to the fact that in both of these languages the two words are of the same gender. *In Hebrew, however, which has no neuter gender, "this" is referred to "bread,"* so that it would be proper to say *Hic* [bread] *est corpus meum.*

Ninety-nine percent of the time, Luther bases his theology on the original Bible languages – Greek and Hebrew, not Latin. *But not here.* He's objecting to the Latin translation – the translation of the Church whose authority he was rejecting. He's dismissing the original translation, the Greek, because it agrees with the Latin. And he's appealing to a different language entirely – Hebrew, which he assumes Christ spoke at the Last Supper (modern scholars believe it more likely was Aramaic) – to undermine the transubstantiation doctrine which he associated with Rome's corruptions of the faith.

My hands shook as I read that passage for the first time. I thought: But that's wrong! *He can't do that!*

I was back in my professional realm. I don't know Greek ... but I'm a writer, and I can research. I spent the next day ransacking the library and the Internet, finding the exact Greek words and learning how the Greek language treats pronouns. When I was done, the evidence was overwhelming: In the language used by the New Testament's divinely inspired authors, Christ's "this" *cannot refer to anything other than "body."* (A straight-across reading of the Greek in an interlinear New Testament reinforces the point: "This is the body of Me.")

In other words ... Rome was right, and Luther was wrong. I no longer had a case against joining the Catholic Church.

Prayer for Unity

I took Communion with my wife for the first time less than two months later. Our oldest son, Jonathan, made his first Communion in December 1998. (Our other son, Joshua, age five, is a couple of years away as of this writing.) I

126

can't begin to express the joy of being fully spiritually united with them – not to mention all the Catholics whose quiet witnesses and utter lack of pressure unquestionably were God's instruments on the way to Rome.

There has been pain, too, and that isn't an unfamiliar story to Christians who have reconciled with Rome. It's one thing for Catholics to ask forgiveness for the events of centuries ago. It's another for Orthodox and Protestants of all stripes to grant it – to put aside the pain and the polemics and humbly, sincerely, thoroughly explore how it all happened, how the other side thinks and what God is saying to His people in these increasingly faithless days.

The Holy Father has called on Catholics to work for the unity of the Church – to join Christ's high-priestly prayer that we all may be one. I pray that Rome and Missouri in particular may be led to forgive each other, to look toward God and His Word with truly unbiased eyes and ask whether they're meant to remain divided. They share far, far more than they know.

After the pope spoke his astonishing words in Denver, I heard Dana sing the World Youth Day's theme song for the first time. It quickly took root in my heart because of its echo – whether intended or not, I don't know – of Luther's alleged "Here I stand" statement at the Diet of Worms. It seems an appropriate way to end this tale:

We are one body, one body in Christ,
And we do not stand alone,
We are one body, one body in Christ,
And He came that we might have life ...

Before beginning his journalism career, Todd von Kampen played piano and sang in high school music groups in western Nebraska. He and his wife, Joan, work together in music ministry at Church of the Blessed Sacrament in Omaha, Neb., where they song-lead, play piano and organ at Sunday Mass and direct seasonal choirs. They have three children, a cat and a house full of books and recordings.

In the Breaking of the Bread

Tim Drake

I was born, baptized, and raised in Minnesota – the land of lakes, lefse, Larsons, lutefisk, and Lutherans. Had I been any more Lutheran, the Evangelical Lutheran Church in America (E.L.C.A.) would have shipped me back to Germany. I expected to be Lutheran for life, but God had other plans. The Holy Spirit took me along a path I never intended to go.

I was born prematurely and baptized two months later at St. John's Evangelical Lutheran Church in St. Paul on November 19, 1967. Growing up, I attended church regularly with my family. We were nominal Lutherans though, and certainly did not attend services each and every Sunday. My mother taught us to pray, and although my early prayer life was dominated by petitionary prayer, I prayed often, especially as I lay waiting to fall asleep each night.

When I was a Lutheran, Holy Communion always meant something very special to me. From my youngest days I always remember the deep reverence during this part of the Lutheran worship service. Up until my college years, in fact, the Lutheran churches I attended still had the congregation approach and kneel at an altar rail to receive Christ's body and blood.

However, two things about communion in the Lutheran Church troubled me. The first was the fact that the churches we attended only had communion on the first Sunday of each month. As Lutherans, not required to attend church faithfully, we often missed the first Sunday. In so doing, it could be months in between receiving Christ in Holy Communion. Secondly, as our church began having communion weekly, although not at every service, I began to sense that perhaps communion was more central to the Church than the Evangelical Lutheran Church in America had made it.

I took religious formation and confirmation seriously. My youth pastor frequently led Bike and Bible -- morning bike rides followed by Bible study.

Aside from an occasional Catholic wedding, I was seldom exposed to the practice of Catholicism. I remember finding the wedding Masses long, the kneeling odd, and the church decorations ornate. Still, somehow I acquired the usual misconceptions about Mary, the Pope, and confession. These were not prejudices I was taught by my parents, but rather misconceptions that were picked up culturally from peers, the media, and through the practice of my Lutheran faith.

At the age of ten, standing in a hallway on my first day in a new grade school, I met Mark. Mark and I became fast and best friends. Mark was Catholic.

At that age, religion wasn't something he and I discussed, but as our relationship developed, we couldn't help but recognize the differences in our lives. Mark and I spent as much time as we could at each other's homes, and on a few occasions attended one another's churches. One night, while I was staying over at his home I discovered a laminated prayer card from Italy sitting on his nightstand. It was a prayer card picturing St. Joseph. I found the artwork and the prayer quite beautiful. After I told him how much I admired the card he generously gave it to me.

After high school, Mark and I journeyed to the same college. Here, I met the second Catholic in my life, a fellow student by the name of Mary. Mary and I became friends during our freshman year. We lived on the same dormitory floor. We enjoyed studying together, going on walks with one another, talking for hours on end, and simply being with one another. By the end of our freshman year we began dating. It wasn't very Lutheran of me, but in college, as in high school, I used the St. Joseph prayer card in times of special need. As an intercessor Joseph never seemed to fail.

In our junior year Mary decided to live off-campus in the Newman Catholic Campus Ministry Center. Partly in response to her, and partly out of my own desire to learn more about my faith, I decided to live in the Lutheran version of the Newman Center – the Lutheran Campus Ministry Center, or Christus House, as a resident peer minister. Mary and I also took part in annual joint ecumenical retreats. This opened us up to discussing matters of faith more seriously.

I was as committed in my Lutheranism as Mary was in her Catholicism. Living in the Christus House meant weekly Wednesday night vespers, Bible studies, quarterly retreats, and the added bonus of reduced rent. At one point during my senior year I even contemplated a vocation as a pastor. I visited Luther Seminary in St. Paul with my campus ministry pastor and sat in on a class taught by professor and author Walter Sundberg.

My courtship with Mary lasted four years. During that time I found the faith of her farm family, their devotion, and traditions particularly attractive. They were truly a faithful family and this showed in their attendance at Mass every Sunday, in the ways in which they prayed together, and in the ways that they made their faith a part of their lives. I found myself drawn to Mary and her family. It was here that I first gained a respect for Catholicism.

As an inter-denominational couple we struggled with the questions all such couples struggle with. What prayers would we say? What church would we attend? How would we raise our children? We found comfort in the similarities of our faith and often prayed the Our Father or common meal prayers together. We wrestled with many issues, and occasionally we argued, but slowly we began to realize that we could work through them, or at least respectfully disagree.

During marriage preparation the priest asked us if we were willing to raise our children Catholic. This promise was one I found difficult both to understand and agree with. I felt slighted, as though my denomination were somehow inferior or less important. I thought to myself, "What if I don't want to?" I certainly didn't want to say "yes" to something that I wasn't sure I wanted to do. Of the two of us, I felt that Mary practiced her faith more than I, and so, reluctantly, I agreed.

Although we didn't have all the issues worked out we were married on July 8, 1989.

It was a mixed ceremony at St. Eloi's Catholic Church in Ghent, Minnesota. We decided not to have a Mass so that my family would not feel uncomfortable. My Lutheran campus ministry pastor gave the homily, while Mary's priest co-celebrated. I particularly remember the "Our Father." The priest, Father Bernie Schriner, asked the wedding party to join hands in a circle near the altar. In a sign of unity, Father Schriner asked that the parishioners hold hands, even across the aisles. A college friend sang a moving rendition of the prayer. Toward the end, overcome with emotion, Father Schriner shouted "Everyone!" and together the congregation sang "For thine is the kingdom, and the power, and the glory, forever. Amen." There was something chilling about it. I remember getting goosebumps and being teary eyed. I looked around and could see tears in the eyes of Mary and some of the other wedding party members. It was a moment of ecumenism at its best, and it foreshadowed what was to come in our marriage.

After our marriage, as before, we would sometimes attend our churches separately. At
other times we would attend one or the other together, or sometimes we would attend both churches each Sunday. We both found this a challenge. Although Mary had been brought up in Catholic grade school she didn't know her faith well enough to be able to explain to me why we had to go to both.

Beginning in 1992 several remarkable things happened. We moved into our first home in St. Paul. It was also at about this time that my Lutheran shell began to crack. I grew disillusioned with the Lutheran parishes we attended. The teachings of the church seemed to vary greatly depending on the individual pastor. I found myself questioning the issue of authority. Who or what gave an individual pastor the right to preach a different doctrine from another pastor?

More out of convenience than anything, I started attending St. Columba Catholic Church, just three blocks from our home, with Mary, and foregoing Lutheran Sunday services, reserving Lutheran services for only special occasions such as Christmas and Easter.

The final blow came when the E.L.C.A. began changing doctrine in regard to sexuality and abortion. The E.L.C.A. had released a draft report in which they had compromised on their opposition to abortion. Whereas the Catholic Church taught that abortion was always wrong, the Lutheran Church had started teaching that it was an unfortunate, but necessary fact of life for some women. Lutheran medical insurance even began paying for abortions for Lutheran pastors. Sitting in church one Sunday I realized that being a Lutheran meant more than simply sitting in the pew. Ultimately, it meant believing everything that the Lutheran Church believes and teaches. Thus began my own walk toward Emmaus.

My Lutheranism contained an active element of rebelliousness. I rejected authority. I questioned everything. I didn't like being told what to do. This was an attitude I found difficult to overcome. When my friend Mark suggested that I watch a videotape of former Protestant minister Scott Hahn, for example, or when he suggested that he would be willing to sponsor me should I decide to go through RCIA, I reacted with rebelliousness, thinking that his efforts were merely to try to "convert" me. This attitude also surfaced in my relationship with Mary. Had she or her family pressured me in any way to convert, I would have dismissed the possibility outright. I never would have considered Catholicism. Thankfully they did not, and so I remained open. It was this strong-headedness that the Spirit had to work with.

Eventually I saw this attitude as an outcome of the Reformation. It was a position that stated that individual judgment takes precedence over any kind of authority. It implied that there was no authority outside of one's self. Therefore, I was free to create a Bible and a religion to suit myself if need be. This is what Luther did. It was an attitude that said that no Pope, no council, no Magisterium, and certainly no Church could dictate how I lived.

While I found myself attracted to Catholicism, I had many questions and doubts. I could not convert because Mary was Catholic. It had to be a decision I came to on my own. What I needed to find was a fellow convert to whom I could talk. Mark and Mary had embraced Catholicism because they were born into it. I desperately wanted to talk to someone who had come to Catholicism on his own. God provided exactly what I needed, but in a most unexpected way.

An Epiphany

Rich Haataja and I first met in the summer of 1985. At the time, I had just graduated from high school. Rich lived nearby, and was married and had two children. I worked as a cashier at Kmart's automotive repair register, and Rich coincidentally had all of his automotive work done at Kmart. We met when he came in to pay his bill. While checking his ID, I noted the name. "Haataja! That's a unique name," I said.

"It's Finnish," he replied. "Yes, I guess it is unique." My brother and I had just met, without realizing it.

Flash forward to 1991. As a writer, I frequently wrote humorous memoir. While at my parents' house one day I innocently asked my father, "Dad, when did you return home from your Air Force service in Guam?"

He responded, "The summer of 1967." I was doing the mathematical equation in my head and, while I am a poor math student, something really wasn't computing. I was born in September of 1967.

So I asked, "Well, you must have come home around Christmas-time or something?"

His response was simply, "No." Rather than jump to any conclusions, I merely pawned the "error" off on my father's poor memory. He had a hard time even keeping his children's names straight. In the end, I wrote a story loosely based on the incident. Titled "I am the Milkman's Son," it tongue-in-cheek told how when you want an important date or the "real" story, you go to your mother. Mothers remember everything.

Almost a year later, in the August of 1992, my father showed up on my doorstep. His presence, unannounced and unaccompanied by my mother, warned me that something was not as it should be. Calmly, yet tearfully, he told me that I was not his son.

An Air Force enlisted man, my father was stationed in Guam immediately after he and my mother were married. He brought papers showing that he had been discharged and returned home from Guam during the summer of 1967. When he came home, he found my mother five months pregnant. I arrived on September 13th. Having grown up with divorced parents himself, he did not want a broken home for me, and so, honorably, he stayed with my mother, albeit with a great deal of pain and bitterness.

To say that such news was shocking is an understatement. Learning the truth turned my whole world upside down. It threw everything I thought I knew into question. Growing up, I had never once questioned whether my parents were not who they said they were. While my younger brother, Jeff, and I shared little resemblance we simply thought that he took after dad and I took after mom. Perhaps even more shocking was to learn that my father had wanted me aborted.

Thankfully, my mother did not.

God, in His wisdom, can bring good even from sin. Learning the truth was a blessing. It helped to explain some of the misdirected hostility I had received from my father as a child, and it helped to explain why my younger brother and I were so different. But, I was also blessed with newly discovered family members.

Not only did I learn about the true identity of my father, Irving, but in learning the truth I also discovered two older half-brothers that I had not known existed. Two months after learning the truth and coming to terms with who I was, I placed a phone call to the first of my half-brothers, Rich. We spoke for a long time and agreed to meet at a nearby restaurant. I was nervous about our meeting and did not know what to expect. Rich admitted that he fully expected to see someone totally unlike him, with red hair and freckles walk into the restaurant claiming to be his brother. Instead, when I walked into the restaurant there was a man facing me who bore an undeniable resemblance. It was as if I was staring into a mirror and looking at myself 13 years older. As we sat eating our hamburgers and comparing stories the waitress asked, "Are you guys brothers?" Here we were, meeting for the first time in our lives, and a stranger could see the resemblance. We laughed, thinking, "If you only knew..."

Four years earlier Rich had had an argument that caused his father, Irving, and him to be estranged. Our meeting inspired Rich to call his father. Early in 1993, Rich took me to meet my father for the first time. My biological father, Irving, took no responsibility for me. An alcoholic, he sat watching television, and talked very little. Yet, meeting him was healing. Meeting him was beneficial if only to realize that our only bond was one of genetics. I came away from that meeting feeling fortunate that I grew up in the family that I had. Several months later Irving died.

In meeting Rich, a unique and inseparable bond was formed. We each felt more complete. Yet our bond was one that was more than genetic. Although thirteen years separated us, we had different mothers, and we grew up in different homes, our looks, voices, personalities, and mannerisms were similar. We shared the same values. We had similar senses of humor. We both shared a passion for motion pictures and pizza.

Most importantly, in Rich, I found the convert I so desperately needed to talk to. Like me, he had grown up Lutheran. His parents' lack of practicing their faith, and a friendship with a priest, led Rich to convert to Catholicism at age 18. Sharing his story with me propelled me to learn more. Learning the truth about my father led me to a far greater Truth.

Overcoming Hurdles

Not long after meeting Rich, a couple of other events pointed me toward the Church. The new *Catechism of the Catholic Church* was published and I purchased a copy. I found it most helpful. When I had a question, it was an excellent place to go for an answer. It also impressed upon me the validity of having all that the Church believes in a single source, and gave meaning to the statement "One holy, Catholic, and apostolic Church." As a Lutheran, I had questioned all authority. Now, as a potential Catholic, I could see the wisdom of the teaching Magisterium.

On September 11, 1994 Archbishop Harry Flynn held a Mass and procession at St. Columba's Church instituting perpetual Eucharistic adoration. Feeling the need to pray more, but not fully understanding the meaning of the Blessed Sacrament, I signed up to pray for one hour each Sunday evening.

Unfortunately, the Rite of Christian Initiation for Adults (RCIA) program at our local parish left much to be desired. The instructor was prone to asking, "So, what questions do you have?" when many of us did not even know what questions to ask. Had it been for RCIA alone I never would have converted. Thankfully, a friend recommended a Fundamentals of Catholicism course at a nearby parish and offered to attend them with me. A faithful and humble priest capable of handling any question put to him taught the class. It didn't take long for the Holy Spirit to work within me. Before long the issues I had long had contention with were no longer issues.

Through an audiotape by former Presbyterian minister Dr. Scott Hahn, I learned of the errors of Luther's rallying cries of *Sola Fide* and *Sola Scriptura*. Although Protestants believe in the Bible as the sole rule of faith, this was a teaching I could find supported nowhere in Scripture. In fact, 2 Thessalonians 2:15, 2 Peter 3:15-17, and the Council of Jerusalem in the book of Acts seemed to suggest that tradition also played a role in faith. Although Lutherans liked to discount Catholic tradition, I saw that they passed along their own tradition through Luther's small catechism.

Moreover, the Good News Bible (American Bible Society, 1976) which I had used throughout confirmation translated Romans 3:28 to say, "For we conclude that a person is put right with God only through faith, and not by doing what the Law commands." By contrast, the Revised Standard Version, which I used throughout my discerning process, translated that verse to read, "For we hold that a man is justified by faith apart from works of law." I learned that Luther had inserted the word "alone" during his translation to justify his position that we are saved by faith "alone." This error of Luther's contradicts James 2:17 which states that "So faith by itself, if it has no works, is dead." I had to agree with Dr. Hahn's assessment that if Luther was wrong on either of his points, the entire church that he founded fell, as well as every split that came later.

During my weekly hour with the Lord in the Blessed Sacrament I read chapter by chapter from a small purple book titled *Surprised by Truth*. Each chapter provided a simple to understand Scriptural basis for all of the Catholic Church's teachings. I also came to understand that the teachings have to be considered as a whole. Picking and choosing does not work because individual Church teachings depend on one another.

Doctrinally, I still had to overcome my major hurdles. They included Mary, papal authority, contraception, communion and confession.

As a Lutheran, I incorrectly believed that Catholics worshipped Mary. I had seen Catholics kneeling before statues of Mary, and I had heard the rosary. I believed both to be forms of worship. However, a closer examination of Scripture cleared up my misunderstandings about Mary.

Mary is clearly prefigured in Genesis 3:15 when God says that He will "put enmity between you and the woman." The title "woman" at first seemed a strange one for Mary, until I discovered Christ using the same title when he addressed his mother at the wedding feast of Cana (John 2:4), and again later from the Cross (John 19:26). The title is again used in Revelation 12: 1-2, 17. Christ is clearly indicating that Mary is the New Eve. Just as Eve was the mother of us all, Mary, as the New Eve, is our Heavenly Mother. Furthermore, the comparison of the Ark of the Covenant, to Mary as the Ark of the New Covenant helped me to understand the Catholic teaching on the Immaculate Conception.

Therefore, Scripture helped me to understand Mary's role in our salvation and the reason for the Catholic Church's well-meant attention to her. It became clear that Catholics do not worship Mary, but venerate (honor) her. I learned that a statue of Mary was no different from a historical statue, and that a prayer card would be no different from carrying a photo of a loved one around in your purse or wallet. I also learned that asking Mary to pray for me was no different than asking a friend or family member to pray for me. The rosary itself, I learned, was scriptural, reminding us of the angel's words to Mary at the Annunciation. The other thing I discovered is that Mary is not, ultimately, the point of Marian devotion. Its object is the fruit of her womb. She always points the way to her Son.

A fresh reading of Matthew helped clear my eyes on the question of papal authority. In Matthew 16: 18-19, Christ states, "And I tell you, you are Peter, and on this rock I will build my church, and the powers of death shall not prevail against it. I will give you the keys of the kingdom of heaven, and whatever you bind on earth shall be bound in heaven, and whatever you loose on earth shall be loosed in heaven." What church was Christ talking about here? It did not appear that he was speaking literally of a physical church. The only explanation that made any sense to me was that he was speaking of the church Christ established, the Catholic Church.

Furthermore, I was confronted by the absurdity of Christ giving the keys to the kingdom of heaven to a man, even one as weak as Peter. Peter is the disciple whom would later deny Christ three times, and yet Christ is entrusting him with the keys to heaven. It makes no sense, and yet in its senselessness it provided meaning to papal authority, which had troubled me for so long. It became obvious to me that if God could inspire fallible men to write an infallible book, guide the Church, and guard heaven, then he could also use a fallible men, such as Peter and all later Popes, to pass on infallible teachings.

Although we had been using NFP in our marriage from the beginning, I had not been convinced that contraception was wrong. Eventually, I discovered that in marriage the husband and wife are joined in a covenant relationship where each says to the other "I am yours and you are mine." Yet, contraceptive use places an artificial barrier between the love of a man and his wife. It is like saying, "I give you all of me, but this one part." Understanding this teaching made it easier to embrace the Church's respect for the sanctity of all human life from conception to a natural death.

One by one, my arguments against the Church melted away. It was as if I had been infused with a complete knowledge and acceptance of the Church and her teachings. I wanted our family to be one spiritually. I was on the road to reconciliation.

Confession remained my last major obstacle, more out of fear than any lack of understanding. It was difficult to overcome my Lutheran belief that we are "dung heaps covered with snow." My priest-teacher compared the Lutheran concept of forgiveness to typing with an old typewriter. If a sin were like a mistake, you could white it out, but you would always be able to tell that the mistake had been made. In contrast, he compared the Catholic idea of forgiveness to using a computer. Confession, he described, was like hitting the delete key. Once the key was struck, you would never be able to tell that the mistake had been made. If this were true, I felt that confession had to be the most powerful and freeing sacrament Christ had given His Church. In addition, John 20: 22-23 and James 5:14-15 helped clear the way for a Scriptural understanding of confession.

On Ash Wednesday I was moved to go to confession. Compiling a laundry list of 27 years worth of sin was a very humbling experience. The Cathedral of St. Paul seemed an appropriate place to go. There, I poured out the sins of my life and was filled with the grace that accompanies the sacrament. It wasn't a lightning bolt of grace, striking me suddenly, but rather a gradual appreciation of the sacrament and its graces. After confession things moved quickly.

I saw converting as a covenant one enters into with God. Like marriage or parenthood, it is not something you can try out beforehand. Once I decided to convert, there was no turning back. It was all or nothing. Either I accepted the Church and her teachings, or I wasn't Catholic. There was no room to pick and choose. RCIA and the Fundamentals classes were very much like marriage preparation coursework and Engaged Encounter. There was only so much prayer, reading, discussion, and discerning I could do. My intellect could only take me so far. Eventually my heart had to follow. Truly, I was in love with God, and was being moved to take a childlike leap. I did not have all the answers. I did not know where it would lead. But I had to trust in God. As the Church teaches, some things have been and will continue to be a mystery. This is what faith is.

The Turning Point

The issue that ultimately led me to my final step in the conversion process was the Eucharist. As early as college, when I would attend Mass with Mary, I began to hunger for the Eucharist. As I sat in the pew, often alone, I wondered how lonely it would be to watch my entire family go up to share in the Lord's meal while I remained behind.

As a Lutheran, I certainly embraced a non-symbolic understanding of Christ's presence in communion. Yet, I was troubled by the infrequency of communion within the Lutheran church. I could clearly see that the highlight of Lutheran worship tended to be Scripture readings and the homily, while the highlight of Catholic worship appeared to be the Eucharist. Adoration of the Blessed Sacrament and John 6:22-71 helped me to understand the difference.

In John 6, Christ says repeatedly that he is the living bread from heaven and that anyone who eats of this bread will live forever. So shocked by this, many of Christ's followers turn away. What does Christ mean? Does he mean he is bread symbolically? If he does, why doesn't Christ chase after them saying, "Wait, wait…you misunderstood me. What I really meant to say is that I am symbolically bread or that I am bread only sometimes." Instead, Christ turns to his disciples and asks, "Will you also go away?"

My time of prayer before the Blessed Sacrament created in me an unquenchable hunger for the Eucharist. I recognized that the Catholic Church's belief in transubstantiation - that the bread and wine become Christ in Body, Blood, Soul and Divinity - was something no other Church offered. I had retained bitter feelings about being unable to receive communion within the Catholic Church. My new understanding helped me to see why non-Catholic reception of our Lord's Body and Blood implied a wholeness that hasn't existed since the Reformation.

The Gospel of Luke's story of Christ's appearance to the two disciples on their way to Emmaus remains one of my favorites. For in this story, more than any other, I can clearly see the pattern of my own journey.

Although Lutherans are not prone to making confessions, I confess that I never understood the Road to Emmaus story. How was it, I wondered, that Christ's own disciples – the men who walked, talked, prayed, and ate with him – could not recognize him? I had heard the familiar explanation that in his risen and glorified state he was different and unrecognizable, but it just didn't hold water for me. It was a passage that completely puzzled me.

In Luke's story, the two disciples do not recognize Jesus. In an effort to reveal Himself, Christ first breaks open Scripture. Luke states that Christ, "…beginning with Moses and all the prophets… interpreted to them what referred to him in all the scriptures" (Luke 24: 27). But, *still*, they do not recognize him. As a Lutheran I felt that I knew Jesus because I was familiar with His Word. Yet, something was clearly missing.

In the story, it is not until Christ breaks bread with his disciples that they come to *know* Him. Week after week I attended my hour of prayer at Eucharistic adoration. It didn't take long for me to figure out Who I was kneeling before. In my own conversion, it was also in the breaking of the bread that I came to *know* Jesus Christ.

Once the disciples recognize Christ, they literally run several miles back to Jerusalem to tell the others. Again, this parallels my own story. Once I had recognized Christ in the "breaking of the bread" I could not be held back. I wanted nothing more than to run to Him as fast as my legs would take me. Therefore, I was unable to wait until Easter to convert and told my pastor that to wait to convert felt as if I was denying Him. And so, on March 19, 1995, the Feast of St. Joseph, gathered with my friends and family and Mary as my sponsor, I professed my belief in the Holy Catholic Church, was confirmed, and accompanied Mary to the Lord's table for the first time since we had begun dating ten years earlier.

Ongoing Conversion

A conversion is a lifelong process, rather than a single event. Just as all conversion stories do not end until we are home with Christ in Heaven, my own story does not end with my conversion.

As a Lutheran, although I believed in Christ, my faith did not hold the fullness of Truth so beautifully expressed in Christ and His Church. Therefore, through my conversion, I Corinthians 7:14 was fulfilled. An unbelieving husband was sanctified by a believing wife. It used to be that both the Lutheran and Catholic Church seriously cautioned against mixed marriages because of the potential for the "danger of loss of faith." While I understand their caution and the potential that mixed marriages have for causing pain, I marvel at the joy that Mary and I now share. Our own mixed marriage not only strengthened my faith, but Mary's as well.

Even more miraculous, God took my love for Mary, combined it with my love for Him, and created new life, not only within me, but within us. Within weeks after my conversion, after a long struggle with infertility, my wife and I learned we were expecting a child. Our joy was compounded in discovering that we would join in the pregnancy of the Holy Family when we learned that our projected due date was Christmas. During the pregnancy Mary and I were fortunate to visit Rome. It truly felt like going "home." Attending Mass in Assisi, I marveled at how universal the Mass was.

Later that year, our son, Elias Joseph Drake, was born on December 27, 1995.

The Eucharist remains central to my spiritual life as a Catholic. Each time I receive Christ, I utter the simple prayer, "Jesus, as I take Your Body into my body, help to make me more like you." Because Christ in the Eucharist is what brought me into the Church, it is the source of my life both within and outside of the Church. I still attend my weekly hour of Eucharistic adoration and continue to be awed that Christ humbles himself and makes himself vulnerable in this Sacrament so that we can be united with Him.

I can now able to look back on these extraordinary events and can clearly see the hand of

God in their timing. I continue to marvel at how in other people's conversion stories, as well as my own, the Holy Spirit provides just what people need when they need it, if they are open. This is, perhaps, what makes conversion stories so extraordinary. While each is distinct, they are also in some ways very much the same.

While at first it may seem odd that God would have Rich and I meet before we actually "met," it makes perfect sense in God's timing. Neither of us knew that the other existed. If God had somehow let us learn the truth at our first meeting, I am not certain that everything would have worked out in the way that it did. Our first meeting took place before college, before I was married, and long before I considered the Catholic faith. I was still spiritually immature at the time. His own conversion would have made little difference to me. However, God put him right back into my life exactly when I needed him.

Had my stepfather not told me the truth, not only would I still be living without the knowledge of my father or my brothers, but I probably would not have met my biological father before his death, I might not have come into the Church, and I would certainly not be doing the work that I am doing today.

Afterword

When I first thought of writing my conversion story I naively envisioned creating something profound, perhaps something that would touch others. Because it is so deeply personal I discovered it to be the most difficult writing I have ever undertaken. As the famous Jewish convert to Catholicism, Dr. Karl Stern, wrote, "How do you begin to write about how you fell in love with God?" To write a conversion story from only the human perspective is to provide an incomplete tale. Clearly, in ways seen and unseen, the Holy Spirit was acting and moving in me, opening my ears, mind, and heart. Likewise, the prayers of my wife Mary, and others known and unknown were being raised in unison to Heaven. As complete as this story may seem, our perspective pales in comparison to the Heavenly events we are unable to relate.

Tim Drake is a full-time Catholic writer. He currently serves as features correspondent with the National Catholic Register and associate editor of Envoy Magazine. Tim lives in St. Cloud, Minnesota with his wife, Mary, and their four children.

Appendices

Appendix A

JOINT DECLARATION ON THE DOCTRINE OF JUSTIFICATION
Lutheran World Federation and the Catholic Church

Preamble

1. The doctrine of justification was of central importance for the Lutheran Reformation of the sixteenth century. It was held to be the "first and chief article"[1] and at the same time the "ruler and judge over all other Christian doctrines."[2] The doctrine of justification was particularly asserted and defended in its Reformation shape and special valuation over against the Roman Catholic Church and theology of that time, which in turn asserted and defended a doctrine of justification of a different character. From the Reformation perspective, justification was the crux of all the disputes. Doctrinal condemnations were put forward both in the Lutheran Confessions[3] and by the Roman Catholic Church's Council of Trent. These condemnations are still valid today and thus have a church-dividing effect.

2. For the Lutheran tradition, the doctrine of justification has retained its special status. Consequently it has also from the beginning occupied an important place in the official Lutheran-Roman Catholic dialogue.

3. Special attention should be drawn to the following reports: "The Gospel and the Church" (1972)[4] and "Church and Justification" (1994)[5] by the Lutheran-Roman Catholic Joint Commission, "Justification by Faith" (1983)[6] of the Lutheran-Roman Catholic dialogue in the USA and "The Condemnations of the Reformation Era - Do They Still Divide?" (1986)[7] by the Ecumenical Working Group of Protestant and Catholic theologians in Germany. Some of these dialogue reports have been officially received by the churches. An important example of such reception is the binding response of the United Evangelical-Lutheran Church of Germany to the "Condemnations" study, made in 1994 at the highest possible level of ecclesiastical recognition together with the other churches of the Evangelical Church in Germany.[8]

4. In their discussion of the doctrine of justification, all the dialogue reports as well as the responses show a high degree of agreement in their approaches and conclusions. The time has therefore come to take stock and to summarize the results of the dialogues on justification so that our churches may be informed about the overall results of this dialogue with the necessary accuracy and brevity, and thereby be enabled to make binding decisions.

I

5. The present Joint Declaration has this intention: namely, to show that on the basis of their dialogue the subscribing Lutheran churches and the Roman Catholic Church[9] are now able to articulate a common understanding of our justification by God's grace through faith in Christ. It does not cover all that either church teaches about justification; it does encompass a consensus on basic truths of the doctrine of justification and shows that the remaining differences in its explication are no longer the occasion for doctrinal condemnations.

6. Our Declaration is not a new, independent presentation alongside the dialogue reports and documents to date, let alone a replacement of them. Rather, as the appendix of sources shows, it makes repeated reference to them and their arguments.

7. Like the dialogues themselves, this Joint Declaration rests on the conviction that in overcoming the earlier controversial questions and doctrinal condemnations, the churches neither take the condemnations lightly nor do they disavow their own past. On the contrary, this Declaration is shaped by the conviction that in their respective histories our churches have come to new insights. Developments have taken place which not only make possible, but also require the churches to examine the divisive questions and condemnations and see them in a new light.

1. Biblical Message of Justification

8. Our common way of listening to the word of God in Scripture has led to such new insights. Together we hear the gospel that "God so loved the world that he gave his only Son, so that everyone who believes in him may not perish but may have eternal life" (*Jn* 3:16). This good news is set forth in Holy Scripture in various ways. In the Old Testament we listen to God's word about human sinfulness (*Ps* 51:1-5; *Dan* 9:5f; *Eccl/Qo* 8:9f; *Ezra* 9:6f) and human disobedience (*Gen* 3:1-19; *Neh* 9:16f,26) as well as of God's "righteousness" (*Isa* 46:13; 51:5-8; 56:1 [cf. 53:11]; *Jer* 9:24) and "judgment" (*Eccl/Qo* 12:14; *Ps* 9:5f; 76:7-9).

9. In the New Testament diverse treatments of "righteousness" and "justification" are found in the writings of Matthew (5:10; 6:33; 21:32), John (16:8-11), Hebrews (5:3; 10:37f), and James (2:14-26).[10] In Paul's letters also, the gift of salvation is described in various ways, among others: "for freedom Christ has set us free" (*Gal* 5:1-13; cf. *Rom* 6:7), "reconciled to God" (2 *Cor* 5:18-21; cf. *Rom* 5:11), "peace with God" (*Rom* 5:1), "new creation" (2 *Cor* 5:17), "alive to God in Christ Jesus" (*Rom* 6:11,23), or "sanctified in Christ Jesus" (cf. 1 *Cor* 1:2; 1:30; 2 *Cor* 1:1). Chief among these is the "justification" of sinful human beings by God's grace through faith (*Rom* 3:23-25), which came into particular prominence in the Reformation period.

10. Paul sets forth the gospel as the power of God for salvation of the person who has fallen under the power of sin, as the message that proclaims that "the righteousness of God is revealed through faith for faith" (*Rom* 1:16f) and that grants "justification" (*Rom* 3:21-31). He proclaims Christ as "our righteousness" (1 *Cor* 1:30), applying to the risen

Lord what Jeremiah proclaimed about God himself (*Jer* 23:6). In Christ's death and resurrection all dimensions of his saving work have their roots for he is "our Lord, who was put to death for our trespasses and raised for our justification" (*Rom* 4:25). All human beings are in need of God's righteousness, "since all have sinned and fall short of the glory of God" (*Rom* 3:23; cf. *Rom* 1:18-3:20; 11:32; *Gal* 3:22). In Galatians (3:6) and Romans (4:3-9), Paul understands Abraham's faith (*Gen* 15:6) as faith in the God who justifies the sinner (*Rom* 4:5) and calls upon the testimony of the Old Testament to undergird his gospel that this righteousness will be reckoned to all who, like Abraham, trust in God's promise. "For the righteous will live by faith (Hab 2:4; cf. *Gal* 3:11; *Rom* 1:17). In Paul's letters, God's righteousness is also God's power for those who have faith (*Rom* 1:16f; 2 *Cor* 5:21). In Christ he makes it our righteousness (2 *Cor* 5:21). Justification becomes ours through Christ Jesus "whom God put forward as a sacrifice of atonement by his blood, effective through faith" (*Rom* 3:25; see 3:21-28). "For by grace you have been saved through faith, and this is not your own doing; it is the gift of God - not the result of works" (*Eph* 2:8f).

11.Justification is the forgiveness of sins (cf. *Rom* 3:23-25; *Acts* 13:39; *Lk* 18:14), liberation from the dominating power of sin and death (*Rom* 5:12-21) and from the curse of the law (*Gal* 3:10-14). It is acceptance into communion with God: already now, but then fully in God's coming kingdom (*Rom* 5:1f). It unites with Christ and with his death and resurrection (*Rom* 6:5). It occurs in the reception of the Holy Spirit in baptism and incorporation into the one body (*Rom* 8:1f, 9f; I *Cor* 12:12f). All this is from God alone, for Christ's sake, by grace, through faith in "the gospel of God's Son" (*Rom* 1:1-3).

12.The justified live by faith that comes from the Word of Christ (*Rom* 10:17) and is active through love (*Gal* 5:6), the fruit of the Spirit (*Gal* 5:22f). But since the justified are assailed from within and without by powers and desires (*Rom* 8:35-39; *Gal* 5:16-21) and fall into sin (1 *Jn* 1:8,10), they must constantly hear God's promises anew, confess their sins (1 *Jn* 1:9), participate in Christ's body and blood, and be exhorted to live righteously in accord with the will of God. That is why the Apostle says to the justified: "Work out your own salvation with fear and trembling; for it is God who is at work in you, enabling you both to will and to work for his good pleasure" (*Phil* 2:12f). But the good news remains: "there is now no condemnation for those who are in Christ Jesus" (*Rom* 8:1), and in whom Christ lives (*Gal* 2:20). Christ's "act of righteousness leads to justification and life for all" (*Rom* 5:18).

2.The Doctrine of Justification as Ecumenical Problem

13.Opposing interpretations and applications of the biblical message of justification were in the sixteenth century a principal cause of the division of the Western church and led as well to doctrinal condemnations. A common understanding of justification is therefore fundamental and indispensable to overcoming that division. By appropriating insights of recent biblical studies and drawing on modern investigations of the history of theology and dogma, the post-Vatican II ecumenical dialogue has led to a notable convergence concerning justification, with the result that this Joint Declaration is able to formulate a consensus on basic truths concerning the doctrine of justification. In light of this consensus, the corresponding doctrinal condemnations of the sixteenth century do not apply to today's partner.

3. The Common Understanding of Justification

14.The Lutheran churches and the Roman Catholic Church have together listened to the good news proclaimed in Holy Scripture. This common listening, together with the theological conversations of recent years, has led to a shared understanding of justification. This encompasses a consensus in the basic truths; the differing explications in particular statements are compatible with it.

15.In faith we together hold the conviction that justification is the work of the triune God. The Father sent his Son into the world to save sinners. The foundation and presupposition of justification is the incarnation, death, and resurrection of Christ. Justification thus means that Christ himself is our righteousness, in which we share through the Holy Spirit in accord with the will of the Father. Together we confess: By grace alone, in faith in Christ's saving work and not because of any merit on our part, we are accepted by God and receive the Holy Spirit, who renews our hearts while equipping and calling us to good works.[11]

16.All people are called by God to salvation in Christ. Through Christ alone are we justified, when we receive this salvation in faith. Faith is itself God's gift through the Holy Spirit who works through word and sacrament in the community of believers and who, at the same time, leads believers into that renewal of life which God will bring to completion in eternal life.

17.We also share the conviction that the message of justification directs us in a special way towards the heart of the New Testament witness to God's saving action in Christ: it tells us that as sinners our new life is solely due to the forgiving and renewing mercy that God imparts as a gift and we receive in faith, and never can merit in any way.

18.Therefore the doctrine of justification, which takes up this message and explicates it, is more than just one part of Christian doctrine. It stands in an essential relation to all truths of faith, which are to be seen as internally related to each other. It is an indispensable criterion which constantly serves to orient all the teaching and practice of our churches to Christ. When Lutherans emphasize the unique significance of this criterion, they do not deny the interrelation and significance of all truths of faith. When Catholics see themselves as bound by several criteria, they do not deny the special function of the message of justification. Lutherans and Catholics share the goal of confessing Christ in all things, who alone is to be trusted above all things as the one Mediator (1 *Tim* 2:5f) through whom God in the Holy Spirit gives himself and pours out his renewing gifts. [cf. Sources for section 3].

4. Explicating the Common Understanding of Justification
4.1 Human Powerlessness and Sin in Relation to Justification

19.We confess together that all persons depend completely on the saving grace of God for their salvation. The freedom they possess in relation to persons and the things of this world is no freedom in relation to salvation, for as sinners they stand under God's judgment and are incapable of turning by themselves to God to seek deliverance, of meriting their justification before God, or of attaining salvation by their own abilities. Justification takes place solely by God's grace. Because Catholics and Lutherans confess this together, it is true to say:

20.When Catholics say that persons "cooperate" in preparing for and accepting justification by consenting to God's justifying action, they see such personal consent as itself an effect of grace, not as an action arising from innate human abilities.

21.According to Lutheran teaching, human beings are incapable of cooperating in their salvation, because as sinners they actively oppose God and his saving action. Lutherans do not deny that a person can reject the working of grace. When they emphasize that a person can only receive (mere passive) justification, they mean thereby to exclude any possibility of contributing to one's own justification, but do not deny that believers are fully involved personally in their faith, which is effected by God's Word. [cf. Sources for 4.1].

4.2 Justification as Forgiveness of Sins and Making Righteous

22.We confess together that God forgives sin by grace and at the same time frees human beings from sin's enslaving power and imparts the gift of new life in Christ. When persons come by faith to share in Christ, God no longer imputes to them their sin and through the Holy Spirit effects in them an active love. These two aspects of God's gracious action are not to be separated, for persons are by faith united with Christ, who in his person is our righteousness (1 *Cor* 1:30): both the forgiveness of sin and the saving presence of God himself. Because Catholics and Lutherans confess this together, it is true to say that:

23.When Lutherans emphasize that the righteousness of Christ is our righteousness, their intention is above all to insist that the sinner is granted righteousness before God in Christ through the declaration of forgiveness and that only in union with Christ is one's life renewed. When they stress that God's grace is forgiving love ("the favor of God"[12]), they do not thereby deny the renewal of the Christian's life. They intend rather to express that justification remains free from human cooperation and is not dependent on the life-renewing effects of grace in human beings.

24.When Catholics emphasize the renewal of the interior person through the reception of grace imparted as a gift to the believer,[13] they wish to insist that God's forgiving grace always brings with it a gift of new life, which in the Holy Spirit becomes effective in active love. They do not thereby deny that God's gift of grace in justification remains independent of human cooperation. [cf. Sources for section 4.2].

4.3 Justification by Faith and through Grace

25. We confess together that sinners are justified by faith in the saving action of God in Christ. By the action of the Holy Spirit in baptism, they are granted the gift of salvation, which lays the basis for the whole Christian life. They place their trust in God's gracious promise by justifying faith, which includes hope in God and love for him. Such a faith is active in love and thus the Christian cannot and should not remain without works. But whatever in the justified precedes or follows the free gift of faith is neither the basis of justification nor merits it.

26. According to Lutheran understanding, God justifies sinners in faith alone (*Sola Fide*). In faith they place their trust wholly in their Creator and Redeemer and thus live in communion with him. God himself effects faith as he brings forth such trust by his creative word. Because God's act is a new creation, it affects all dimensions of the person and leads to a life in hope and love. In the doctrine of "justification by faith alone," a distinction but not a separation is made between justification itself and the renewal of one's way of life that necessarily follows from justification and without which faith does not exist. Thereby the basis is indicated from which the renewal of life proceeds, for it comes forth from the love of God imparted to the person in justification. Justification and renewal are joined in Christ, who is present in faith.

27. The Catholic understanding also sees faith as fundamental in justification. For without faith, no justification can take place. Persons are justified through baptism as hearers of the word and believers in it. The justification of sinners is forgiveness of sins and being made righteous by justifying grace, which makes us children of God. In justification the righteous receive from Christ faith, hope, and love and are thereby taken into communion with him.[14] This new personal relation to God is grounded totally on God's graciousness and remains constantly dependent on the salvific and creative working of this gracious God, who remains true to himself, so that one can rely upon him. Thus justifying grace never becomes a human possession to which one could appeal over against God. While Catholic teaching emphasizes the renewal of life by justifying grace, this renewal in faith, hope, and love is always dependent on God's unfathomable grace and contributes nothing to justification about which one could boast before God (*Rom* 3:27). [See Sources for section 4.3].

4.4 The Justified as Sinner

28. We confess together that in baptism the Holy Spirit unites one with Christ, justifies, and truly renews the person. But the justified must all through life constantly look to God's unconditional justifying grace. They also are continuously exposed to the power of sin still pressing its attacks (cf. *Rom* 6:12-14) and are not exempt from a lifelong struggle against the contradiction to God within the selfish desires of the old Adam (cf. *Gal* 5:16;

Rom 7:7-10). The justified also must ask God daily for forgiveness as in the Lord's Prayer (*Mt.* 6:12; 1 *Jn* 1:9), are ever again called to conversion and penance, and are ever again granted forgiveness.

29.Lutherans understand this condition of the Christian as a being "at the same time righteous and sinner." Believers are totally righteous, in that God forgives their sins through Word and Sacrament and grants the righteousness of Christ which they appropriate in faith. In Christ, they are made just before God. Looking at themselves through the law, however, they recognize that they remain also totally sinners. Sin still lives in them (1 *Jn* 1:8; *Rom* 7:17,20), for they repeatedly turn to false gods and do not love God with that undivided love which God requires as their Creator (*Deut* 6:5; *Mt* 22:36-40 pr.). This contradiction to God is as such truly sin. Nevertheless, the enslaving power of sin is broken on the basis of the merit of Christ. It no longer is a sin that "rules" the Christian for it is itself "ruled" by Christ with whom the justified are bound in faith. In this life, then, Christians can in part lead a just life.

Despite sin, the Christian is no longer separated from God, because in the daily return to baptism, the person who has been born anew by baptism and the Holy Spirit has this sin forgiven. Thus this sin no longer brings damnation and eternal death.[15] Thus, when Lutherans say that justified persons are also sinners and that their opposition to God is truly sin, they do not deny that, despite this sin, they are not separated from God and that this sin is a "ruled" sin. In these affirmations, they are in agreement with Roman Catholics, despite the difference in understanding sin in the justified.

30.Catholics hold that the grace of Jesus Christ imparted in baptism takes away all that is sin "in the proper sense" and that is "worthy of damnation" (*Rom* 8:1).[16] There does, however, remain in the person an inclination (concupiscence) which comes from sin and presses toward sin. Since, according to Catholic conviction, human sins always involve a personal element and since this element is lacking in this inclination, Catholics do not see this inclination as sin in an authentic sense. They do not thereby deny that this inclination does not correspond to God's original design for humanity and that it is objectively in contradiction to God and remains one's enemy in lifelong struggle. Grateful for deliverance by Christ, they underscore that this inclination in contradiction to God does not merit the punishment of eternal death[17] and does not separate the justified person from God. But when individuals voluntarily separate themselves from God, it is not enough to return to observing the commandments, for they must receive pardon and peace in the Sacrament of Reconciliation through the word of forgiveness imparted to them in virtue of God's reconciling work in Christ. [See Sources for section 4.4].

4.5 Law and Gospel

31.We confess together that persons are justified by faith in the gospel "apart from works prescribed by the law" (*Rom* 3:28). Christ has fulfilled the law and by his death and resurrection has overcome it as a way to salvation. We also confess that God's commandments retain their validity for the justified and that Christ has by his teaching and example expressed God's will which is a standard for the conduct of the justified also.

32. Lutherans state that the distinction and right ordering of law and gospel is essential for the understanding of justification. In its theological use, the law is demand and accusation. Throughout their lives, all persons, Christians also, in that they are sinners, stand under this accusation which uncovers their sin so that, in faith in the gospel, they will turn unreservedly to the mercy of God in Christ, which alone justifies them.

33. Because the law as a way to salvation has been fulfilled and overcome through the gospel, Catholics can say that Christ is not a lawgiver in the manner of Moses. When Catholics emphasize that the righteous are bound to observe God's commandments, they do not thereby deny that through Jesus Christ God has mercifully promised to his children the grace of eternal life.[18] [See Sources for section 4.5].

4.6 Assurance of Salvation

34. We confess together that the faithful can rely on the mercy and promises of God. In spite of their own weakness and the manifold threats to their faith, on the strength of Christ's death and resurrection they can build on the effective promise of God's grace in Word and Sacrament and so be sure of this grace.

35. This was emphasized in a particular way by the Reformers: in the midst of temptation, believers should not look to themselves but look solely to Christ and trust only him. In trust in God's promise they are assured of their salvation, but are never secure looking at themselves.

36. Catholics can share the concern of the Reformers to ground faith in the objective reality of Christ's promise, to look away from one's own experience, and to trust in Christ's forgiving word alone (cf. *Mt* 16:19; 18:18). With the Second Vatican Council, Catholics state: to have faith is to entrust oneself totally to God,[19] who liberates us from the darkness of sin and death and awakens us to eternal life.[20] In this sense, one cannot believe in God and at the same time consider the divine promise untrustworthy. No one may doubt God's mercy and Christ's merit. Every person, however, may be concerned about his salvation when he looks upon his own weaknesses and shortcomings. Recognizing his own failures, however, the believer may yet be certain that God intends his salvation. [See Sources for section 4.6].

4.7 The Good Works of the Justified

37. We confess together that good works - a Christian life lived in faith, hope and love – follow justification and are its fruits. When the justified live in Christ and act in the grace they receive, they bring forth, in biblical terms, good fruit. Since Christians struggle against sin their entire lives, this consequence of justification is also for them an

obligation they must fulfill. Thus both Jesus and the apostolic Scriptures admonish Christians to bring forth the works of love.

38.According to Catholic understanding, good works, made possible by grace and the working of the Holy Spirit, contribute to growth in grace, so that the righteousness that comes from God is preserved and communion with Christ is deepened. When Catholics affirm the "meritorious" character of good works, they wish to say that, according to the biblical witness, a reward in heaven is promised to these works. Their intention is to emphasize the responsibility of persons for their actions, not to contest the character of those works as gifts, or far less to deny that justification always remains the unmerited gift of grace.

39.The concept of a preservation of grace and a growth in grace and faith is also held by Lutherans. They do emphasize that righteousness as acceptance by God and sharing in the righteousness of Christ is always complete. At the same time, they state that there can be growth in its effects in Christian living. When they view the good works of Christians as the fruits and signs of justification and not as one's own "merits", they nevertheless also understand eternal life in accord with the New Testament as unmerited "reward" in the sense of the fulfillment of God's promise to the believer. [See Sources for section 4.7].

5. The Significance and Scope of the Consensus Reached

40.The understanding of the doctrine of justification set forth in this Declaration shows that a consensus in basic truths of the doctrine of justification exists between Lutherans and Catholics. In light of this consensus the remaining differences of language, theological elaboration, and emphasis in the understanding of justification described in paras. 18 to 39 are acceptable. Therefore the Lutheran and the Catholic explications of justification are in their difference open to one another and do not destroy the consensus regarding the basic truths.

41.Thus the doctrinal condemnations of the 16th century, in so far as they relate to the doctrine of justification, appear in a new light: The teaching of the Lutheran churches presented in this Declaration does not fall under the condemnations from the Council of Trent. The condemnations in the Lutheran Confessions do not apply to the teaching of the Roman Catholic Church presented in this Declaration.

42.Nothing is thereby taken away from the seriousness of the condemnations related to the doctrine of justification. Some were not simply pointless. They remain for us "salutary warnings" to which we must attend in our teaching and practice.[21]

43.Our consensus in basic truths of the doctrine of justification must come to influence the life and teachings of our churches. Here it must prove itself. In this respect, there are still questions of varying importance which need further clarification. These include, among other topics, the relationship between the Word of God and church doctrine, as well as ecclesiology, ecclesial authority, church unity, ministry, the sacraments, and the relation between justification and social ethics. We are convinced that the consensus we have reached offers a solid basis for this clarification. The Lutheran churches and the Roman Catholic Church will continue to strive together to deepen this common understanding of justification and to make it bear fruit in the life and teaching of the churches.

44.We give thanks to the Lord for this decisive step forward on the way to overcoming the division of the church. We ask the Holy Spirit to lead us further toward that visible unity which is Christ's will.

APPENDIX
Resources for the Joint Declaration on the Doctrine of Justification

In parts 3 and 4 of the "Joint Declaration" formulations from different Lutheran-Catholic dialogues are referred to. They are the following documents:

"All Under One Christ," Statement on the Augsburg Confession by the Roman Catholic/Lutheran Joint Commission, 1980, in: Growth in Agreement, edited by Harding Meyer and Lukas Vischer, New York/Ramsey, Geneva, 1984, 241-247.

Denzinger-Schönmetzer, Enchiridion symbolorum ...32nd to 36th edition (hereafter: DS). Denzinger-Hünermann, Enchiridion symbolorum ...since the 37th edition (hereafter: DH). Evaluation of the Pontifical Council for Promoting Christian Unity of the Study Lehrverurteilungen - kirchentrennend?, Vatican, 1992, unpublished document (hereafter: PCPCU). Justification by Faith, Lutherans and Catholics in Dialogue VII, Minneapolis, 1985 (hereafter: USA).

Position Paper of the Joint Committee of the United Evangelical Lutheran Church of Germany and the LWF German National Committee regarding the document "The Condemnations of the Reformation Era.Do They Still Divide?" in: Lehrverurteilungen im Gespräch, Göttingen, 1993 (hereafter: VELKD).
The Condemnations of the Reformation Era. Do they Still Divide? Edited by Karl Lehmann and Wolfhart Pannenberg, Minneapolis, 1990 (hereafter: LV:E)

For 3: The Common Understanding of Justification (paras 17 and 18) (LV:E 68f; VELKD 95)
- "... a faith centered and forensically conceived picture of justification is of major importance for Paul and, in a sense, for the Bible as a whole, although it is by no means the only biblical or Pauline way of representing God's saving work" (USA, no. 146).

- "Catholics as well as Lutherans can acknowledge the need to test the practices, structures, and theologies of the church by the extent to which they help or hinder 'the proclamation of God's free and merciful promises in Christ Jesus which can be rightly received only through faith' (para. 28)" (USA, no. 153).

X

Regarding the "fundamental affirmation" (USA, no. 157; cf. 4) it is said:

- "This affirmation, like the Reformation doctrine of justification by faith alone, serves as a criterion for judging all church practices, structures, and traditions precisely because its counterpart is 'Christ alone' (solus Christus). He alone is to be ultimately trusted as the one mediator through whom God in the Holy Spirit pours out his saving gifts. All of us in this dialogue affirm that all Christian teachings, practices, and offices should so function as to foster 'the obedience of faith' (*Rom.* 1:5) in God's saving action in Christ Jesus alone through the Holy Spirit, for the salvation of the faithful and the praise and honor of the heavenly Father" (USA, no. 160).

- "For that reason, the doctrine of justification - and, above all, its biblical foundation - will always retain a special function in the church. That function is continually to remind Christians that we sinners live solely from the forgiving love of God, which we merely allow to be bestowed on us, but which we in no way - in however modified a form - 'earn' or are able to tie down to any preconditions or postconditions. The doctrine of justification therefore becomes the touchstone for testing at all times whether a particular interpretation of our relationship to God can claim the name of 'Christian.' At the same time, it becomes the touchstone for the church, for testing at all times whether its proclamation and its praxis correspond to what has been given to it by its Lord" (LV:E 69).

- "An agreement on the fact that the doctrine of justification is significant not only as one doctrinal component within the whole of our church's teaching, but also as the touchstone for testing the whole doctrine and practice of our churches, is - from a Lutheran point of view - fundamental progress in the ecumenical dialogue between our churches. It cannot be welcomed enough" (VELKD 95, 20-26; cf. 157).

- "For Lutherans and Catholics, the doctrine of justification has a different status in the hierarchy of truth; but both sides agree that the doctrine of justification has its specific function in the fact that it is 'the touchstone for testing at all times whether a particular interpretation of our relationship to God can claim the name of "Christian". At the same time it becomes the touchstone for the church, for testing at all times whether its proclamation and its praxis correspond to what has been given to it by its Lord' (LV:E 69). The criteriological significance of the doctrine of justification for sacramentology, ecclesiology and ethical teachings still deserves to be studied further" (PCPCU 96).

For 4.1: Human Powerlessness and Sin in Relation to Justification (paras 19-21) (LV:E 42ff; 46; VELKD 77-81; 83f)

- "Those in whom sin reigns can do nothing to merit justification, which is the free gift of God's grace. Even the beginnings of justification, for example, repentance, prayer for grace, and desire for forgiveness, must be God's work in us" (USA, no. 156.3).

- "*Both* are concerned to make it clear that ... human beings cannot ... cast a sideways glance at their own endeavors ... But a response is not a 'work.' The response of faith is itself brought about through the uncoercible word of promise which comes to human beings from outside themselves. There can be '*co*operation' only in the sense that in faith the heart is involved, when the Word touches it and creates faith" (LV:E 46f).

- "Where, however, Lutheran teaching construes the relation of God to his human creatures in justification with such emphasis on the divine 'monergism' or the sole efficacy of Christ in such a way, that the person's willing acceptance of God's grace - which is itself a gift of God - has no essential role in justification, then the Tridentine canons 4, 5, 6 and 9 still constitute a notable doctrinal difference on justification" (PCPCU 22).

-"The strict emphasis on the passivity of human beings concerning their justification never meant, on the Lutheran side, to contest the full personal participation in believing; rather it meant to exclude any cooperation in the event of justification itself. Justification is the work of Christ alone, the work of grace alone" (VELKD 84,3-8).

For 4.2: Justification as Forgiveness of Sins and Making Righteous (paras. 22-24) (USA, nos. 98-101; LV:E 47ff; VELKD 84ff; cf. also the quotations for 4.3)

- "By justification we are both declared and made righteous. Justification, therefore, is not a legal fiction. God, in justifying, effects what he promises; he forgives sin and makes us truly righteous" (USA, no. 156,5).

- "Protestant theology does not overlook what Catholic doctrine stresses: the creative and renewing character of God's love; nor does it maintain ..God's impotence toward a sin which is 'merely' forgiven in justification but which is not truly abolished in its power to divide the sinner from God" (LV:E 49).

- "The Lutheran doctrine has never understood the 'crediting of Christ's justification' as without effect on the life of the faithful, because Christ's word achieves what it promises. Accordingly the Lutheran doctrine understands grace as God's favor, but nevertheless as effective power ..'for where there is forgiveness of sins, there is also life and salvation'" (VELKD 86,15-23).

- "Catholic doctrine does not overlook what Protestant theology stresses: the personal character of grace, and its link with the Word; nor does it maintain ..grace as an objective 'possession' (even if a conferred possession) on the part of the human being - something over which he can dispose" (LV:E 49).

For 4.3: Justification by Faith and through Grace (paras.25-27) (USA, nos. 105ff; LV:E 49-53; VELKD 87-90)

- "If we translate from one language to another, then Protestant talk about justification through faith corresponds to Catholic talk about justification through grace; and on the other hand, Protestant doctrine understands substantially under the one word 'faith' what Catholic doctrine (following 1 *Cor*. 13:13) sums up in the triad of 'faith, hope, and love'" (LV:E 52).

- "We emphasize that faith in the sense of the first commandment always means love to God and hope in him and is expressed in the love to the neighbour" (VELKD 89,8-11).

- "Catholics ..teach as do Lutherans, that nothing prior to the free gift of faith merits justification and that all of God's saving gifts come through Christ alone" (USA, no. 105).

- "The Reformers ..understood faith as the forgiveness and fellowship with Christ effected by the word of promise itself .. This is the ground for the new being, through which the flesh is dead to sin and the new man or woman in Christ has life (*Sola Fide per Christum*). But even if this faith necessarily makes the human being new, the Christian builds his confidence, not on his own new life, but solely on God's gracious promise. Acceptance in Christ is sufficient, if 'faith' is understood as 'trust in the promise' (fides promissionis)" (LV:E 50).

- Cf. The Council of Trent, Session 6, Chap. 7: "Consequently, in the process of justification, together with the forgiveness of sins a person receives, through Jesus Christ into whom he is grafted, all these infused at the same time: faith, hope and charity" (DH 1530).

- "According to Protestant interpretation, the faith that clings unconditionally to God's promise in Word and Sacrament is sufficient for righteousness before God, so that the renewal of the human being, without which there can be no faith, does not in itself make any contribution to justification" (LV:E 52).

- "As Lutherans we maintain the distinction between justification and sanctification, of faith and works, which however implies no separation" (VELKD 89,6-8).

- "Catholic doctrine knows itself to be at one with the Protestant concern in emphasizing that the renewal of the human being does not 'contribute' to justification, and is certainly not a contribution to which he could make any appeal before God. Nevertheless it feels compelled to stress the renewal of the human being through justifying grace, for the sake of acknowledging God's newly creating power; although this renewal in faith, hope, and love is certainly nothing but a response to God's unfathomable grace" (LV:E 52f).

- "Today Catholics can appreciate the Reformer's efforts to ground faith in the objective reality of Christ's promise, 'whatsoever you loose on earth ....' and to focus believers on the specific word of absolution from sins. ..Luther's original concern to teach people to look away from their experience, and to rely on Christ alone and his word of forgiveness [is not to be condemned]" (PCPCU 24).

XIII

- A mutual condemnation regarding the understanding of the assurance of salvation "can even less provide grounds for mutual objection today - particularly if we start from the foundation of a biblically renewed concept of faith. For a person can certainly lose or renounce faith, and self-commitment to God and his word of promise. But if he believes in this sense, he *cannot at the same time* believe that God is unreliable in his word of promise. In this sense it is true today also that - in Luther's words - faith *is* the assurance of salvation" (LV:E 56).

- With reference to the concept of faith of Vatican II, see Dogmatic Constitution on Divine Revelation, no. 5: "'The obedience of faith' ..must be given to God who reveals, an obedience by which man entrusts his whole self freely to God, offering 'the full submission of intellect and will to God who reveals,' and freely assenting to the truth revealed by Him."

- "The Lutheran distinction between the certitude (certitudo) of faith which looks alone to Christ and earthly security (securitas), which is based on the human being, has not been dealt with clearly enough in the LV. The question whether a Christian "has believed fully and completely" (LV:E 53) does not arise for the Lutheran understanding, since faith never reflects on itself, but depends completely on God, whose grace is bestowed through word and sacrament, thus from outside (extra nos)" (VELKD 92,2-9).

For 4.7: The Good Works of the Justified (paras.37-39) (LV:E 66ff, VELKD 90ff)

- "But the Council excludes the possibility of earning *grace* - that is, justification - (can. 2; DS 1552) and bases the earning or merit of *eternal life* on the gift of grace itself, through membership in Christ (can. 32: DS 1582). Good works are 'merits' as a *gift*. Although the Reformers attack 'Godless trust' in one's own works, the Council explicitly excludes any notion of a claim or any false security (cap. 16: DS 1548f). It is evident ..that the Council wishes to establish a link with Augustine, who introduced the concept of merit, in order to express the responsibility of human beings, in spite of the 'bestowed' character of good works" (LV:E 66).

- If we understand the language of "cause" in Canon 24 in more personal terms, as it is done in chapter 16 of the Decree on Justification, where the idea of communion with Christ is foundational, then we can describe the Catholic doctrine on merit as it is done in the first sentence of the second paragraph of 4.7: growth in grace, perseverance in righteousness received from God and a deeper communion with Christ.

- "Many antitheses could be overcome if the misleading word 'merit' were simply to be viewed and thought about in connection with the true sense of the biblical term 'wage' or reward" (LV:E 67).

- "The Lutheran confessions stress that the justified person is responsible not to lose the grace received but to live in it ..Thus the confessions can speak of a preservation of grace and a growth in it. If righteousness in Canon 24 is understood in the sense that it affects human beings, then it does not strike to us. But if 'righteousness' in Canon 24 refers to the Christian's acceptance by God, it strikes to us; for this righteousness is always perfect; compared with it the works of Christians are only 'fruits' and 'signs'" (VELKD 94,2-14).

- "Concerning Canon 26, we refer to the Apology where eternal life is described as reward: '..We grant that eternal life is a reward because it is something that is owed - not because of our merits but because of the promise'" (VELKD 94,20-24).

[1]The Smalcald Articles, II,1; Book of Concord, 292.
[2]"Rector et judex super omnia genera doctrinarum" Weimar Edition of Luther's Works (WA), 39,I,205.
[3]It should be noted that some Lutheran churches include only the Augsburg Confession and Luther's Small Catechism among their binding confessions. These texts contain no condemnations about justification in relation to the Roman Catholic Church.
[4]Report of the Joint Lutheran-Roman Catholic Study Commission, published in Growth in Agreement (New York; Geneva, 1984), pp. 168-189.
[5]Published by the Lutheran World Federation (Geneva, 1994).
[6]Lutheran and Catholics in Dialogue VII (Minneapolis, 1985).
[7]Minneapolis, 1990.
[8]"Gemeinsame Stellungnahme der Arnoldshainer Konferenz, der Vereinigten Kirche und des Deutschen Nationalkomitees des Lutherischen Weltbundes zum Dokument 'Lehrverurteilungen - kirchentrennend?'," Ökumenische Rundschau 44 (1995): 99-102; See also the position papers which underlie this resolution, in Lehrverurteilungen im Gespräch, Die ersten offiziellen Stellungnahmen aus den evangelischen Kirchen in Deutschland (Göttingen: Vandenhoeck & Ruprecht, 1993).
[9]The word "church" is used in this Declaration to reflect the self-understandings of the participating churches, without intending to resolve all the ecclesiological issues related to this term.
[10]Cf. "Malta Report," paras. 26-30; Justification by Faith, paras. 122-147. At the request of the US dialogue on justification, the non-Pauline New Testament texts were addressed in Righteousness in the New Testament, by John Reumann, with responses by Joseph A. Fitzmyer and Jerome D. Quinn (Philadelphia; New York:1982), pp. 124-180. The results of this study were summarized in the dialogue report Justification by Faith in paras. 139-142.
[11]"All Under One Christ," para. 14, in Growth in Agreement, 241-247.
[12]Cf. WA 8:106; American Edition 32:227.
[13]Cf. DS 1528
[14]Cf. DS 1530.
[15]Cf. Apology II:38-45; Book of Concord, 105f.
[16]Cf. DS 1515.
[17]Cf. DS 1515.
[18]Cf. DS 1545.
[19]Cf. DV 5.
[20]Cf. DV 5.
[21]Condemnations of the Reformation Era, 27.

Appendix B

OFFICIAL COMMON STATEMENT

The Catholic Church and The World Lutheran Federation

1. On the basis of the agreements reached in the Joint Declaration regarding the doctrine of Justification, the Lutheran World Federation and the Catholic Church declare together: "The understanding of the doctrine of justification set forth in this Declaration shows that a consensus in basic truths of the doctrine of justification exists between Lutherans and Catholics" (JD 40). On the basis of this consensus the Lutheran World Federation and the Catholic Church declare together: "The teaching of the Lutheran churches presented in this Declaration does not fall under the condemnations from the Council of Trent. The condemnations in the Lutheran Confessions do not apply to the teaching of the Roman Catholic Church presented in this Declaration" (JD 41).

2. With reference to the Resolution on the Joint Declaration by the Council of the Lutheran World Federation of 16 June 1998 and the response to the Joint Declaration by the Catholic Church of 25 June 1998 and to the questions raised by both of them, the annexed statement (called "Annex") further substantiates the consensus reached in the Joint Declaration; thus it becomes clear that the earlier mutual doctrinal condemnations do not apply to the teaching of the dialogue partners as presented in the Joint Declaration.

3. The two partners in dialogue are committed to continued and deepened study of the biblical foundations of the doctrine of justification. They will also seek further common understanding of the doctrine of justification, also beyond what is dealt with in the Joint Declaration and the annexed substantiating statement. Based on the consensus reached, continued dialogue is required specifically on the issues mentioned especially in the Joint Declaration itself (JD 43) as requiring further clarification, in order to reach full church communion, a unity in diversity, in which remaining differences would be "reconciled" and no longer have a divisive force. Lutherans and Catholics will continue their efforts ecumenically in their common witness to interpret the message of justification in language relevant for human beings today, and with reference both to individual and social concerns of our times.

By this act of signing The Catholic Church and The Lutheran World Federation confirm the Joint Declaration on the Doctrine of Justification in its entirety.

Appendix C

ANNEX TO COMMON STATEMENT
EXPLAINING TERMS OF JOINT DECLARATION
The Catholic Church and The World Lutheran Federation

1. The following elucidations underline the consensus reached in the Joint Declaration on the Doctrine of Justification (JD) regarding basic truths of justification; thus it becomes clear that the mutual condemnations of former times do not apply to the Catholic and Lutheran doctrines of justification as they are presented in the Joint Declaration.

2. "Together we confess: By grace alone, in faith in Christ's saving work and not because of any merit on our part, we are accepted by God and receive the Holy Spirit, who renews our hearts while equipping and calling us to good works" (JD 15).

A) "We confess together that God forgives sin by grace and at the same time frees human beings from sin's enslaving power (...)" (JD 22). Justification is forgiveness of sins and being made righteous, through which God "imparts the gift of new life in Christ" (JD 22). "Since we are justified by faith, we have peace with God" (Rom 5:1). We are "called children of God; and that is what we are" (1 Jn 3:1). We are truly and inwardly renewed by the action of the Holy Spirit, remaining always dependent on his work in us. "So if anyone is in Christ, there is a new creation: everything old has passed away; see, everything has become new!" (2 Cor 5:17). The justified do not remain sinners in this sense.

Yet we would be wrong were we to say that we are without sin (1 Jn 1:8-10, cf. JD 28). "All of us make many mistakes" (Jas 3:2). "Who is aware of his unwitting sins? Cleanse me of many secret faults" (Ps 19:12). And when we pray, we can only say, like the tax collector, "God, be merciful to me, a sinner" (Lk 18:13). This is expressed in a variety of ways in our liturgies. Together we hear the exhortation "Therefore, do not let sin exercise dominion in your mortal bodies, to make you obey their passions" (Rom 6:12). This recalls to us the persisting danger which comes from the power of sin and its action in Christians. To this extent, Lutherans and Catholics can together understand the Christian as simul justus et peccator, despite their different approaches to this subject as expressed in JD 29-30.

B) The concept of "concupiscence" is used in different senses on the Catholic and Lutheran sides. In the Lutheran Confessional writings concupiscence is understood as the self-seeking desire of the human being which in light of the Law, spiritually understood, is regarded as sin. In the Catholic understanding concupiscence is an inclination, remaining in human beings even after baptism, which comes from sin and presses towards sin. Despite the differences involved here, it can be recognized from a Lutheran perspective that desire can become the opening through which sin attacks. Due to the power of sin the entire human being carries the tendency to oppose God. This tendency, according to both

Lutheran and Catholic conception, "does not correspond to God's original design for humanity" (JD 30) . Sin has a personal character and, as such, leads to separation from God. It is the selfish desire of the old person and the lack of trust and love toward God.

The reality of salvation in baptism and the peril from the power of sin can be expressed in such a way that, on the one hand, the forgiveness of sins and renewal of humanity in Christ by baptism is emphasised and, on the other hand, it can be seen that the justified also "are continuously exposed to the power of sin still pressing its attacks (cf. Rom 6: 12-14) and are not exempt from a lifelong struggle against the contradiction to God (...)" (JD 28).

C) Justification takes place "by grace alone" (JD 15 and 16), by faith alone, the person is justified "apart from works" (Rom 3:28, cf. JD 25). "Grace creates faith not only when faith begins in a person but as long as faith lasts" (Thomas Aquinas, S. Th II/II 4, 4 ad 3). The working of God's grace does not exclude human action: God effects everything, the willing and the achievement, therefore we are called to strive (cf. Phil 2:12 ff.). "As soon as the Holy Spirit has initiated his work of regeneration and renewal in us through the Word and the holy sacraments, it is certain that we can and must cooperate by the power of the Holy Spirit ..." (The Formula of Concord, FC SD II, 64f; BSLK 897, 37ff).

D) Grace as fellowship of the justified with God in faith, hope and love is always received from the salvific and creative work of God (cf. JD 27). But it is nevertheless the responsibility of the justified not to waste this grace but to live in it. The exhortation to do good works is the exhortation to practice the faith (cf. BSLK 197,45). The good works of the justified "should be done in order to confirm their call, that is, lest they fall from their call by sinning again" (Apol. XX,13, BSLK 316,18-24; with reference to 2 Pet. 1:10. Cf. also FC SD IV,33; BSLK 948,9-23). In this sense Lutherans and Catholics can understand together what is said about the "preservation of grace" in JD 38 and 39. Certainly, "whatever in the justified precedes or follows the free gift of faith is neither the basis of justification nor merits it" (JD 25).

E) By justification we are unconditionally brought into communion with God. This includes the promise of eternal life: "If we have been united with him in a death like his, we will certainly be united with him in a resurrection like his" (Rom 6:5, cf. Jn 3:36, Rom 8:17). In the final judgement, the justified will be judged also on their works (cf. Mt 16:27; 25:31-46; Rom 2:16; 14:12; 1 Cor 3:8; 2 Cor 5:10, etc.). We face a judgement in which God's gracious sentence will approve anything in our life and action that corresponds to his will. However, everything in our life that is wrong will be uncovered and will not enter eternal life. The Formula of Concord also states: "It is God's will and express command that believers should do good works which the Holy Spirit works in them, and God is willing to be pleased with them for Christ's sake and he promises to reward them gloriously in this and in the future life" (FC SD IV,38). Any reward is a reward of grace, on which we have no claim.

3) The doctrine of justification is measure or touchstone for the Christian faith. No teaching may contradict this criterion. In this sense, the doctrine of justification is an "indispensable criterion which constantly serves to orient all the teaching and practice of our churches to Christ" (JD 18). As such, it has its truth and specific meaning within the overall context of the Church's fundamental Trinitarian confession of faith. We "share the goal of confessing Christ in all things, who is to be trusted above all things as the one Mediator (1 Tim 2:5-6) through whom God in the Holy Spirit gives himself and pours out his renewing gifts" (JD 18).

4) The Response of the Catholic Church does not intend to put in question the authority of Lutheran Synods or of the Lutheran World Federation. The Catholic Church and the Lutheran World Federation began the dialogue and have taken it forward as partners with equal rights ("par cum pari"). Notwithstanding different conceptions of authority in the Church, each partner respects the other partner's ordered process of reaching doctrinal decisions.

Appendix D

PRESENTATION OF THE JOINT STATEMENT
Edward Cardinal Cassidy
President of the Pontifical Council for Promoting Christian Unity

1. In June of last year, both the Lutheran World Federation and the Catholic Church officially responded to the Joint Declaration on the Doctrine of Justification that had been prepared by the Joint Lutheran-Catholic Dialogue Commission. Following two distinct processes of reception, both the Lutheran World Federation and the Catholic Church were able to declare that a consensus had indeed been reached in the Joint Declaration "in basic truths of the doctrine of justification".

2. In making this statement, both the Catholic Church and the Lutheran World Federation indicated some aspects of the doctrine of justification that required further study. The "Clarifications" of the Catholic Church, however, seemed in the view of the Lutheran partner to leave some doubt as to the nature and the extent of the approval of the Joint Declaration on the part of the Catholic partner. This resulted in a number of statements being made even in the press and a sense of disappointment by both partners.

3. The Secretary-General of the Lutheran World Federation and myself, in consultation with those responsible with us for pursuing this matter, set about finding a way in which to affirm the consensus reached and overcome the doubts that had arisen.

4. The document that we are making public today is the fruit of those discussions. It consists of two parts: an Official Common Statement by the Lutheran World Federation and the Catholic Church to be signed together with the Joint Declaration on the Doctrine of Justification and an Annex.

5. The Official Common Statement explains clearly and unequivocally just what the two partners understand by their act of signing the Joint Declaration. The two partners declare together:

- that a consensus has indeed been reached in basic truths of the doctrine of justification as set forth in the Joint Declaration and on the basis of this consensus they declare together "The teaching of the Lutheran churches presented in this Declaration does not fall under the condemnations of the Council of Trent. The condemnations in the Lutheran Confessions do not apply to the teachings of the Roman Catholic Church presented in this Declaration";
- with reference to the questions raised by the responses to the Joint Declaration, the Statement explains that the attached Annex "further substantiates the consensus reached in the Joint Declaration and thus it becomes clear that the earlier mutual condemnations do not apply to the teaching of the dialogue partners as presented in the Joint Declaration";

XX

- In the third paragraph, the Statement sets out future work that the two partners intend to pursue: "continued and deepened study of the biblical foundations of the doctrine of justification", which did not seem to have been given sufficient attention in the Joint Declaration; "to seek further common understanding of the doctrine of justification, also beyond what is dealt with in the Joint Declaration and in the annexed substantiating statement". Some of these issues are mentioned in the Joint Declaration itself (JD 43) as requiring further clarification in order to reach full church communion. Finally, the two partners declare that they "will continue their efforts ecumenically in their common witness to interpret the message of justification in language relevant for human beings today, and with reference both to individual and social concerns of our times".

6. The Annex, as I have stated, "further substantiates the consensus reached in the Joint Declaration". In brief, it takes up those questions that were causing some uncertainty on the part of one or other of the two partners and without altering the Joint Declaration, removes that uncertainty. A study of the questions raised by the two dialogue partners in their respective responses, side by side with the Official Common Statement and its Annex will show how those questions have been dealt with to the satisfaction of both partners.

7. On the Catholic side, the Official Common Statement and the Annex have been approved by the Pontifical Council for Promoting Christian Unity and by the Congregation for the Doctrine of Faith. His Holiness Pope John Paul II has been informed accordingly and has given his blessing for the signing of the Joint Declaration on the Doctrine of Justification, together with the Official Common Statement with its attached Annex on the date and in the place to be decided by the two partners.

RESPONSES OF THE CATHOLIC CHURCH TO THE JOINT DECLARATION OF THE CATHOLIC CHURCH AND THE LUTHERAN WORLD FEDERATION ON THE DOCTRINE OF JUSTIFICATION
Pontifical Council for Promoting Christian Unity

Declaration

The "Joint Declaration of the Catholic Church and the Lutheran World Federation on the Doctrine of Justification" represents a significant progress in mutual understanding and in the coming together in dialogue of the parties concerned; it shows that there are many points of convergence between the Catholic position and the Lutheran position on a question that has been for centuries so controversial. It can certainly be affirmed that a high degree of agreement has been reached, as regards both the approach to the question and the judgement it merits.[1] It is rightly stated that there is "a consensus in basic truths of the doctrine of justification".[2]

The Catholic Church is, however, of the opinion that we cannot yet speak of a consensus such as would eliminate every difference between Catholics and Lutherans in the understanding of justification. The Joint Declaration itself refers to certain of these differences. On some points the positions are, in fact, still divergent. So, on the basis of the agreement already reached on many aspects, the Catholic Church intends to contribute towards overcoming the divergencies that still exist by suggesting, below, in order of importance, a list of points that constitute still an obstacle to agreement between the Catholic Church and the Lutheran World Federation on all the fundamental truths concerning justification. The Catholic Church hopes that the following indications may be an encouragement to continue study of these questions in the same fraternal spirit that, in recent times, has characterized the dialogue between the Catholic Church and the Lutheran World Federation.

Clarifications

1. The major difficulties preventing an affirmation of total consensus between the parties on the theme of justification arise in paragraph 4.4 *The Justified as Sinner* (nn. 28-30). Even taking into account the differences, legitimate in themselves, that come from different theological approaches to the content of faith, from a Catholic point of view the title is already a cause of perplexity. According, indeed, to the doctrine of the Catholic Church, in baptism everything that is really sin is taken away, and so, in those who are born anew there is nothing that is hateful to God.[3] It follows that the concupiscence that remains in the baptized is not, properly speaking, sin. For Catholics, therefore, the formula *"at the same time righteous and sinner"*, as it is explained at the beginning of n. 29 (*"Believers are totally righteous, in that God forgives their sins through Word and*

Sacrament.... Looking at themselves ... however, they recognize that they remain also totally sinners. Sin still lives in them ") is not acceptable. This statement does not, in fact, seem compatible with the renewal and sanctification of the interior man of which the Council of Trent speaks.[4] The expression "opposition to God" (Gottwidrigkeit) that is used in nn. 28-30 is understood differently by Lutherans and by Catholics, and so becomes, in fact, equivocal. In this same sense, there can be ambiguity for a Catholic in the sentence of n. 22, ..."*God no longer imputes to them their sin and through the Holy Spirit effects in them an active love*", because man's interior transformation is not clearly seen. So, for all these reasons, it remains difficult to see how, in the current state of the presentation given in the Joint Declaration, we can say that this doctrine on "*simul iustus et peccator*" is not touched by the anathemas of the Tridentine decree on original sin and justification.

2. Another difficulty arises in n. 18 of the Joint Declaration, where a clear difference appears in the importance, for Catholics and for Lutherans, of the doctrine of justification as criterion for the life and practice of the Church.

Whereas for Lutherans this doctrine has taken on an altogether particular significance, for the Catholic Church the message of justification, according to Scripture and already from the time of the Fathers, has to be organically integrated into the fundamental criterion of the "*regula fidei*", that is, the confession of the one God in three persons, Christologically centered and rooted in the living Church and its sacramental life.

3. As stated in n. 17 of the Joint Declaration, Lutherans and Catholics share the common conviction that the new life comes from divine mercy and not from any merit of ours. It must, however, be remembered - as stated in 2 Cor 5:17 - that this divine mercy brings about a new creation and so makes man capable of responding to God's gift, of cooperating with grace. In this regard, the Catholic Church notes with satisfaction that n. 21, in conformity with can. 4 of the Decree on Justification of the Council of Trent (DS 1554) states that man can refuse grace; but it must also be affirmed that, with this freedom to refuse, there is also a new capacity to adhere to the divine will, a capacity rightly called "*cooperatio*". This new capacity given in the new creation does not allow us to use in this context the expression "*mere passive*" (n. 21). On the other hand, the fact that this capacity has the character of a gift is well expressed in chap. 5 (DS 1525) of the Tridentine Decree when it says: "*ita ut tangente Deo cor hominis per Spiritus Sancti illuminationem, neque homo ipse nihil omnino agat, inspirationem illam recipiens, quippe qui illam et abicere potest, neque tamen sine gratia Dei movere se ad iustitiam coram illo libera sua voluntate possit*".

In reality, also on the Lutheran side, there is the affirmation, in n. 21, of a full personal involvement in faith *("believers are fully involved personally in their faith")*. A clarification would, however, be necessary as to the compatibility of this involvement with the reception "*mere passive*" of justification, in order to determine more exactly the degree of consensus with the Catholic doctrine. As for the final sentence of n. 24: "*God's gift of grace in justification remains independent of human cooperation*", this must be understood in the sense that the gifts of God's grace do not depend on the works of man, but not in the sense that justification can take place without human cooperation. The sentence of n. 19 according to which man's freedom *"is no freedom in relation to salvation"* must, similarly, be related to the impossibility for man to reach justification by his own efforts.

The Catholic Church maintains, moreover, that the good works of the justified are always the fruit of grace. But at the same time, and without in any way diminishing the totally divine initiative,[5] they are also the fruit of man, justified and interiorly transformed. We can therefore say that eternal life is, at one and the same time, grace and the reward given by God for good works and merits.[6] This doctrine results from the interior transformation of man to which we referred in n. 1 of this "Note". These clarifications are a help for a right understanding, from the Catholic point of view, of paragraph 4.7 (nn. 37-39) on the good works of the justified.

4. In pursuing this study further, it will be necessary to treat also the sacrament of penance, which is mentioned in n. 30 of the Joint Declaration. According to the Council of Trent, in fact,[7] through this sacrament the sinner can be justified anew (*rursus iustificari*): this implies the possibility, by means of this sacrament, as distinct from that of baptism, to recover lost justice.[8] These aspects are not all sufficiently noted in the above-mentioned n. 30.

5. These remarks are intended as a more precise explanation of the teaching of the Catholic Church with regard to the points on which complete agreement has not been reached; they are also meant to complete some of the paragraphs explaining Catholic doctrine, in order to bring out more clearly the degree of consensus that has been reached. The level of agreement is high, but it does not yet allow us to affirm that all the differences separating Catholics and Lutherans in the doctrine concerning justification are simply a question of emphasis or language. Some of these differences concern aspects of substance and are therefore not all mutually compatible, as affirmed on the contrary in n. 40.

If, moreover, it is true that in those truths on which a consensus has been reached the condemnations of the Council of Trent no longer apply, the divergencies on other points must, on the contrary, be overcome before we can affirm, as is done generically in n. 41, that these points no longer incur the condemnations of the Council of Trent. That applies in the first place to the doctrine on *"simul iustus et peccator"* (cf. n. 1, above).

6. We need finally to note, from the point of view of their representative quality, the different character of the two signatories of this Joint Declaration. The Catholic Church recognizes the great effort made by the Lutheran World Federation in order to arrive, through consultation of the Synods, at a " *magnus consensus*", and so to give a true ecclesial value to its signature; there remains, however, the question of the real authority of such a synodal consensus, today and also tomorrow, in the life and doctrine of the Lutheran community.

Prospects for future work

7. The Catholic Church wishes to reiterate its hope that this important step forward towards agreement in doctrine on justification may be followed by further studies that will make possible a satisfactory clarification of the divergencies that still exist. Particularly desirable would be a deeper reflection on the biblical foundation that is the common basis of the doctrine on justification both for Catholics and for Lutherans. This reflection should be extended to the New Testament as a whole and not only to the Pauline writings. If it is true, indeed, that St Paul is the New Testament author who has had most to say on this subject, and this fact calls for a certain preferential attention, substantial references to this theme are not lacking also in the other New Testament writings. As for the various ways in which Paul describes man's new condition, as mentioned in the Joint Declaration, we could add the categories of sonship and of heirs (Gal 4:4-7; Rom 8:14-17). Consideration of all these elements will be a great help for mutual understanding and will make it possible to resolve the divergences that still exist in the doctrine on justification.

8. Finally, it should be a common concern of Lutherans and Catholics to find a language which can make the doctrine on justification more intelligible also for men and women of our day. The fundamental truths of the salvation given by Christ and received in faith, of the primacy of grace over every human initiative, of the gift of the Holy Spirit which makes us capable of living according to our condition as children of God, and so on. These are essential aspects of the Christian message that should be a light for the believers of all times.

This Note, which constitutes the official Catholic Response to the text of the Joint Declaration, has been prepared by common agreement between the Congregation for the Doctrine of the Faith and the Pontifical Council for Promoting Christian Unity. It is signed by the President of the same Pontifical Council, which is directly responsible for the ecumenical dialogue.

Notes

[1] Cf. "Joint Declaration", n. 4: "ein hohes Mass an gemeinsamer Ausrichtung und gemeinsamem Urteil".

[2] Ibid., n. 5: "einen Konsens in Grundwahrheiten der Rechtfertigungslehre" (cf. nn. 13; 40; 43).

[3] Cf. Council of Trent, Decree on Original Sin (DS 1515).

[4] Cf. Council of Trent, Decree on Justification, chap. 8: "... *iustificatio ... quae non est sola peccatorum remissio, sed et sanctificatio et renovatio interioris hominis"* (DS 1528); cf. also can. 11 (DS 1561).

[5] Cf. Council of Trent, Decree on Justification, chap. 16 (DS 1546), which quotes Jn 15:5: the vine and the branches.

[6] Cf. ibid., DS 1545; and can. 26 (DS 1576).

[7] Ibid., chap. 14 (cf. DS 1542).

[8] Cf. ibid., can. 29 (DS 1579); Decree on the Sacrament of Penance, chap. 2 (DS 1671); can. 2 (DS 1702).

XXVI

How to Contact the Contributors

Father Larry Blake
Email: larry.blake@sthubert.org

Arthur Bowman
Email: abowmanmn@earthlink.net

James Cope
P.O. Box 586
St. Paris, OH 43072
Phone: 937-663-4460
Email: jcope@main-net.com

Tim Drake
2009 13th Street South
Saint Cloud, MN 56301
Phone: 320-230-1881
Email: timd@astound.net

Jennifer Ferrara
Jferrara@fast.net

Anthony Gerring
1057 Winchester Avenue
Lincoln Park, MI 48146
Phone: (313) 389-3523
Agerring@juno.com

Marie Hosdil
Email: emhosdil@1st.net

Patricia Sodano Ireland
irelands1@home.com

Todd von Kampen
Email: toddvk@mitec.net

Sally Nelson
LeSainteBaume@aol.com

Audrey Zech
1539 Fulham Street
St. Pual, MN 55108
Azech@luthcrsem.edu

Organizations to Help in the Journey

Catholic Answers

Catholic Answers is the largest Catholic apologetics and evangelization organization in North America. They promote the Catholic faith through books, booklets, tracts, magazines, tapes, and television and radio appearances. Their lay staff includes people who have always been Catholic as well as Catholic reverts and converts. Their staff apologists answer questions about the faith and give parish seminars. Whatever Catholic question you have, Catholic Answers has the answer.

2020 Gillespie Way, El Cajon, CA 92020
Inquiries: 619-387-7200 Fax: 619-387-0042
www.catholic.com

Envoy Magazine

Envoy.magazine is the award winning bi-monthly journal of Catholic apologetics and evangelization, edited by Patrick Madrid (*Surprised by Truth, Pope Fiction, Any Friend of God is a Friend of Mine*).

PO Box 1117, Steubenville, OH 43952
800-55-ENVOY
www.envoymagazine.com

Coming Home Network International

The Coming Home Network International provides fellowship, encouragement and support for Protestant pastors and laymen who are somewhere along the journey or have already been received into the Catholic Church. The network is committed to assisting and standing beside all inquirers, serving as a friend and an advocate.

P.O. Box 8290, Zanesville, OH 43702
800-664-5110
www.chnetwork.org

Catholics United for the Faith

CUF is an international lay apostolate building on the teachings of Jesus Chirst and His Church. They publish *Lay Witness Magazine*, a series of *Faith Facts* dealing with common questions about the Church, and staff a 1-800 hotline that individuals can use to help answer their questions about the faith. Their *Faith Facts* can also be downloaded from their website.

827 North Fourth Street
Steubenville, OH 43952
1-800-MY-FAITH (800) 693-2484
www.cuf.org

Mary Foundation

The Mary Foundation is an excellent resource for free resources about the Catholic faith. They distribute audio tapes about the faith, CDs, and novels.
www.CatholiCity.com

ABOUT THE AUTHOR

Tim Drake is a full-time Catholic writer. A history teacher by training, he serves as features correspondent with the *National Catholic Register* and as associate editor of *Envoy Magazine*. He has published more than 200 articles in publications such as *Catholic Faith and Family*, *Be*, *Gilbert!*, *Lay Witness*, *Catholic World Report*, e3mil.com, the Catholic Marketing Network Trade Journal, and *Columbia Magazine*.

Printed in the United States
708100003B